JOSEPH CONRAD'S FICTION

A *Study in Literary Growth*

JOSEPH CONRAD'S FICTION

A Study in Literary Growth

JOHN A. PALMER

Cornell University Press

ITHACA, NEW YORK

Acknowledgments

For permission to quote from the works and letters of Joseph Conrad, I am indebted to J. M. Dent & Sons, Ltd., and the Trustees of the Joseph Conrad Estate. My debt to Conrad's critics and biographers will be obvious from the notes and text themselves.

I owe thanks to friends and colleagues who read the manuscript and made suggestions: William M. Sale, Jr., Walter Slatoff, Robert Greenberg, and others; and to W. R. Keast, whose generosity as English Department Chairman at Cornell gave me free time to think about Conrad. I have profited from the guidance of Cornell University Press, and from the criticisms of their anonymous reader. Betty Slater and Tom Yeager, who helped prepare the manuscript, also deserve thanks. My greatest debt, of course, is to Jean Steinbeck Palmer, whose continuous help and encouragement have almost reached the point of co-authorship.

J. A. P.

Los Angeles, California
March 1968

[v]

Acknowledgements

Contents

Contents

Introduction:

The Growth of Conrad's Art

So many critics have discussed Joseph Conrad in recent years that anyone proposing still another full-length study must consider whether there really is room for it—whether the main lines of Conrad criticism have not already been laid down and extended as far as possible, and in some cases perhaps farther than desirable. With works in the field so brilliant as Albert Guerard's *Conrad the Novelist* and so painstaking as Jocelyn Baines's *Joseph Conrad* and Norman Sherry's *Conrad's Eastern World*, Conrad studies have reached a high level of sophistication.

Yet recent Conrad criticism has shown two tendencies that demand further study. The first of these is the inclination to abandon what Guerard has called the "old" view of Conrad, as a simple rational man with a conservative ethic and a love of the sea, and to stress instead the psychological and symbolic subtleties of his fiction. Guerard himself has found a "temperamental evasiveness" and a repeated use of the archetypal "night journey" in Conrad; other critics have found Christian and classical mythology, a persistent misogyny, and even "hidden symbolic intentions." Without disputing these discoveries, I still think the best way of approaching his work is the "old" one, at least insofar as it takes a set of moral attitudes and psycho-moral dilemmas as its starting point: the fundamental notions Conrad himself points to in such phrases as "a few very simple ideas" and "*les valeurs idéales.*" Not that Conrad's work is simple. But its psychological, philosophical, and symbolic subtleties are secondary to his central moral interest, and largely derivative from it. To adopt such a point of view not only makes possible a more coherent reading than we now have of many individual works, but provides also a firmer base for seeing Conrad's work as a whole—a task not yet satisfactorily accomplished, despite persuasive efforts by Guerard, Douglas Hewitt, Thomas Moser, Bernard Meyer, and others.

The second questionable tendency of recent criticism, then, is the growing inclination to view Conrad's career as a case of achievement and decline. Almost everyone seems to agree that half a dozen novels and stories toward the middle of Conrad's career—*Lord Jim, Nostromo,* perhaps "The Secret Sharer" and a few others—are his best, and that most of his later efforts, including in particular *Chance, Victory, The Arrow of Gold,* and *The Rover,* are markedly inferior: sentimental, melodramatic, falsely "affirmative," and marked by creative exhaustion. In its extreme form, this view denies almost all value to these later works, and attempts to discover the moral, psychological, and biographical causes of Conrad's deterioration. A few cautionary voices have been heard; but no one has really come to grips with the suppositions underlying the achievement-and-decline theory, or offered a better way of describing Conrad's career. The result has been to impose a false symmetry on the Conrad canon: to undervalue some works and overvalue others, and to blur the distinctions whereby we might see how Conrad's later works do and do not represent a decline. The present study will suggest that Conrad's career may more usefully be viewed as one of successive major achievements, each preceded by a period of experiment and partial success; and that his later work is much better than commonly supposed—so much so, in fact, that "achievement and decline" is rather a misleading label.

In a Bibliographical Note at the end of this volume, I have discussed briefly the major sources of the achievement-and-decline theory. Among them are the very finest books on Conrad—Guerard's *Conrad the Novelist*, for example, and Bernard Meyer's *Joseph Conrad: A Psychoanalytic Biography*. Guerard's studies of such early works as "Heart of Darkness" and *The Nigger of the 'Narcissus'* are classics in the field; and Moser and Meyer have given us valuable tools for dismantling some of Conrad's more spectacular failures. But when their particular analytic methods are carried over to works like *Nostromo* and *Victory*—so that *Nostromo* can be held out as Conrad's supreme achievement, or *Victory* seen as a "love" story—the results are simply unsatisfactory. "Love," or more exactly sexual and romantic relationships, serves primarily a symbolic purpose in Conrad's later work; realistic psychology and the normal sense of probability are subordinated to rhetorical and allegorical structures; and to view this fiction as "popular romance" is to seek unity and integrity where they cannot possibly be found. The stock characters and romantic clichés of *Chance* are a part of the book's irony, elements of that chivalric vision represented by Anthony ("The Knight") and Flora ("The Damsel"), and effectively undercut by Marlow. Similarly, the blacks and whites of *Victory*, the "romantic" conception of Lena and the book's melodramatic ending, are functions of the mode of allegory and fable that determines the novel's methods. *Victory* is the paradigm of Conrad's final moral and philosophical attitude, dealing with total commitment and total withdrawal, and with the problems of knowledge, belief, and feeling bearing upon that problem of commitment: the culmination of lines of intellectual and technical growth that had begun all the way back with *Almayer's Folly*. The real questions the critic must face are whether the substance of the novel actually requires Conrad's peculiar non-

realistic techniques, and whether they are sufficiently developed
to yield the full pleasures of that kind of fictional art. The
present study will answer a qualified "yes" to both questions; but
in any case, it is clear that the achievement-and-decline critics'
view of the later fiction needs some revision: not in the spirit of
controversy, but with the purpose of establishing a more generous point of view toward our common object of interest.

One trouble with valid negative criticisms of literary works,
especially when they are buttressed by powerful psychoanalytic
insights like Meyer's, is that they are likely to focus repeatedly on
the same kind of artistic difficulty, so that the reader tends to
forget the works' general richness and complexity. Reading
Meyer and Moser, one begins to feel that Conrad was wholly a
psychic cripple, and that his private symbology reflected nothing
more than his own inner conflicts. But again, the real question is
how much significant external reference Conrad did manage,
despite his sexual fears and other inner obstacles. In seeking
after this esthetic coherence, the present study will focus more
on Conrad's successes—those works in which his creative energies emerge comparatively unhindered—than his failures, and
will, by and large, silently ignore those fetishes and conflicts
identified so persuasively by Moser and Meyer. In the balance of
these two points of view, it is hoped, there will be a fairer
assessment of Conrad—a considerable softening of the lines of
achievement and decline, and a more complex picture of his
artistic growth.

The view proposed here is that Conrad's career shows a progress-of-awareness that divides itself into three distinct stages:
beginning with the presocial dilemmas of private honor and
individual fidelity standing at the center of the early works;
expanding, with *Nostromo,* to a consideration of the individual
in society and the moral contradictions imposed by social idealism; and extending finally, with *Chance* and *Victory,* to the
theoretical and metaphysical bases of any moral commitment.
Conrad begins at the center, with a fully developed ethic, and

gradually moves toward the periphery of his total vision, exploring its social and metaphysical associations as he goes, and bringing more and more of that vision into developed artistic form, so that he can terminate finally in the relative calm and controlled awareness of his last works. As this progress-of-awareness proceeds, Conrad's technical ingenuity keeps pace, lagging at first when some genuinely new subject or theme is approached, and then devising the techniques that will go to its center and provide the control it needs. Thus in each of his major periods, smaller patterns of growth may also be seen, with the outstanding achievement of each period coming toward its close—a fact that dictates, in turn, the order in which the stories and novels may best be discussed, if the shape of Conrad's career is to be clearly marked. The method will be to discuss the higher achievements of each period first, and then return to the earlier works to examine their thematic and technical growth toward these later achievements. Mere chronology is violated in this way, but in the service of clarity.

This line of Conrad's growth—both intellectual and technical —comes to an end with *Victory*, and the works that follow are largely anticlimactic. In *Victory* Conrad seems finally to have resolved the moral and philosophical perplexities that had motivated his fiction from the beginning (or to have achieved finally their full dramatic resolution in his art, which for a novelist may be the same thing); and with this principal spring of his creative effort stilled, the works that followed were simply less urgent, their subjects themselves suggesting a calmer and more intellectually conscious approach to his work. But even here, we must be careful not to dwell too exclusively on the negative. The diminution of social context and of normal psychological cause and effect in these works, for example, may be just one more way in which Conrad's later work prefigures modern existentialist fiction, and thus be related to a significant strain of recent Conrad criticism. And many of the relaxed techniques of these later works, such as the comparatively simple descriptive style and symbolic delicacy of *The Rover,* may be the correlates of Conrad's maturity—a stylistic affirmation of the commitment to human community that had been so sorely tested in the earlier fiction. In any case, their loss of quality probably can be traced not so much to failing powers as to the consciously nostalgic nature of Conrad's final works—a seeking for subjects, as it were, after the great major subject had been closed. These later books are difficult to judge, and the problem is made even harder in two instances by the fragmentary nature of *Suspense* and the complicated history of *The Rescue.*

The details of Conrad's creative journey will appear in the following discussion, and will define a talent capable of continuing growth through the worst vicissitudes of public reputation and private anxiety. But it will be useful to identify in advance some fundamental relationships among Conrad's three major periods. Conrad's central moral concerns remain the same throughout his career—individual responsibility; self-knowledge; man's near inability to cope with (or even discover) his own darkness, and yet the necessity of his doing so. In this sense, Heyst's (or Lena's) victory is simply the converse of Almayer's folly. But the range of significant action gradually widens for Conrad's protagonists, as social and philosophical issues impinge more and more on his moral consciousness, so that by the time of *Nostromo* his attention has shifted away from individual regression and infidelity, toward the follies of doctrinaire political action in its service to some remote "ideal": a service which is essentially divisive, and thereby destroys the fidelity of one human to another; and which places expediency above moral principle, and thereby sacrifices the individual to the group. Many writers have seen that Conrad is deeply skeptical of all political idealism. But what is too rarely stressed is that this attitude is at bottom an ironic inversion of his more basic commitments: his scorn for political institutions is implicit in the value he places on the individual, and on the individual's paradox-ridden obligation to meet the darkness within himself; and his scorn for abstract doctrine is implicit in his intellectual skepticism. The subjects of *Chance* and *Victory* are implicit also in these early moral commitments. In their symbolic examination of the very preconditions of individual responsibility, these later novels bring into the foreground the metaphysical and epistemological skepticism which had always been in the background of Conrad's fiction, serving as an ironic counterpoint to his protagonists' struggles for dignity and significance. In his final declaration for "life" despite the threats posed by human society and by an enigmatic universe, Conrad merely reaffirms his earliest values. And all his major works after *Lord Jim* may be seen as logical extensions of these commitments, exploring either their social implications or their broad philosophical assumptions. To see these basic relationships among Conrad's works helps to resolve the usual critical indignation over the famous passage in *A Personal Record*: "Those who read me know my conviction that the world, the temporal world, rests on a few very simple ideas; so simple that they must be as old as the hills" (p. xix). Significantly, this statement is associated in its immediate context both with a rejection of revolutionary idealism and with the hope that the reader will find a "coherent, justifiable personality" behind "books so fundamentally dissimilar as, for instance, 'Almayer's Folly' and 'The Secret Agent.'" Conrad's perception of what is involved in a commitment to these "few very simple ideas"—their psychological, social, and philosophical implications—is of course complex, and the narrative and symbolic superstructure he builds upon that commitment cannot be understood by looking at the foundation alone. But this is not the same as denying that the foundation exists.

I have undertaken, then, two tasks here: to identify the deepest thematic centers of Conrad's work, and to see how his most characteristic techniques—the involved narrator, the time shift, the use of symbolic description, and so on—reflect these deep concerns. Done carefully enough and in sufficient detail, this kind of analysis will reveal the pattern of growth described briefly above, and will help to resolve some of the strange anomalies of Conrad criticism—the continuing ambivalence over *Nostromo*, for example. At the same time, the scope of this study imposes some limits and raises some obvious hazards. In drawing upon the available criticism and scholarship, much of value must be passed by because of its level of detail; seductive comparisons with Henry James, Flaubert, Hardy, Crane, Dostoevski, Faulkner, Melville, and others must remain unexplored, along with the question of Conrad's influence and intellectual relation to his times. Moreover, *The Inheritors, Romance,* and *The Rescue* raise separate problems and would require too extended a discussion here; they have accordingly been omitted, along with some of Conrad's lesser short stories. Finally, there is always the danger that the critic interested in general patterns will violate the integrity of individual works, and miss the value of off-center masterpieces. I have tried to obviate that danger by referring the reader rather generously to other discussions of Conrad, and by providing fairly detailed analyses of such pivotal works as *Lord Jim,* "The Secret Sharer," *The Secret Agent, Victory,* and *Nostromo.* And it is hoped that enough has been said about each of Conrad's major works to indicate what are, at least for one reader, its chief pleasures—since only as it bears finally upon that question is a critical study justified at all.

JOSEPH CONRAD'S FICTION

A *Study in Literary Growth*

1

The Early Marlow Tales

It is obviously best if you can contrive to be without views at all; your business with the world is rendering, not alteration. . . . If, however, your yearning to amend the human race is so great that you cannot possibly keep your fingers out of the watch-springs there is a device that you can adopt. . . . You must then invent, justify, and set going in your novel a character who can convincingly express your views. . . . You thus have an admirable opportunity of expressing with emphasis quite a number of views through the mouth of the character whom you have so carefully "justified" as yourself. Quite a number of views!
—Ford Madox Ford, in *Joseph Conrad: A Personal Remembrance*

Looking back on his early fiction from the vantage point of 1917, Conrad recalls that "['Youth'] marks the first appearance in the world of the man Marlow, with whom my relations have grown very intimate in the course of years," a characteristic remark which gently underplays the moral identity between author and narrator: "He haunts my hours of solitude, when, in silence, we lay our heads together in great comfort and harmony. . . . I don't think that either of us would care much to survive the other. . . . A most discreet, understanding man" (*Youth*, pp. v–vi). Anyone who would understand Conrad's early fiction

must grasp at once this deep affinity between Conrad and Marlow; there are no more important works in the canon than *Lord
Jim* and "Heart of Darkness," and no aspect of them more
important than Marlow's role.

So much has been written on Conrad's early Marlow tales that
it is probably impossible now to say anything really new about
them. But it may be possible to gain some fresh insight, at least,
and to provide a focal point for this earlier criticism, by returning
once again to their most striking feature—the use of Marlow as
inner narrator—and reconsidering the esthetic purposes of that
tactic. In all the stories in which he appears, Marlow must be
taken as a choral character in the fullest sense—for all practical
purposes the voice of Conrad himself; and Marlow's meditative
history—not the train of physical events reflected in that history
—must be taken as the reader's primary object of interest. These
simple-sounding propositions have seemed obviously true to
some readers, and obviously false to others; but they are really
not obvious in any sense; the evidence bearing on them is complex, and their implications surprisingly varied. When discussions of the Marlow tales go wrong, it seems to me, it is usually
through their failure to attend closely enough to certain features
of Marlow's narration, or to accept his affirmations as thematically definitive. Instead of viewing Marlow's reflections as the
substance of these stories, Conrad's most influential critics have
tended to see them merely as a device, or point of view, or
meditative smoke screen thrown up between the reader and the
facts for the purposes of mystery and irony. The result has been
to introduce irrelevancies, or even at times to convert virtues into
defects—to miss the ironies of "Youth," for example, and see it as
a mere lyric tribute to youthful illusion; [1] or to complain about
the adjectival vagueness of certain parts of "Heart of Darkness";
or to attempt to discuss Jim outside the moral framework so

---

[1] A recent writer's phrase, "existential comedy," seems more exactly to
capture the story's tone (J. Oates Smith, "The Existential Comedy of
Conrad's 'Youth,' " *Renascence*, XVIII [Fall 1963], 22–28).

carefully set up by Marlow and Stein. Marlow's impressionistic methods, his dislocations of chronology, his paradoxes and abstractions, and the like, do tend to drive the impatient reader through the narrative surface in search of the hard facts that seem to lie behind it; but this search is a mistake. Marlow's meditation is itself the hard fact of the story.[2]

The following discussion of the early Marlow tales (postponing Chance) will, then, have several purposes: to explore the identification between Conrad and Marlow and assess its importance; to examine the technical and thematic reasons for the use of Marlow, and for other features of the early Marlow stories which bear heavily on Conrad's artistic growth; and finally to perceive as clearly as possible the ethical commitments implicit in these works. Lord Jim and "Heart of Darkness," which represent the finest achievement of Conrad's early period, seem to end in paradox and dilemma; yet they sustain a core of affirmative meaning, and provide the philosophical and moral base from which the rest of his work must be viewed.

The early Marlow tales are of such importance, in fact, that all the work preceding them may be seen as a kind of prelude. In his exploration of the spiritual dilemmas of his early works,

[2] An occasional article stresses this point: see W. Y. Tindall, "Apology for Marlow," in R. C. Rathburn and M. Steinmann, Jr., eds., From Jane Austen to Joseph Conrad (Minneapolis: University of Minnesota Press, 1959), pp. 274–285, reprinted in Bruce Harkness, ed., Conrad's 'Heart of Darkness' and the Critics (San Francisco: Wadsworth, 1960), pp. 123–133; Raymond Gates Malbone, " 'How to Be': Marlow's Quest in Lord Jim," Twentieth Century Literature, X (January 1965), 172–180; and John Oliver Perry, "Action, Vision, or Voice: The Moral Dilemmas in Conrad's Tale-telling," Modern Fiction Studies, X (Spring 1964), 3–14. Limitations of space and context, however, usually preclude much development. One major critic who suggests its importance is Zabel, in his acknowledgment that Conrad's major contribution to modern fictional method is "his imposition of the processes and structures of the moral experience . . . on the form of the plot" (The Portable Conrad [New York: Viking, 1947], p. 26); but it is unclear whether Zabel would have been willing to view Marlow consistently as protagonist.

Conrad gradually writes his way toward Marlow: his protagonists grow steadily in stature as his awareness of the complexity of his central subject grows; and as he works toward a purer vision of this central moral core his techniques become more advanced also, so that even from the technical standpoint the early works may be said to exhibit the evolution of Marlow. Not until "Heart of Darkness" and *Lord Jim* does Conrad perfect the fictional rhetoric that will give free play to his meditative bent, and not until then does he fully test the rigidity and optimism of his moral presuppositions. Almayer commits simple folly, through avarice and ambition; Willems betrays his kind more subtly and under the impetus of a more nearly universal instinct; but both are easily condemned for it and made objects of satire. Only with Kurtz and Jim does Conrad approach what, in his special frame of reference, must be the final tragic irony—that a man of stature and self-consciously heroic intentions must nevertheless inhabit a world that will drive him to betrayal beyond his will, and hold him responsible for it. This early growth may be seen clearly, however, only in the light supplied by Marlow himself, and must therefore await the next chapter.

There is plenty of external evidence of the identity of Conrad and Marlow, most of it too well known to need repetition. Conrad's biographers acknowledge the point,[3] and Conrad insists upon it in his Author's Note: " 'Youth' is a feat of memory . . . a record of experience. . . . 'Heart of Darkness' is experience, too; but it is experience pushed a little (and only very little) beyond the actual facts of the case. . . . That sombre theme had to be given a sinister resonance, a tonality of its own, a continued vibration that, I hoped, would hang in the air and dwell on the

[3] G. Jean-Aubry, *The Sea Dreamer: A Definitive Biography of Joseph Conrad*, trans. by Helen Sebba (Garden City, N.Y.: Doubleday, 1957); Jocelyn Baines, *Joseph Conrad: A Critical Biography* (New York: McGraw-Hill, 1960); and other biographical sources provide information relating to the "factual" identity of Conrad and Marlow.

ear after the last note had been struck" (p. vii). Clearly, Conrad wished to take responsibility for the meditative and didactic components of Marlow's narratives, as well as their factual content. Zabel and others have observed that beyond any mere factual parallels between Conrad's life and works, the real *donnée* of his fiction is in any case always his own experience of physical and psychic distraction, so that the spiritual histories of his protagonists are never wholly imaginary. On these grounds alone, one would expect the mediating voice projected in the fiction to be, with whatever dramatic limitations, the meditative projection of Conrad himself. A variety of evidence confirms this expectation: Marlow's language and opinions tally so closely with Conrad's as to suggest a deliberate projection of the author into his character (significantly, the intellectual refinement Marlow undergoes between *Lord Jim* and *Chance* parallels Conrad's own growth during these years). A few examples from *Lord Jim* will suffice to show this point: Marlow's references to "a few simple notions you must cling to if you want to live decently" (p. 43) and to "fidelity to a certain standard of conduct" (p. 50), both closely duplicated in the well-known Preface to *A Personal Record*; his explanation that "I am trying to interpret for you into slow speech the instantaneous effect of visual impressions" (p. 48), so sharply reminiscent of the Preface to *The Nigger of the 'Narcissus'*; his repeated use of key words like "illusion" and "idea"; and the like.

That Marlow represented a major discovery for Conrad is suggested by the relative ease with which the early Marlow tales were written, once the inner narrator had been invented—a piece of Conrad's history sharply outlined by John D. Gordan in *Joseph Conrad: The Making of a Novelist*. As Conrad himself recalls in his Author's Note, he had begun *Lord Jim* as a short story about the *Patna* episode, and then, encountering difficulty after about twenty pages, had interrupted the novel to write "Youth" and "Heart of Darkness." Only after finishing these stories was he able to go ahead with the longer work; only then did he perceive "that the pilgrim ship episode was a good start-ing-point for a free and wandering tale" (*Lord Jim,* p. viii). The inference is inescapable that Marlow had come as an illumina-tion to Conrad: that the plastic possibility represented by an "oral" narrator had freed his tale from conventional rhetorical patterns, and *enabled* it to be "free and wandering." The varie-ties of emphasis made possible by such a narrator allowed Con-rad to escape his habitual redundancy, and forestalled the neces-sity for heavy cutting: "The corrections in the manuscript of *Lord Jim* [actually] enlarged the text"; and although the serial was carefully revised, as usual, for the first edition, Conrad seemed to feel that "the first edition was as perfect a text as he could achieve. The definitive edition differed from the first scarcely at all." [4] For such a persistent reviser as Conrad, this attitude was a notable change. And finally, all the Marlow tales involve such a variety of artifices tending to "justify" Marlow as a choral voice that the reader must suppose Conrad to have been deeply concerned in gaining the reader's trust for his inner narrator. Because Conrad's fiction cannot be properly understood without first assessing the framework of moral and philosophical ideas Marlow sets up, and because *Lord Jim* in particular cannot be understood without judging the propriety of Marlow's sub-mission to Stein, it is necessary to examine these choral devices carefully.

In general, the strategy of any author who has been deprived both of the formal choric elements of early drama (and their formal analogues, like the prologue and epilogue) and of the free authorial presence one finds in a novelist like, say, Trollope, is somehow to render dramatically the conditions of valid judg-ment—to establish, on behalf of some choral character, condi-tions which would normally, in nondramatic or nonnarrative contexts, persuade a listener of a speaker's objectivity and accu-racy. These conditions may be of two kinds—either the logical

---

[4] John Dozier Gordan, *Joseph Conrad: The Making of a Novelist* (Cambridge: Harvard University Press, 1940), pp. 156 ff.

conditions of valid judgment, like disinterestedness and native intelligence; or conditions external to the judgment which induce a reader to accept it, but may not necessarily be good reasons for doing so. In the work of writers with complex ethical and metaphysical commitments—Shakespeare is probably the supreme example—one finds an astonishing variety and range of choral devices and choral characters, and techniques for justifying them. From the Fool and Touchstone and Thersites and Mistress Quickly up through the social spectrum to Enobarbus and Kent and Horatio and the Archbishop of Canterbury, one finds characters and speeches wholly or partly choral, and in each case a subtle internal rhetoric to elicit (and, of course, also often to limit) the audience's affirmative response to them.

Moving away from an age of poetry and drama toward an age of prose narrative, away from a metaphysical substructure and a religious ethic toward a more naturalistic world-view and a secular ethic, one finds a steady diminution of the choric elements in both drama and fiction (this is a radical simplification of both intellectual and literary history, yet is accurate enough as a description of a broad central tendency). Novels which persist in having choral work done by the author himself may move sharply toward the pole of pure exposition, as for example *The Egoist*, which may be read as an extended illustration of Meredith's theory of comedy; or a straightforward thesis novel like *The Grapes of Wrath*, where a melodramatic and rhetorical structure is supplemented with expository chapters. At the other end of the scale may be the subtlest choral devices, like those used to justify the viewpoint of first-person narrators inside the frame of the novel, who may explicate symbolism, render judgments, and explore dramatic ironies; and who must often mark the limits of their judgment by restricting their own affirmations and involving themselves in paradoxes and dilemmas. The first chapter of *Moby-Dick*, from which so much of the book ultimately takes its meaning, is intimately concerned with validating the choral voice of Ishmael: an educated man who yet can rise

above the dry-land pedantries of mere schoolteaching; one motivated not by a desire for shipboard status or money, but rather by
high curiosity; an Old Testament wanderer and observer of men
whose first utterance has a prophetic intrusiveness; a man well-
versed in mariner's lore who can construct a careful inductive
argument justifying the sea as a source of symbolic truth—Ishmael is all these things and more, and the reader is willing to
follow him through the maze of *Moby-Dick* and study his cosmological and ethical asides with care, as clues to the book's total
meaning.

Ian Watt has remarked that some of Conrad's early lyrical
flights are like a Greek chorus, in their formal qualities and
placement. Holding out against the modern critical tendency to
seek the sharp image and eschew the abstract, Watt finds even
Conrad's purple prose a viable stylistic mode; and in any case, as
he says, Conrad's art may simply have demanded an occasional
chiaroscuro effect, the rhythmical abstract playing against the
disciplined concrete.[5] I find these analogies fascinating, and we
may perhaps go even further: if some passages of *The Nigger of
the 'Narcissus'* sound like a Greek chorus, some passages of
Almayer's Folly sound like *fin de siècle* lyrics disembodied from
any dramatic structure whatever. It really is not too fanciful to
say that in the early phase of his career Conrad recapitulates
some very broad tendencies in literary history, learning to write
increasingly organic works and to bring his moralistic impulses
under the protection of modern symbolic and rhetorical methods.
The final emergence of Marlow, at the end of this process,
enables both lyricist and chorus to pass into a fully internalized
choral voice; and Conrad is able for the first time to write novels
which are both contemporary and in the great ethical tradition of
English fiction.

Marlow is a housebroken Ishmael: like Ishmael, he is a seaman in a world where shipboard society is a symbol of all human

[5] Ian Watt, "Conrad Criticism and *The Nigger of the 'Narcissus,'*"
Nineteenth-Century Fiction, XII (March 1958), 262.

life; his motives are never commercial or merely prudential, but rather spiritual; he combines a learned vocabulary with the skepticism and irony of hard experience; he has voyaged alone to dark places and returned to tell the tale; and like Ishmael, he provides the reader a moral (and ultimately a metaphysical) framework for his tale. But it is only in terms of the imagery and the specific dramatic situations of Conrad's stories that one can see the force of these remarks.

The best place to begin any discussion of the Marlow stories is with the "frame" surrounding Marlow's own narrative, since it is here that Conrad makes his most concentrated effort to "justify" Marlow. An important feature of both "Youth" and "Heart of Darkness," for example, is the exact composition of Marlow's audience, and their reaction to his tale. In both cases, the audience represents a spectrum of social types and values; implicit in their appreciation of Marlow is an admission that his point of view somehow transcends their own partial ones. To brighten this spotlighting of Marlow and divert attention from the personalities of his auditors to their functions as representatives of a moral spectrum, Conrad refrains from giving them names: "the director had been a *Conway* boy, the accountant had served four years at sea, the lawyer—a fine crusted Tory, High Churchman, the best of old fellows, the soul of honour—had been chief officer in the P. & O. service in the good old days" (*Youth*, p. 3). Here, of course, "the man of finance, the man of accounts, the man of law" (p. 42) have the further status of having been seamen, so that their grudging nods of agreement with Marlow are even more significant; and their final acknowledgement of the meaning of his tale, as in the famous last sentence of "Heart of Darkness," acts as a powerful persuasion on the reader.

The frame narrator's descriptions of Marlow are significant in themselves, of course. In "Heart of Darkness," Marlow is first seen sitting "cross-legged right aft, leaning against the mizzenmast. He had sunken cheeks, a yellow complexion, a straight back, an ascetic aspect, and, with his arms dropped, the palms of hands outwards, resembled an idol" (p. 46); at the end, he is found once again "in the pose of a meditating Buddha" (p. 162). Some attempt has been made to read Marlow's experience in light of these Oriental suggestions; however valid this reading, Marlow is at least depicted as an unworldly and meditative figure in the highest sense—one whose posture contrasts sharply with that of the Director, standing in a nautical pose looking seaward; or the Lawyer, lying comfortably cushioned on deck; or the Accountant, toying with the mathematical bones from his domino box. Marlow's gaze is inward, his abstraction from the physical world complete; and his first speech ("And this also has been one of the dark places of the earth"—p. 48) emerges suddenly, as if conjoined with some silent meditation. The Oriental overtones, whatever else they do, grant Marlow a kind of wisdom more ancient than the Renaissance wisdom implicit in the frame narrator's rhapsody on the Thames, and set him apart from his thoroughly English audience. Marlow the bachelor, the wanderer, the uninvited guest, the seaman superior to his class —this is the teller-of-tales whose sensibility and involuted purity of judgment so intrigue and exasperate his auditors. The meaning of Marlow's stories, says the frame narrator of "Heart of Darkness," is like "one of these misty halos that sometimes are made visible by the spectral illumination of moonshine" (p. 48)—a piece of ironic diffidence on Conrad's part which suggests that the "adjectival vagueness" of parts of "Heart of Darkness" is intentional, and places those readers who object to that "vagueness" in the same class with Marlow's auditors: more accustomed to tales which have "a direct simplicity, the whole meaning of which lies within the shell of a cracked nut" (p. 48).

Lord Jim does not have a "frame" in the same sense, but uses similar techniques to justify Marlow. The rhetoric begins as soon as Marlow enters:

Jim's eyes, wandering in the intervals of his answers, rested upon a white man who sat apart from the others, with his face worn and clouded, but with quiet eyes that glanced straight, interested and clear. . . . The glance directed at him was not the fascinated stare of the others. It was an act of intelligent volition. . . .

And later on, many times, in distant parts of the world, Marlow showed himself willing to remember Jim, to remember him at length, in detail and audibly.

. . . With the very first word uttered Marlow's body, extended at rest in the seat, would become very still, as though his spirit had winged its way back into the lapse of time and were speaking through his lips from the past. (pp. 32–33)

Here are a surprising variety of implications: Marlow's vision is clear and intelligent, despite the wear of hard experience (itself, of course, a condition of sound judgment), and his memory firm and articulate; Jim is one of his favorite subjects, and a variety of audiences have applauded Marlow's account of him; Marlow strikes one immediately (even in moments of high personal crisis) as a man of superior perception; in telling his tale he is likely to go into a trancelike state suggestive of mediums, sleep-walkers, and other time-honored oracles of literature.

Symbolic overtones of this kind are reinforced throughout Marlow's tale, especially in its first twenty or thirty pages—establishing firmly not only most of the logical conditions of sound judgment, but certain extralogically persuasive circumstances as well. Marlow's fitness as a spiritual counselor, for example (the counselor of his audience, as much as of Jim), is attested not only by the universal effort of other men to unload their troubles on him, but also, and more importantly, by his self-confessed knowledge of his own inner darkness. Ironically, he bemoans "the kind of thing that by devious, unexpected, truly diabolical ways causes me to run up against men with soft spots, with hard spots, with hidden plague spots, by Jove! and loosens their tongues at the sight of me for their infernal confidences; as though, forsooth, I had no confidences to make to myself, as though—God help me!—I didn't have enough confidential information about myself to harrow my own soul till the end of my appointed time" (p. 34). Marlow's descriptions of waterfront society display a keen power of observation, and his irony here suggests the skeptical manner which is itself a condition of truth (or more accurately, like the ironic manner generally, is persuasive because it implies both a subtlety of intellect and a resistance to facile commitment). In still another passage—we are still in the first eight or ten pages of Marlow's narrative—Marlow suggests a further reason for his own authority:

There are times when a man must act as though life were equally sweet in any company. I've known such a time, and, what's more, I shan't now pretend to pull a long face over my necessity, because a good many of that bad company from want of moral—moral—what shall I say?—posture, or from some other equally profound cause, were twice as instructive and twenty times more amusing than the usual respectable thief of commerce you fellows ask to sit at your table without any real necessity—from habit, from cowardice, from good-nature, from a hundred sneaking and inadequate reasons. (p. 41)

And finally, of course, in speaking here with the Fool's privileged tongue, and reviling the values and understanding of his auditors, Marlow assumes the choral authority of the wholly dissociated voice. In sum, the early Marlow tales hold their narrator out as a trustworthy spiritual guide, one whose judgment about his own experiences is likely to be both subtle and sound, and whose irony, perversity, and "evasiveness," where they do exist, represent essential hesitations in the face of profound dilemmas. Marlow's increasing flexibility from "Youth" to "Heart of Darkness" to Lord Jim, and the growing subtlety of choral techniques in these works, illustrate the facility with which Conrad learned from practical experiment, even when his works were spaced closely together. And in Marlow's very character and narrative habits lies much of the meaning of the early fiction.

To acknowledge the choral authority of Marlow, however, is to take only a first step toward defining his full esthetic function.

It is commonly observed that Marlow allows Conrad "freedom of presence" and provides the focal center of a single consciousness for bringing together diverse materials; and the great craftsman Henry James admired simply the amount of "doing" Marlow made possible: a "prolonged hovering flight of the subjective over the outstretched ground of the case exposed." [6] But two further points, I think, are more important: first, that Marlow allows Conrad an efficient means of fulfilling some of his basic esthetic aims; and second, that by placing the narrating consciousness within a larger framework, Conrad was able for the first time to draw attention to the primary object of interest in his early fiction—the *processes* of moral discovery and self-exploration. This latter point explains, in fact, why Marlow so frequently withholds his judgment, or contradicts himself, or indulges in ironies at his own expense: his moral knowledge and knowledge of himself are continually expanding, so that while each stage of his awareness, with its element of judgment, is warranted at the time, the later stages revise and supersede the earlier. Marlow's self-contradictions and hesitations thus constitute an assertion of the possibility of spiritual growth, and in that assertion lies much of the affirmative meaning of "Heart of Darkness" and *Lord Jim*.

Any discussion of Conrad's early esthetic aims must of course begin with the famous Preface to *The Nigger of the 'Narcissus'*, not only because it is Conrad's most extended theoretical discussion of his own aims, but because its date makes it especially important for any analysis of the earlier fiction. There is no need to dwell on this familiar document, but two points do need to be recalled: first, that art must make its basic appeal through the senses; and second, that it must somehow reveal the inner truth of the experience thus sensuously recorded. Fiction must "aspire to the plasticity of sculpture, to the colour of painting, and to the magic suggestiveness of music. . . . By the power of the written

[6] Henry James, "The New Novel, 1914," in *Notes on Novelists* (New York: Scribner's, 1914), p. 348.

word to make you hear, to make you feel . . . before all, to make you *see*" (pp. ix–x). This assertion must in the first place be taken literally; the preponderantly visual imagery of Conrad's work would be enough to confirm it, even without the existence of similar remarks in his letters and elsewhere. Gordan underscores the importance of the visual sense to Conrad when he tells of Conrad's continual effort to visualize his own material—by forcing Mrs. Conrad to act out scenes, for example, or by drawing pictures of his own characters and settings: Nina Almayer in red and black ink, or a detailed floor plan of Doña Rita's house.[7] At the same time, Conrad's intentions are obviously not those of a documentary realist: "To snatch . . . a passing phase of life, is only the beginning of the task. The task . . . is to hold up unquestioningly, without choice and without fear, the rescued fragment before all eyes in the light of a sincere mood. It is to show its vibration, its colour, its form; and through its movement, its form, and its colour, reveal the substance of its truth—disclose its inspiring secret: the stress and passion within the core of each convincing moment" (p. x). Like Maupassant, "a great artist, who sees the essential in everything,"[8] Conrad is concerned with the symbolic qualities of experience. To this end he makes use not only of color, form, and movement; but also shifts of perspective, stylistic and tonal variations, conjunctions of disparate experiences, and innumerable other devices. And all of these devices are made easier by the presence of Marlow, who can stand as mediator between the reader and a range of physical fact, elicit and define its meanings, and finally communicate an experience which is both perceptual and meditative. The situations Marlow observes cannot finally be judged apart from the symbolic construction he gives them, since it is precisely that evocation of meaning which is Conrad's primary purpose.

No one really knows how Conrad took the idea that some

[7] Gordan, *Joseph Conrad*, pp. 105–106.

[8] G. Jean-Aubry, *Joseph Conrad: Life and Letters* (Garden City, N.Y.: Doubleday, Page, 1927), I, p. 265.

"rescued fragment" of life might hold a substantial truth or "inspiring secret" independent of the "truth" arbitrarily given it by the artist. It is a commonplace of Conrad criticism that he was in some sense a symbolist, and that the Preface is a kind of personal manifesto (perhaps stimulated by his annoyance at being lumped with the more genuinely "impressionistic" Stephen Crane [9]). But the whole question of "symbolism" is obscure and difficult. In writers with transcendental leanings the symbolism of physical fact is supposed in some sense to be "objective"; other writers may create a world of symbols which is consciously arbitrary. Conrad appears neither so theoretical as the one nor so private as the other; it is usually possible, in fact, to analyze the overtones of his descriptive passages into their components of connotation, abstract statement, conscious analogy, and the like.[10] He seems sometimes to suggest that the symbolic rendering of experience is the simple *fiat* of the observer, as when he remarks again of Maupassant that "he thinks sufficiently to concrete his fearless conclusions in illuminative instances" (*Notes on Life and Letters*, p. 31);[11] and the conscious artifice of much of his later work, in which he has passed beyond symbolism to allegory, is obvious. But when a novelist feels the need to theorize about his mimetic object, important issues may be at stake; and it is best to proceed with caution in summarizing his ideas.

In the course of a recent (and brilliant) chapter on Conrad,[12]

[9] Bruce Johnson, "Joseph Conrad and Crane's *Red Badge of Courage*," *Papers of the Michigan Academy of Science, Arts, and Letters*, XLVIII (1963), 649–655.

[10] Watt, "Conrad Criticism and *The Nigger of the 'Narcissus,'* " explores some related issues. I agree with Watt that in this phase of his career Conrad's symbolism is generally "exoteric," and his thematic roots ethical, rather than "mythical."

[11] Baines offers a shrewd and concise summary of the French influences on Conrad (*Joseph Conrad*, pp. 144–148).

[12] J. Hillis Miller, *Poets of Reality: Six Twentieth-Century Writers* (Cambridge, Mass.: Belknap Press, 1965), pp. 13–67.

J. Hillis Miller suggests that what Conrad may have wanted his readers to "see" was some field of reality beyond the merely illusive, the perceptually habitual or metaphorically conventional ranges of sensory objects to which they were accustomed: for Miller, ultimately, the "darkness," since he sees Conrad chiefly as an exponent of modern nihilism (a suggestion to which we must return later). Without putting the point entirely in terms of this dark transcendentalism, it is certainly possible to discriminate between the symbolic use of concretes and Conrad's effort to render sensory experience so precisely that it gives rise to its own strange intuitions and emotional nuances. I have wanted, by and large, to avoid questions of ontology except where they bear very directly on unusual aspects of Conrad's diction, or on his characters' struggles to record reality; and for this reason I have used the word "symbolic" so broadly as to include both Miller's kind of "seeing" and the more traditional ways of extracting meaning from, or instilling meaning in, sensory descriptions. But the distinction is important in any assessment of Conrad's place in the development of modern literature, and it may be that despite his later allegorical methods, Conrad's primary esthetic is founded on the kind of metaphysical, if not moral, nihilism that Miller finds in his work.

In any case, transferring the burden of a symbolic reading to Marlow tends to obviate some of this question. The reader can grant the reality of Marlow's experience, and assent to his conclusions, and even accept the symbolic language in which he communicates that experience, without being forced to accept the objective validity of his symbolism, as if the meanings he attached to things inhered in them independently of his own reflection, and might be apprehended by any sensitive observer. The reader can grant the symbolic process, in other words, without committing himself to any single symbolic system or ontological premise. Without an internal narrator, on the other hand, the intuitive or interpretative component of the narrative must seem arbitrary; existing side by side with unquestionable sensory reports, it seems to claim the same inflexible objectivity. Much of the excessively "romantic" or exotic cast of Conrad's early work is the result of his effort to create symbolic moods and overtones by a kind of sly hinting-around in the imagery. And since, as Gordan has shown, Conrad was greatly concerned with excising redundancies and prolix passages of analysis in his early work, more of the burden of meditative meaning was thrown onto natural description than it could persuasively carry.[13] But put the whole story in quotation marks and hand it over to an internal narrator, and the tale itself becomes an object of perception, so that no matter how fanciful Marlow may become, the fundamental criterion of realism is never violated. The efficiency of getting from fact to meaning is considerably increased by this method: Marlow not only can be prolix and redundant; he can cajole the reader with argument, make mistakes, reinterpret a part of his experience, employ irony at the reader's expense, use the "as if" construction and confess his own whimsy—in short, build up the symbolic structure in any number of ways that would seem mere perversity or uncertainty of control in an "omniscient" author. As has already been pointed out, Conrad felt far less need to revise the Marlow stories than the earlier ones. And when one thinks of chapters like "Cetology" and "The Whiteness of the Whale" in *Moby-Dick*, the analogy between Marlow and Ishmael is once again illuminating.

Less important, perhaps, but just as noticeable to the reader who has been exposed to the romantic excesses of Conrad's earlier style, is still another advantage Marlow gives Conrad: a sort of colloquial freedom that enables Conrad to capture very directly the symbolic qualities of an immediate sensory experience. Take for example a brief passage from "Youth," whose style is often excessively lyrical (wherever Conrad is interested in generating the ironic sentimentality that gives the story its peculiar flavor), but is elsewhere remarkably plastic to the inno-

---

[13] Gordan, *Joseph Conrad,* pp. 116 ff.

cent experience of the young Marlow. Here is how the older Marlow describes part of a harbor scene near the beginning of his tale: "The steam-colliers were going in and out in the darkness with their lights burning bright, a great plashing of propellers, rattling of winches, and a lot of hailing on the pier-heads" (p. 8). The words gather lyric force both by their controlled alliteration and by the mere denotative strengths of the words themselves—the sharp contrast between darkness and light that is always an important kind of image in Conrad, and forceful kinesthetic and sound words like "burning," "plashing," and "rattling." At the same time, the series is so constructed that its affirmative quality is gradually undercut by an increasing incertitude as to exactly what is being perceived: the steam-colliers with their bright lights and plashing propellers are clearly visible and audible, but the grammatical subjects of "rattling" are lost in the darkness, and both the subjects and objects of "hailing" disappear, so that the verbal stands out alone in a somewhat unnatural construction, just as the disembodied shouting itself does in the boy's experience. The sentence is precisely true to the young protagonist's "seeing," yet its syntactical mysteries foreshadow the antiromantic discoveries to follow. Small subtleties of this kind do not yield easily to heavy analytic equipment, but they do illustrate the sensory "rightness" made possible by the flexibility of Marlow's "oral" style.

These brief technical considerations serve merely to reinforce what should be clear in any case from the broad masses and structures of the Marlow tales themselves: that the reader ought to focus his attention on Marlow's consciousness rather than on the physical events he reports. In all the works in which he appears (even *Chance*), Marlow is protagonist; his narrative is not merely an impressionistic rendering of the artistic object, it *is* the object: a meditative projection of remembered experience in a morally significant pattern. Whether he is recounting his own history or someone else's, Marlow repeatedly calls attention to his narrative as a symbolic construct, and tries continually to give the most precise definition to his own states of mind. In a later story, "The Secret Sharer," where the symbolism is so closely structured as to be nearly allegorical, almost everyone has seen that the drama is the psychic drama of the narrator. The same holds true of the early Marlow tales, and considerable insight can be gained by keeping the point in mind.

Albert Guerard uses the excellent word "psycho-moral" to specify the sort of spiritual conflict Conrad's early fiction dramatizes, a term which places proper emphasis on the moral center of Conrad's early consciousness, while recognizing the psychological complexity of the issues with which his work deals. The ultimate issues for Conrad are those conflicts recognized and resolved only in the depths of self-understanding; even to recognize them constitutes a spiritual growth. It follows that his protagonists, or the symbolic figures present to his narrators' awareness—the Marlows, Jims, Kurtzes, Heysts—are usually men of superior sensitivity, capable of a growth in self-understanding. Committed to some course of worldly action, or observing it, they discover in themselves a complexity of motivation and responsibility they had not initially been aware of. And the judgment of inferior men upon their behavior (or upon the behavior of those they observe) is inevitably partial and insensitive. In its lowest form, this exterior judgment assumes the character of total hostility. The hotelkeeper Schomberg, with his Teutonic density of perception, is the most obvious example; here Conrad is reduced to a satirical portrait only occasionally relieved by milder ironies or touches of pathos. One of Marlow's most important jobs is to provide a focal point for these incomplete assessments of figures like Jim and Kurtz, and to synthesize and transcend them. As will be shown, this process gives certain parts of *Lord Jim* a surprisingly orderly rhetorical structure.

Self-understanding is no mere matter of solemn reasoning or visceral realism for Conrad, however; his moral universe is Swiftian, with Yahoos like Schomberg and Chester and Verloc to be scorned equally with the advocates of a utopian idealism. Conrad's mistrust of facile theorizing, especially of a social-idealistic kind, permeates his work, revealing itself not only in explicit statements and in the satire of such works as *The Secret Agent*, but inadvertently in many passages of imagery as well. Marlow's moral discoveries, and Kurtz's, and Heyst's, depend far less on intelligence than on a direct confrontation of inner truths reflected in outward circumstances; it is this feature of Conrad's work that makes Zabel's term "recognition" so appropriate, and the methods of symbolism, in the broad sense specified earlier, so congenial to Conrad. If Conrad's work is finally affirmative, it is in spite of, or perhaps ultimately because of, the darkness of man's motives and of his reason.

A skepticism toward human understanding is common enough, of course, in "naturalistic" fiction, and Conrad's early work shows other affinities with naturalism, in a loose, nontheoretical form. It is partly this conscious development of metaphysical background, in fact, which makes *Lord Jim* important not only as the best of Conrad's early novels, but as a central document in understanding the development of his later fiction; for many of the ideas implicit in the early Marlovian universe emerge more consciously and more centrally in works like *Chance* and *Victory*. Jim's dilemma aboard the *Patna* is at once universalized and made infinitely more complex than any formal Court of Inquiry might comprehend, by the book's early descriptive passages:

Every morning the sun, as if keeping pace in his revolutions with the progress of the pilgrimage, emerged with a silent burst of light exactly at the same distance astern of the ship, caught up with her at noon, pouring the concentrated fire of his rays on the pious purposes of the men, glided past on his descent, and sank mysteriously into the sea evening after evening, preserving the same distance ahead of her advancing bows . . . and a faint hum, a low murmur of sad voices, alone revealed the presence of a crowd of people upon the great blaze of the ocean. Such were the days, still, hot, heavy,

disappearing one by one into the past, as if falling into an abyss for
ever open in the wake of the ship; and the ship, lonely under a wisp
of smoke, held on her steadfast way black and smouldering in a
luminous immensity, as if scorched by a flame flicked at her from a
heaven without pity. (p. 16)[14]

Placed in a position of supreme responsibility toward a human
cargo in an indifferent universe, Jim discovers the fundamental
paradox of moral responsibility. Hidden in night's "benediction,"
in its geometrical perfection and hardness and coldness—qualities which give Jim, as they are later to give the narrator of "The
Secret Sharer," a conviction of peace and rational control—lies
the sunken derelict which strikes the *Patna* from beneath the
sea's surface and introduces an endless chain of serpent-imagery
into Marlow's account. Like Kurtz, Jim is victim of a weakness
and symbol of a guilt which are universal: "From weakness
unknown, but perhaps suspected, as in some parts of the world
you suspect a deadly snake in every bush—from weakness that
may lie hidden . . . repressed or maybe ignored more than half a
lifetime, not one of us is safe" (p. 43). These dimensions of Jim's
dilemma help to give Stein's puzzling "destructive element" its
meaning, and grant Jim some of his symbolic stature.

Symbolic stature is not moral stature, however; and no reader
of *Lord Jim* can evade some well-worn questions: What is the
precise quality of Jim's guilt, and does he or does he not redeem

[14] The sea is of course a microcosm for Conrad. Marlow draws the
analogy in "Youth," when he speaks of "the fellowship of the craft, which
no amount of enthusiasm for yachting, cruising, and so on can give, since
one is only the amusement of life and the other is life itself" (p. 3). But
even this very natural aspect of Conrad's symbolic system took some time
to emerge into consciousness, and was not really explicit until the *Nigger*
and "Youth." Thereafter much of his fiction is built upon it—notably
Lord Jim, Chance, "The Secret Sharer," and *The Shadow-Line*—and the
reader is always well advised to be alert to it: *Nostromo,* for example,
which is no sea story, nevertheless draws its title from a shore figure who
supervises transactions between land and sea, and whose experience may
be seen partly in those terms.

himself on Patusan? Or more exactly, how are Marlow's concepts of moral heroism, of guilt and fidelity and responsibility to
the human community, made more profound by his study of
Jim's case? To answer these questions requires an analysis of
some crucial passages and value-structures in Lord Jim. But by
way of anticipating some key ideas, one may just point out, first,
that if the deepest premise of Lord Jim (and "Heart of Darkness" as well) is a kind of metaphysical pessimism, its final
conclusion is spiritually affirmative; and second, that the values
which survive the agonizing test of Marlow's identification with
Jim and Kurtz are essentially individual and prepolitical—un-
shakable duties toward the human community at large, rather
than the moral implications of some social ideal.

It will be necessary in Chapters 3 and 4 to develop this last
point in some detail; for it is important to see that in Nostromo
Conrad enters a new moral field. Jim's social policies on Patusan
—the ideas and values he brings to the arbitration of neighborly
disputes, and the like—are simply extensions of prepolitical
virtues; similarly, although the outer perimeter of "Heart of
Darkness" is defined by a notion of civilized advance in the
service of political ideals, the core of its meaning is in Kurtz's
subcivic reversion to savagery, and the terms of Marlow's experience in the end become such prepolitical terms as "truth" and
"illusion." The conscious parallels with descents into hell and
the Oriental overtones take the reader instantly beneath the
mere historical surface of the Congo exploration; and the story is
freed from the dilemmas of social idealism by tactics which
render its key figures supranational: Marlow is set apart from his
English audience, Kurtz and the Harlequin are politically synthetic. The same device is found in Lord Jim: the cargo of
pilgrims undertake their voyage on a ship "owned by a Chinaman, chartered by an Arab, and commanded by a sort of rene-
gade New South Wales German" (p. 14). As Marlow says of
Jim and Gentleman Brown, facing each other finally across a

muddy creek-bed in Patusan, they stand "on the opposite poles of that conception of life which includes all mankind" (p. 381).

The precise quality of the spiritual affirmation in Conrad's early fiction is of course notoriously difficult to define. Most of Conrad's critics have accepted the idea of his "evasiveness"; and Zabel and others have related this to his technical performance: "The devices he employed—the time-shift, the plot-inversion and dislocation, the repetition of motifs, the use of interlocutors and other agencies for realistic and analytical observation, his highly specialized use of indirection . . . seem to have originated in profoundly habitual, deeply ingrained, almost incurably obsessional tendencies of his character." Even so, Zabel finds Conrad able to sustain a core of affirmation: "The nature of illusion is probed, the residue of truth is sublimated, the operations of intelligence and consciousness are tested, until finally, out of that vaporous haze of skepticism . . . a hard irreducible center of moral certitude and human conviction is arrived at." [15] But Albert Guerard, probably the most brilliant and influential of the critics, sees Conrad's indirection and complexity as founded ultimately on a set of inward conflicts that made affirmation impossible: a conviction that ethical matters are simple, coupled with an extraordinary awareness of ethical complexities; a strong idealism, coupled with a distrust of idealism; an ironic skepticism, coupled with a fear of the intellect; an introspective drive toward the unconscious, coupled with a distrust of the unconscious; a fidelity to the individual, coupled with a fidelity to the law which so often is at odds with the individual.

As has been suggested, however, Conrad's technical indirections may also be seen as legitimate extensions of meaning, and many of his apparent conflicts are resolved in a higher synthesis of moral attitudes. The duty of the individual, given the human community and the enigmatic universe it inhabits, is not a very

[15] Zabel, ed., The Portable Conrad, pp. 32, 38.

difficult matter, since it rests on adherence to the "few very simple ideas" which are in themselves so plain as to be almost platitudinous; but fulfilling these duties, given the depth of circumstance and psychological force the moral agent may face, is tremendously complex, leading ultimately to the dilemma-ridden opposition of duty and survival. Again, a mistrust of political and social idealism is not only consistent with, but ultimately founded on, a commitment to the moral status of the individual —far from being in "conflict," these two attitudes are closely congruent. Correlatively, a fidelity to law—the conservative law of the Western liberal tradition—is an essential part of the belief in the moral dignity of the individual, since the law exists to preserve the *status quo* against authoritarian idealisms, and to guarantee a social framework in which the free moral agent can operate. A consideration of logical types will remove any notion that Conrad's "fear" of the intellect is somehow inconsistent with his own intellectualized skepticism. ("It is impossible to know anything," Conrad remarks jocularly in one of his letters, "tho' it is possible to believe a thing or two." [16]) And finally, Conrad's introspective drive toward the subrational sources of his own being—the direction of such stories as "Heart of Darkness" and "The Secret Sharer"—is no doubt laden with mistrust, as well as fear, anxiety, disbelief, and other forms of civilized resistance to premoral forces, exactly the sort of resistance Marlow often finds in his audiences. The "evasiveness" in such stories is not a way of obscuring their meaning, and need not be seen as anything "obsessional"; it is more exactly an essential part of the meaning. "The Secret Sharer," which dramatizes the transcendence of such conflict, is accordingly far less "evasive" in its techniques.[17]

[16] Aubry, *Life and Letters,* I, p. 208.

[17] A highly informed study of Conrad's power of affirmation is Ian Watt, "Joseph Conrad: Alienation and Commitment," in H. S. Davies and George Watson, eds., *The English Mind* (Cambridge: At the University Press, 1964), pp. 257–278. Watt's article analyzes Conrad's commitment to "solidarity" as a counterbalance to the alienation of the

Conrad's "conflicts," then, may more usefully be seen as elements of a complex affirmation whose ultimate bearing is moral or critical. So long as they are understood as part of the fiction's meaning, and not as prior psychological conditions which cause an otherwise mysterious technical performance, it is useful to acknowledge them. But it is a mistake to view them as obstacles for Conrad; at most, his reservations would have made creation difficult only until he had found the form and dramatic situation that would enable him to articulate them and examine their sources; and that appears to have been exactly what happened with the discovery of Marlow.

J. Hillis Miller's recent discussion of Conrad as an exponent of "modern perspectivism and nihilism" [18] is perhaps the most instructive study of Conrad's struggle to sustain some sort of spiritual affirmation, and of the fragmentation of point of view and the breakdown of denotative language resulting from that struggle. For present purposes, however, we need to discriminate between kinds of nihilism. Even if Conrad is, as Miller argues, a metaphysical nihilist, finding only a pervasive "darkness" behind illusive appearances, he still is not an ethical nihilist. As Conrad well knew, the tale-teller's clarification of meanings, even dark meanings, is a small advance over futility. And even the relativist who proclaims himself the measure of all things must presuppose a reality worth measuring and an activity of valuation significant in itself. Conrad manages a bit more than this—a simple, com-

---

modern mind. Watt is not concerned to trace the exact terms in which Conrad focused either his skepticism or his moral response, but it should be pointed out that "solidarity" implies an acceptance of those notorious "few very simple ideas" which form the core of Conrad's ethical beliefs.

[18] Miller, *Poets of Reality*, p. 6. Like all studies which take metaphysical themes as primary in Conrad, Miller's slightly distorts the intentions of individual works. But he clarifies most of the important concepts and motifs in Conrad: darkness and light, form and chaos, the relation between "reality" and language, and the like; and his chapter is an excellent Introduction for the reader in need of an anchor among the changing tides of Conrad criticism.

munally oriented, and broadly "existential" ethical response to "darkness." Conrad refines and clarifies this response as his career develops: from *Lord Jim's* paradoxical romantic-realism to the allegorized existential response of the later work, in which Conrad's symbolism is sufficiently mixed and ironic to negate any single cosmological language, but structured so as to sustain a simple prepolitical ethos. It may be that Conrad's black metaphysics gives him his significance in modern literature, and that he *ought* not to have kept referring to positive human values, knowing what he knew about the impossibility of final truths; but Conrad persistently refused to acquiesce, and it is the ethical themes, ultimately, that unify his fiction. A study which proposes to examine the growth of Conrad's central themes and techniques must accordingly focus on the psycho-moral explorations of Marlow and Conrad's other protagonists, and set the broader philosophic question aside.

What, then, does Marlow make of Jim, as a moral case? And what aspects of the novel's technique are made more exciting by a full awareness of Marlow's purpose? The first thing to stress, surely, is that whatever the particular dimensions of Jim's existence—and they are spiritually complex—he is, in those dimensions, a superior being, elevated through the rhetorical exaggeration surrounding him, and through Marlow's perception of his abnormal capacity for idealistic achievement and idealistic folly. To see Jim and Kurtz as alienated from humanity, or merely pathological, is wholly to invert their characters; for the truth is that they are grand projections of weaknesses and strengths shared by all men. As with Kurtz, Marlow gradually identifies with Jim, and stresses repeatedly that Jim is "one of us." And because Jim is so clearly a symbolic figure in Marlow's meditation, and not a realistically drawn character, any psychological approach, as if Jim were a case history of neurotic egoism or immaturity, must subordinate itself to the meanings Marlow finds in his story. Marlow himself warns the reader of the inadequacy of the "normal" frame of reference in judging Jim; and any reader who would simply condemn him adopts a view as partial and as limited as a Chester or a Brierly or a Schomberg. The question is not what the reader, peering through Marlow's haze of cigar smoke and irony, will make of Jim, but rather what, finally, Marlow makes of Jim. And the answer, very broadly, is that although Marlow does comment irritably on Jim's egoism, and does identity his idealism with romantic innocence and immaturity, he perceives at the same time the symbolic validity of such idealism. This ambivalence toward Jim defines in dramatic and concretely meditative form, in fact, precisely the paradoxes expressed more abstractly by Stein.[19]

It is this final quality of paradox and ambivalence which leads Marlow to say, at the end of the oral portion of his tale, that he sees Jim standing at "the heart of a vast enigma . . . a tiny white speck, that seemed to catch all the light left in a darkened world" (p. 336). And Marlow's response to Jewel's reiterated analysis of Jim's motives—" 'you always leave us—for your own ends' " (p. 348)—furnishes a key to the breadth and depth of that enigma: "She had said he had been driven away from her by a dream,—and there was no answer one could make her—there seemed to be no forgiveness for such a transgression. And yet is not mankind itself, pushing on its blind way, driven by a dream of its

---

[19] A variety of external evidence shows Conrad's own positive attitude toward Jim. His textual revisions suggest an effort to win sympathy for Jim, without sacrificing the character's essential romantic weakness; and he gives Jim several of his own experiences and habits (see Gordan, *Joseph Conrad*, pp. 59, 169–172). Bernard C. Meyer, M.D., *Joseph Conrad: A Psychoanalytic Biography* (Princeton: Princeton University Press, 1967), pp. 61 ff., gives further evidence of Conrad's identification with Jim. Source studies by Gordan, Jerry Allen, Norman Sherry, and others have shown that Jim was probably modeled on two or three real-life figures of considerable stature and achievement. Baines, *Joseph Conrad*, pp. 252–255, gives a brief summary of sources for *Lord Jim;* Sherry's more recent *Conrad's Eastern World* (Cambridge: At the University Press, 1966) is the most comprehensive treatment.

greatness and its power upon the dark paths of excessive cruelty and of excessive devotion?" (pp. 349–350). Jim's dilemma is thus set finally at the center of all human endeavor.

It is easy to assemble passages underscoring Jim's stature: "He was like a figure set up on a pedestal, to represent in his persistent youth the power, and perhaps the virtues, of races that never grow old, that have emerged from the gloom" (p. 265); "the mystery of his attitude got hold of me as though he had been an individual in the forefront of his kind, as if the obscure truth involved were momentous enough to affect mankind's conception of itself" (p. 93); and the like. But more interesting are the simple narrative devices Conrad uses to this same end. During the inquiry into the *Patna* episode, for example, "complete strangers would accost each other familiarly, just for the sake of easing their minds on the subject: every confounded loafer in the town came in for a harvest of drinks over this affair: you heard of it in the harbour office, at every ship-broker's, at your agent's, from whites, from natives, from half-castes, from the very boatmen squatting half-naked on the stone steps as you went up—by Jove!" (p. 36). The Oriental case-of-law that counterpoints Marlow's first meeting with Jim is a case of "fear" and "falsehood," thus duplicating on a more trivial level precisely the moral vectors of Jim's own case. The very persistence of the *Patna* story in Eastern seaports attests to its symbolic quality, until finally terms like "legend" and "myth" begin to enter Marlow's account, and he hears from the Patusan fisher-folk that "the tide had turned two hours before its time" (p. 242) to help Jim reach his destination.

Jim's romantic success on Patusan parallels Kurtz's abominable success at the other end of the moral spectrum; both occur in an isolated and morally primitive setting, and both elevate their creators to near-supernatural status. Just as Kurtz exaggerates his lusts and his hellish kingship of ivory, so Jim exalts his sense of honor and his Lordship over the natives. Each finds in his isolation the chance to assert and expand some set of normal human impulses, and to perform on a scale not permitted to ordinary mortals; and thus, while it is important to see that they retain their essential humanity, they also become mythic or symbolic for those who view them. If Kurtz in the Congo finds his way to the heart of darkness, and sees finally the horror of his own savagery, Jim conversely finds his way to the heart of romance, with its beatific illusions: "With every instant he was penetrating deeper into the impossible world of romantic achievements. He got to the heart of it at last! A strange look of beatitude overspread his features, his eyes sparkled. . . . He had penetrated to the very heart—to the very heart. It was an ecstatic smile that your faces—or mine either—will never wear, my dear boys" (pp. 83–84). It is of course precisely the dark amorality of mankind—that aspect of the destructive element represented not only by Jim's uncontrollable fear aboard the *Patna* but also by his double Gentleman Brown—that does Jim in. Attention to the diction Marlow uses in describing these dark forces and feelings will underscore the point: a "horror" in Jim's weakness, "spectral horror" and "corruption" in the old Chief Engineer with his pink toads, a hint of "secret abominations" in the *Patna*'s crew's behavior, and so on; terms so crucially significant in "Heart of Darkness" that they can hardly be accidental here. Conrad's protagonists explore different regions of reality, but they move in the same universe of darkness and light; and taken together they dramatize something like the existential dilemma which has been said to characterize the experience of modern man: they are absolutists in an enigmatic world which permits only passing and partial triumphs.

Lord Jim is the end of a process of moral inquiry for Conrad. The romantic sensibility with which he had begun in *Almayer's Folly* has by this time been severely eroded: the pure idealism of a Jim, however heroic, has been acknowledged as unviable; and the final sad wave of Stein's hand at his butterflies is a final relinquishment, for Conrad, of that species of romanticism. The symbolic method itself tends to yield dialectical oppositions (be-

tween butterflies and beetles, for example) rather than solutions.
But there is, as Zabel says, a hard diminished core of conclusion
remaining in Conrad, even after the destructive enigmas of Jim
and Kurtz have been recorded. The terms in which Marlow
himself records this response are usually the symbolic terms of
Jim's particular history, and are usually woven together with a
narrative thread. Hence the reader, like Marlow, must turn to
Stein for a more abstract choral statement. As other writers have
pointed out, Stein is a Renaissance man, a godlike figure created
nowhere else in Conrad's fiction; this hyperbolical character, as
well as the extraordinarily artificial framework in which Marlow
places him and his incredible thumbnail biography, provide precisely the one-step-more away from realism Conrad needs to
highlight his choral function. The Stein episode occasionally
seems absurd simply because Conrad makes a too-conscious effort
to spotlight Stein's formulation in such a way that it will not get
lost in Marlow's more prolix and circling meditation. Having
been carefully "justified" as a choral figure himself, Marlow
passes this status on to Stein (who is, by the way, the only choral
commentator Marlow encounters in *Lord Jim* whom he has to
seek; all the others he meets by chance). Stein's "intelligent good
nature," "his massive and lofty forehead" and "student's face,"
his "resolute searching glance" (cp. Marlow at the Court of
Inquiry), his "intrepidity of spirit" and "physical courage," all
qualify him as final choral authority in *Lord Jim* (pp. 202–203);
and the biographical parallels between his own life and Jim's life
guarantee the "recognition" of Jim that Marlow must win
through more extended rhetorical methods. Most important of
all, perhaps, in view of the metaphysics implicit in *Lord Jim*'s
early descriptive passages and occasionally more abstractly in
Marlow's asides—Stein is a naturalist, who considers man an
"amazing" specimen, and who reappears in the last sentence of
the book, among his butterfly cases.

All this choral distancing has another advantage, of course: it
enables Marlow to examine Stein's paradoxes without being

attacked by his hearers, since he is merely reporting the mysterious wisdom of a higher voice. On the level of plot, Stein gives Jim his new chance on Patusan. On another level, he offers Marlow a philosophical resolution of Jim's problem:

"Yes! Very funny this terrible thing is. A man that is born falls into a dream like a man who falls into the sea. If he tries to climb out into the air as inexperienced people endeavour to do, he drowns—*nicht war?* . . . No! I tell you! The way is to the destructive element submit yourself, and with the exertions of your hands and feet in the water make the deep, deep sea keep you up. So if you ask me—how to be?"

His voice leaped up extraordinarily strong, as though away there in the dusk he had been inspired by some whisper of knowledge. "I will tell you! For that, too, there is only one way."

But here, at the crux of the matter,

the austere exaltation of a certitude seen in the dusk vanished from his face. The hand that had been pointing at my breast fell, and by-and-by, coming a step nearer, he laid it gently on my shoulder. There were things, he said mournfully, that perhaps could never be told. . . . "And yet it is true—it is true. In the destructive element immerse." . . . He spoke in a subdued tone, without looking at me, one hand on each side of his face. "That was the way. To follow the dream, and again to follow the dream—and so—*ewig—usque ad finem.* . . ." (pp. 214–215)

This is an obscurely metaphorical answer to the question "how to be," and it may be so deeply rooted in intense personal experience that its essential grounds can never be "told"; but it does not seem the mere confusion and uncertainty so often attributed to Conrad.

Conrad's dramatic emphasis on the difficulty of rising to a full perception of the affirmation crystallized in Stein's paradoxes, and his manipulation of language patterns to heighten this difficulty, introduce a further obscurity into what Stein is saying. But setting aside for the moment this dramatic and technical obscurity, it is possible to paraphrase the affirmation at the crux of Conrad's moral vision. Robert Penn Warren has done so excellently:

Conrad's scepticism is ultimately but a "reasonable" recognition of the fact that man is a natural creature who can rest on no revealed values and can look forward to neither individual immortality nor racial survival. But reason, in this sense, is the denial of life and energy, for against all reason man insists, as man, on creating and trying to live by certain values. These values are, to use Conrad's word, "illusions," but the last wisdom is for man to realize that though his values are illusions, the illusion is necessary, is infinitely precious, is the mark of his human achievement, and is, in the end, his only truth.[20]

This admirable summary throws considerable light on some of the most puzzling passages in the early Conrad: the enigmatic final scene of "Heart of Darkness," for example. The stress Marlow places on the *saving* value of certain untruths, the positive value of illusions, is nowhere more important than in reading this final scene; Marlow affirms his fellowship with Kurtz, but he acknowledges also an affinity with Kurtz's white "Intended," just as he later is to affirm his fellowship with a Jim who is not unlike her—or to put it perhaps more exactly, it is Marlow's identification with Kurtz which enables him to respond appropriately both to the infernal Venus and to the terrestrial Venus in Kurtz's life.

And it is precisely this duality of impulse which makes it so difficult to judge Jim's case. Jim fails to sustain his greatest illusion about himself aboard the *Patna*, but his defeat is the product of forces equally necessary and equally human. Conversely, he is defeated on Patusan through too *rigorously* sustaining the same sort of illusion, but this time applied more broadly: the romantic view of human nature, applied not only to his own

[20] *Nostromo*, with Introduction by R. P. Warren (New York: Modern Library, 1951), p. xxiii. Introduction reprinted from *Sewanee Review*, LIX (Summer 1951), 363–391.

character, but to the Gentleman Browns and Corneliuses as well. It is finally Jim's radical generosity which defeats him, his persistent idealism and refusal to take prudent account of the destructive element, even after meeting it deep within himself. If in the first half of the book Jim learns acutely the cost of lost honor, in his final self-immolation he learns acutely the cost of sustaining honor, when honor is defined with the Platonic rigor his peculiar temperament forces him to bring to the term. "To the destructive element submit yourself," Stein tells Marlow, "and with the exertions of your hands and feet" make it keep you up—follow the dream, but at the same time, by whatever means, wrest survival from those nonideal, amoral, or immoral forces which threaten the individual dreamer, his safety and his concept of himself. In refusing to exert himself, even when those dark forces appear in the person of Gentleman Brown, Jim tries to climb into the air, and inevitably drowns.

Complementing this view of Jim's moral stature are partial views rendered by figures more limited in their own moral sensibility. Most of these figures precede the entrance of Stein, and their ultimate effect is to underscore the importance of his view; one of their primary purposes, in fact, is to lead Marlow's hearers along a path of understanding toward Stein's perplexing and halting assurances. The French Lieutenant Marlow meets in a cafe in Sydney, for example, offers certainly a bit of the truth— that although every man's courage has a breaking-point, and honor and duty are often no more than a public ritual, one still is not relieved of the obligation; and that in any case life without honor may not be worth much, a discovery that Jim makes repeatedly for himself. Conrad and Marlow do not turn their eyes away from the comedy of Jim's weakness. Jim is doomed to the memory of his role in a grotesque farce: the fat Captain and his fellows desperately attempting to get the boat over the side, their bravado after their escape, and the like; and if Jim is redeemed to some extent because he, unlike the others, perceives these ironies and is pained by them, they are no less ugly for that. Captain Brierly, the "fortunate man of the earth," whose suicide is itself a grim commentary on Jim; Chester the guano entrepreneur, whose moral response to Jim's problem (exile him from humanity, and leave him sitting in the sun on some remote island, up to his knees in guano) is wholly inverted; and the gross and bestial Schomberg, whose awareness of Jim's problem is not even moral—all offer judgments which Marlow can reject or refine or synthesize on his way toward his own final vision of Jim.

This bringing together of partial points of view, symbolic mirrors for Marlow along his own route of growth, is perhaps the most important aspect of *Lord Jim's* structure. Much of the novel's well-known digressiveness and disrupted chronology are products of this rhetorical necessity; the external chronology of physical fact is superseded by an inner chronology of psycho-moral insight. One source of confusion in *Lord Jim*, for example, is that Marlow may report in the same breath not only his initial reaction to some partially choral voice or event, but also his matured and retrospective reaction, so that the reader is confronted with what appears to be an ironic incongruence. But if one keeps in mind both the dramatic Marlow who makes discoveries and the narrating Marlow who gives all those discoveries rhetorical shape and meaning (as one must do also in reading "Heart of Darkness" and "Youth"), this source of difficulty disappears. It is important to distinguish the retrospective view of Jim from the succession of earlier and less lenient views Marlow reports himself as having held, since it is his final conclusions that give the book its shape and meaning. This rhetorical complexity is of course not the only reason for *Lord Jim's* digressive quality: some of it reflects merely the random association of a deepening self-knowledge; some of it contributes to suspense; some of it creates irony through juxtaposition; and so on. But the rhetorical and logical patterns implicit in the novel are probably the most important source of its structural peculiarities.

Consider, for example, the sequence of scenes which begins with the elderly French Lieutenant and terminates finally in the new chance provided by Stein. All this arises rhetorically from the question posed by the Lieutenant—with honor lost, what makes life worthwhile?—and represents a series of possible answers to the Lieutenant's question. The first of these, Brierly's plan of simple escape from the final judgment of the Court of Inquiry (paralleling, of course, his own self-destructive evasion of an inner Court of Inquiry) is rejected by Jim out of hand as a failure to accept the necessary consequences of his act. Chester's solution, an attempt to capitalize on Jim's alienation, is rejected by Marlow with equal sharpness. But then Jim moves on to some more plausible and tolerable answers. He is offered affection and security and moderate position with the affluent Mr. Denver; having rejected these median values, he is welcomed as an exceptionally able employee by Egstrom and Blake, in the most important maritime job he can be permitted to do, but is driven on again by the consciousness of his dishonor; and "there were many others of this sort," Marlow tells us, "more than I could count on the fingers of my two hands" (p. 197). On Jim's principles, none of these solutions will work, since they are "merely opportunities to earn his bread" (p. 202). The only real possibility for him is the entirely new chance provided by Stein in the remote world of Patusan.

Far from being the highest choral figure in the book, it is the French Lieutenant's chief function merely to formulate the question which sets off this series, and simultaneously, by a too stolidly simple affirmation of the "few very simple ideas," to impel Marlow-Conrad toward a subtler and more complexly qualified moral view. There is no doubt, of course, that the French Lieutenant represents an important stage in Marlow's awareness, a step toward Stein. We see in the scene with the French Lieutenant a device visible in both *Lord Jim* and "Heart of Darkness": a pulling-together, in abstract form, of insights and convictions which had, until that point, been only hesitant and too closely concrete for Marlow to generalize satisfactorily. In interaction with the symbol that is Jim, Marlow's insights tend to be exploratory and contradictory; in succeeding scenes with more-or-less choral commentators, where Marlow talks *about,* and not *to,* Jim, he may with the help of these interlocutors draw his hesitant insights together. And so it is with the French Lieutenant; he articulates for Marlow both the universality of cowardice and the necessity of honor in the presence of fear; and so far as it goes, this is no doubt valid both psychologically and morally. But Marlow is able to recognize that Jim's case is too complex to yield to this simple formulation. He points out to the Lieutenant that Jim aboard the *Patna* had had none of the normal public inducements toward a persistence in his duty, and that the whole question of honor might reduce itself in the end to not having one's fear found out: " 'This, monsieur,' " replies the Lieutenant, " 'is too fine for me—much above me—I don't think about it' " (pp. 147, 148–149). On the level of symbolic description, so important to Conrad in indicating the validity of choral and partly choral views, we see the Lieutenant "sitting drowsily" with his shoulder-straps "a bit tarnished," speaking "with a curious mixture of unconcern and thoughtfulness" (p. 138); and it is of course significant in Conrad's universe that this elderly judge of Jim is no more than a third lieutenant. When the Lieutenant admits, in a position of high emphasis at the end of a chapter, that " 'there are many things in this incident of my life . . . which have remained obscure' " (p. 142), the reader and Marlow are inclined to agree. Still, if the French Lieutenant's authority is gently undercut by Marlow, there remains a hard core of realism in what he says; his moral premises persist throughout the book, and it is more accurate to say that they are refined and superseded than that they are abandoned.

The common feature of rhetorical structures like these in *Lord Jim* is that they represent a series of partial approaches or responses to the same reference point, usually ranked in the order of their dignity. Another one occurs early in the book, a spec-

trum of responses to the monstrous test of duty aboard the *Patna*
which appear in the space of twenty-three pages in the precise
order of their validity, and terminate finally in Marlow's first
direct confrontation of Jim. Each of these responses is a type of
running away, of evading the ultimate issue; in the end, as
Marlow says, Jim is the only man willing and able to face it. The
swinish Teutonic Captain of the *Patna* squeezes his greasy bulk
into a gharry and leaves town. The Second Engineer also escapes
—into a hospital and faint delirium, an indication that he is at
least a little troubled. The Chief Engineer, a figure who displays
enough anxiety to win some half-comic sympathy from Marlow,
escapes into an alcoholic world inhabited by giant pink toads
which render, unconsciously, the terror only Jim has stature
enough to acknowledge consciously ("'Bash in the head of the
first that stirs,'" says the Engineer—p. 54). Finally, Captain
Brierly, an inherently more courageous and more complex man,
perceiving the personal bearing of Jim's experience, escapes into
death, but with the classic heroic gesture of suicide; and in his
halting articulation of his own sense of guilt wins a genuine if
ironic sympathy from Marlow. By the time Marlow is ready to
talk to Jim, devices of this kind ought to have persuaded the
reader of Jim's moral stature, and to have ruled out any facile
condemnation. Marlow's own judgment undergoes a complex
rhetorical progress—from his preliminary questions at the beginning of the novel ("Is he silly? is he callous?"—p. 41); through
his first hesitant admission that there might be some extenuation
for Jim, and a gradual discovery of it; through a puzzled acknowledgment that his own powers are inadequate to judge the
case; through a conscious identification of his own ego with
Jim's; and ultimately to a feeling that "he exerted himself to
soothe me as though he had been the more mature of the two"
(p. 241). And although Marlow's complexly ironic respect for
Jim is firmly established by the middle of the book and the scene
with Stein, his understanding grows to the end.

The bifurcation of *Lord Jim* into two apparently discrete parts (what Edward Garnett called the book's "plague spot" [21]) can also be accounted for by the rhetorical design of Marlow's psycho-moral journey. The *Patna* episode only halfway reveals the fundamental dilemma arising from Jim's experience; if his romantic conception of himself fails aboard the *Patna* through a weakness of will, and if simple persistence in a self-glorifying kind of idealism might have led him to the supreme untested success of a Brierly, there seems to be no dilemma. But the inadequacy of Jim's idealism is more complex than that. For if aboard the *Patna* he is unable to carry out one part of Stein's advice, to "follow the dream," on Patusan he is unable to carry out the other part—to immerse himself sufficiently in the destructive element to make it keep him up. Thus Stein's paradox, which stands at the physical center of *Lord Jim*, serves to connect and unite the two halves. As Marlow points out, Jim begins his significant experience in the second half of the book by taking "the second desperate leap of his life—the leap that landed him into the life of Patusan" (p. 380); and this paralleling is carried out in numerous details, not the least of which is the fact that "Patusan" is a near-anagram of *"Patna."*

So much of the book's fundamental vision has become clear during the *Patna* episode, however, and in Stein's abstract summing-up, that even Marlow admits that "there remains . . . little to be told" of Jim (p. 224). Yet for the structural balance he needs to establish the moral significance of the Patusan episode, Conrad draws it out to equal length—with the result that it becomes relatively thin, and drives him back toward the redundancy of his earlier work. Marlow speaks of his "last word" some two hundred pages from the end (p. 225). He cuts off his oral tale eighty pages from the end, and is succeeded once again by the frame narrator (p. 337). And the reader is assured repeatedly that the end is not far off: only a "few pages" remain (p. 342), "to make a long story short" (p. 359), "henceforth events move fast without a check" (p. 389), and so on. Much of the second part is of course organic to the novel. Like the artificially clear moral construct of the *Patna,* the corrupt society of Patusan is symbolically simple, with its fear, fraud, wife-beating, and brass pots; and Jim's storybook success in inverting this moral structure —with his "Homeric" peals of laughter and his white semigodliness—is essential to Conrad's plot. Through the exaggeration of detail made possible by this social context and by Jim's isolation, Conrad is able to dramatize him as a leader-toward-light (so long as the destructive element permits) by placing him on that borderline between light and darkness, form and chaos, the civilized and the primitive, projected ideal and sensual impulse, that furnishes symbolic clarification in so much of his work. Narrative elements associated with this symbolic development are also important here—the gradual emergence in Cornelius and Gentleman Brown, for example, of the forces that will destroy Jim's excessive idealism; or the demand of Jewel and Tamb' Itam for a strength of passional commitment in Jim that they, who are on more intimate terms with the powers of darkness, can see as a pragmatic necessity. But much of the material in the second half of the book does seem defiantly, sometimes almost comically, to resist integration into its central moral idea.[22]

Precision of language is perhaps the best index of a writer's growth, and before leaving the early Marlow tales, it will be useful to examine two significant aspects of Conrad's style during this period. The first of these is a close control of specific image and symbol, and the second is a deliberate use of mysti-

[22] Elliott B. Gose, Jr., has offered a Jungian reading of *Lord Jim* which provides a wealth of suggestion about the book's structural divisions and some of its imagery. Conrad was probably less aware of mythical material than Gose makes him; but his article does seem to throw considerable light on the strange symbolic exaggerations of the Patusan episode, and helps account for those passages which resist integration into more conventional readings. ("Pure Exercise of Imagination: Archetypal Symbolism in *Lord Jim,*" *PMLA,* LXXIX [March 1964], 137–147.)

fying abstractions. This latter device, in fact, has been at the center of some sharp controversy, and no writer on Conrad ought to escape without giving his view of it.

The most obvious image-pattern in Lord Jim is perhaps the animal-imagery. Beginning with Jim's comparison of the Patna to a snake at the Court of Inquiry, this strain is elaborated and reinforced by a species of incremental repetition (the redundancy made more plausible by Marlow's "oral" presence) to create a sense of that prehuman or precivilized inner darkness which victimizes Jim and helps define Stein's "destructive element." The Chief Engineer flees from "a legion of centipedes" (p. 49); reports that the Patna was " 'full of reptiles' " (p. 51); and, clawing Marlow with his "tentacle" and letting out a "wolfish howl," reports the existence of " 'millions of pink toads' " under his bed, " 'all pink—as big as mastiffs, with an eye on the top of the head and claws all round their ugly mouths' " (pp. 52–53), an irruption of fear and disintegration of form much like that at the heart of Kurtz's darkness. Jim's mistaken notion that Marlow has called him a "cur" is, of course, the pivotal point of his first confrontation with Marlow; and Marlow's later remark that Jim was "at bay" (p. 75) adds a thin layer of irony to Jim's "error." Later (in an account which, it will be remembered, is rendered by Marlow, but must have come originally from Jim) the reader sees the crew of the Patna "grovelling on all-fours . . . snarling at each other venomously, ready to kill, ready to weep, and only kept from flying at each other's throats by the fear of death" (p. 96); he hears the crew in the life boat: " 'Yap! yap! Bow-ow-ow-ow-ow! Yap! yap!' " (p. 118); hears Jim called a " 'skunk' " (p. 118) and the Captain a " 'beast' " (p. 119); and sees the imagery extended finally, in a kind of evolutionary regression, to the Captain's " 'fishy eyes' " and turtle-like neck (p. 126). The meaning of all this is underscored by Gentleman Brown, who is described as "like some man-beast of folklore" (p. 372). Like Screwtape, Brown keeps reiterating his hunger and his "mad self-love" (p. 383) as opposed to Jim's mad benevo-

lence; and is advised by a "demon" (p. 386). This strain of
metaphor, which is fairly obvious, would not deserve extended
discussion except that it reappears in Conrad's work from time to
time—as in the swine-imagery associated with Verloc in *The
Secret Agent*—and is finally erected into a symbolic-metaphysi-
cal principle in *Victory*, with the apelike Pedro and the catlike
Ricardo. Similarly, the utter inversion of values which is implicit
in Mr. Jones's ethos in *Victory*, and makes that book's jungle
scene so grotesquely comic, is seen in a less rigid way in the
behavior of the *Patna's* crew: their repeated request to the dead
man to jump; their delight in the mistaken notion that the
Patna, with all its human cargo, has sunk; and so on. And of
course Cornelius, that "loathsome insect" whose abjectness
permeates "all his acts and passions and emotions," and who
skulks on the outskirts of Jim's story, "enigmatical and unclean,
tainting the fragrance of its youth and of its naiveness" (p. 286),
displays the same inversion of motive, abjectness being the moral
opposite of Jim's romantic self-assertion. In the early Marlow
tales Conrad was able for the first time to structure such bodies
of imagery sharply enough to relate them clearly to dominant
motifs: to disorder, regression, and value-inversion, for example.
And it is just at that crux of meaning where Marlow's explorations merge into Stein's straightforward thematic statements that
the animal-imagery of the *Patna* scenes merges into the conscious symbolism of butterfly and beetle: early precursors of the
allegorical symbolism that will come to express Conrad's final
resolutions.[23]

At the opposite end of the spectrum from these concrete
images are Marlow's high abstractions, used sometimes in his
explanatory comment, and sometimes in reported dialogue.

[23] Some of these details are pursued in Stanton de Voren Hoffman,
"Conrad's Menagerie: Animal Imagery and Theme," *Bucknell Review,*
XII (1964), 59–71; and Tony Tanner, "Butterflies and Beetles—Conrad's Two Truths," *Chicago Review,* XVI (Winter-Spring 1963),
123–140.

Readers frequently have seen this abstractness as a technical failure, when measured against the consistent concreteness of such works as "Typhoon" and *The Shadow-Line*. This reaction misses a crucial point about Marlow's narratives, however; and to explore it is to encounter some of the most important dimensions both of *Lord Jim* and of "Heart of Darkness." The point is that Marlow's attempts to formulate his experience abstractly are part of the experience itself. The use of general terms as counters to control or capture the mysteries he faces—an effort sometimes futile and almost always charged with irony—is part of the concrete dramatization of spiritual growth. General terms which are admittedly too vague to be of much help in conceptualizing the situations of Jim and Kurtz may nonetheless be sharply specific terms in Marlow's meditation; their failure as conceptual tools for Marlow is sometimes the central point of a scene in the drama of his growth. To complain about the final ambiguities or obscurities of *Lord Jim* or "Heart of Darkness" is to suppose that the dilemmas posed by these works must have clear forms and specific solutions, and that the reader would not have failed, as Conrad has, in finding them.

There is a good deal of evidence, especially in *Lord Jim,* that the inconclusive, enigmatic quality of the Marlow stories—whatever it is in Stein's summing-up that can "never be told"—is wholly intentional on Conrad's part; and that far from betraying his inability to come concretely to grips with his subject, it represents his way of dramatizing a high epistemological point much like that of the religious mystic when he maintains the ineffability of his experience. One indication of this is the syntactical progression in the speech of major characters as the perception of spiritual mystery is approached more closely. Jim, the unqualified romantic who perforce "sees" these things most immediately and overwhelmingly, is "inarticulate" and halting in his speech—"there was a high seriousness in his stammerings," says Marlow (p. 248). Stein, who is also "romantic" but who "exists" for Marlow in a sense that Jim does not, and is therefore one step farther away from the immediate perception of mystery, is not quite incoherent, as Jim sometimes is, but is paradoxical and opaquely metaphorical in his speech, and despite his learning, persists in a Germanic reshuffling of normal English syntax. Marlow himself is merely unpredictably ironic and associative. And finally the frame narrator, with his consecutive and logically organized account, returns us to the coherent norms of commonsense usage. The crucial moments of Jim's experience are themselves paradoxical: " 'I had jumped. . . . It seems' " (p. 111); " 'Isn't it awful a man should be driven to do a thing like that—and be responsible?' " (p. 119); and so on. And if Marlow himself gradually rises to a perception of the meaning and implications of remarks like these, he warns the reader repeatedly that the perception is arduous and fleeting.

It is common to object to "Heart of Darkness" on the grounds of its evasiveness, its emotional insistence on mysteries the author is unable to produce, its redundancy in the use of words like "inscrutable" and "unspeakable," its sacrifice of objective precision for atmospheric effect, and so on. Yet here again the vagueness and abstract elaboration are the concrete particulars of a represented experience; this paradox, in fact, is one source of the story's irony. What we are shown in *exact* terms is that much of Marlow's experience cannot immediately be comprehended in *specific* terms, that confusion and hypothetical abstractness are part of a civilized resistance to the forces of darkness. Marlow's whimsical indirection, fragmentation, hesitancy, and the like, tend to increase as he proceeds up the river. The final term of this series is "the horror!"—Kurtz's final summary of his own experience. But Conrad is well aware of the generality of this term: Kurtz cries out as "at some image, at some vision," suggesting a sharply defined visual experience, unspecifiable by the civilized vocabulary but nonetheless a "supreme moment of complete knowledge" (p. 149). (An analogue, in *Lord Jim*, is Jim's near speechlessness at the climax of his confrontation with Gentleman Brown.) The tension between the implied experience and the diction used to report it (as in the more obvious cases of Kafka and Poe) heightens the reader's sense of horror. To object to Kurtz's final ejaculation is much like insisting pedantically that the mystical experience must be effable to be meaningful; the two are at opposite ends of the continuum of value, but are equally resistant to words.[24]

This point about Marlow's diction in "Heart of Darkness" leads in turn to an observation about the story's major strains of imagery. The light-and-darkness imagery has been thoroughly discussed elsewhere; few readers in any case are likely to miss such a striking metaphor, although it is easy to miss some of its subtleties. But there is another dimension of the imagery just as important: if Marlow's journey up the Congo is away from light and toward darkness, it is also away from form and toward chaos, just as the reptiles in the delirium of the Chief Engineer progress steadily toward his fantastic pink toads. From its outer shell of humanitarian idealism the story progresses to Marlow's reliance on his own skill and craft, to the enigmatic and seductive behavior of the natives, to Kurtz's lusts and a wordless "Intended," and finally to some unspecifiable "horror"; from its outer shell of carefully formulated commercial plan to its inner core of indiscriminate greed; from its outer shell of civilized

[24] Marlow's linguistic mysteries have also received recent attention: e.g., James Guetti, " 'Heart of Darkness' and the Failure of the Imagination," *Sewanee Review*, LXXIII (Summer 1965), 488–504; Perry, "Action, Vision, or Voice: The Moral Dilemmas in Conrad's Tale-telling," 3–14; and Miller, *Poets of Reality*, pp. 36–39, *et passim*. Guetti's treatment of Conrad in his recent *The Limits of Metaphor* (Ithaca: Cornell University Press, 1967), pp. 46–68, is a revised version of the *Sewanee Review* article. Guetti's and Miller's books provide the best discussion, though neither, I think, finally asks the essential question: whether, and under what conditions, moral affirmation is possible despite the circumambient darkness and the breakdown of conceptual language. An interesting addendum here is Edward W. Said's claim, in *Joseph Conrad and the Fiction of Autobiography* (Cambridge: Harvard University Press, 1966), of external evidence that "truth for Conrad was . . . the negation of intellectual differentiation" (pp. 137–138).

constructs (passionless marble buildings, steamships and railroads) toward mere raw material (rank vegetation and stockpiled ivory). Sometimes the light-darkness and form-chaos imagery are strikingly conjoined, as when Marlow sees two women in a Brussels office giving form to black wool by knitting it, or when he meets the Harlequin, who both in speech and in costume exhibits a partial disintegration of normal form and a step away from simple nationality toward the dark universality of Kurtz. As other writers have observed, the destruction of form often has its comic side in Conrad, yielding the grotesqueries of the *Patna* episode or the bottomless pails of "Heart of Darkness" (and this, by the way, is one more of Conrad's affinities with Faulkner). As his career progresses, Conrad gains increasing control over this aspect of his symbolic system, using it to excellent advantage in such works as "The Duel" and *The Secret Agent,* and exploiting it fully in the jungle scene of *Victory.*

Despite his acknowledgment of impenetrable mysteries at the extremes of moral experience, however, Conrad's chief interest in these early works is psycho-moral; Marlow's metaphysical and epistemological asides do little more than embroider the central experience, and help to deepen the paradoxical tone of his final affirmations. With *Chance* and *Victory,* Conrad will bring these theoretical ideas more clearly into the narrative foreground, and give his affirmations a more philosophical and even existential cast. To return to Conrad's own words about Maupassant, he has at this point succeeded chiefly in exploring and developing his own ethical consciousness "sufficiently to concrete his fearless conclusions in illuminative instances." Further growth, as we shall see, will force Conrad into new fields of value and new techniques. But first we must turn to his earliest work, and trace the development of a highly original narrative art.

2

Almayer to Jim—
The Growth of a Theme

The study . . . is based fundamentally on *Almayer's Folly*, *The Nigger of the "Narcissus"* and *Lord Jim* because these novels have most to reveal. In the first Conrad was a carefree amateur; in the second he made himself a professional; and in the third he wrote with the resolution of an established professional. The distinctions are not arbitrary. . . . *Almayer's Folly*, *The Nigger*, and *Lord Jim* were landmarks in the making of a novelist.
—John Dozier Gordan, in *Joseph Conrad: The Making of a Novelist*

In his first Author's Note, written in 1895 for *Almayer's Folly*, Conrad sets out to defend "that literature which preys on strange people and prowls in far-off countries . . . amongst honest cannibals and the more sophisticated pioneers of our glorious virtues," and in so doing anticipates all the themes that are to dominate his fiction until the appearance of *Nostromo*, almost a decade later: "There is a bond between us and that humanity so far away. . . . I am content to sympathize with common mortals, no matter where they live; in houses or in tents, in the streets under a fog, or in the forests behind the dark line of dismal mangroves that fringe the vast solitude of the sea. For, their land

—like ours—lies under the inscrutable eyes of the Most High.
Their hearts—like ours—must endure the load of the gifts from
Heaven: the curse of facts and the blessing of illusions, the
bitterness of our wisdom and the deceptive consolation of our
folly" (pp. vii–viii). Here are those moral and morally relevant
ideas Conrad's early fiction would struggle to dramatize: the
metaphysical skepticism, the conflict of illusion and harsh fact,
the assertion of human solidarity and the recognition of human
darkness. In studying the growth of these ideas and of the
techniques which give them expression, the reader finds illuminating parallels among Conrad's early works, and begins to perceive the long creative process that finally yielded the Marlow
tales.

The most important of these parallels, of course, lies in the
character of Conrad's protagonists: all of them are incipient
Kurtzes or Jims, or bear a generic relationship to the Marlow
who studies Kurtz and Jim and identifies with them. Almayer,
Willems, the crew of the *Narcissus*, all make voyages of self-discovery; and in their comparative stature lies the clearest index to
Conrad's own growth of awareness. From the foolish wealth-
dream of an Almayer, through the degraded passion of a Willems, to the high romantic illusion of a Tuan Jim, the motive
force of Conrad's fiction is broadened to become a moral and
epistemological universal. Sometimes, unfortunately, Conrad's
protagonists gain stature even as a novel progresses, so that
Almayer's Folly in the end rises to a genuine pathos which is
inconsistent with the earlier treatment of Almayer; and Conrad
must occasionally excuse himself for what seems a too-sudden
perception on Willems' part: "He was not, of course, able to
discern clearly the causes of his misery; but there are none so
ignorant as not to know suffering, none so simple as not to feel
and suffer from the shock of warring impulses" (*Outcast*, p.
129). It is in this psycho-moral dimension of Conrad's fiction
that his early creative history lies. *Almayer's Folly, An Outcast of
the Islands,* and *The Nigger of the 'Narcissus'* reveal all the

elements of "Heart of Darkness" and *Lord Jim,* but lack the sophisticated development of the later works, and are, finally, less rigorous tests of Conrad's moral commitments: the "Hope" which echoes from the black forest at the end of *Outcast* and the nostalgic affirmation of the *Nigger's* final pages are clearly not so hard won as Marlow's final judgments of Kurtz and Jim. And since the level of awareness of Conrad's fiction is so intimately bound up with his narrative techniques ("It is in those matters gradually, but never completely, mastered that the history of my books really consists" [1]), his technical and moral growth must be studied as a single object of interest.

Another obvious way Conrad's fiction gains between *Almayer's Folly* and *Lord Jim* is in its power and economy of description. Critics have always noted the excessive lushness and fertility of the Malayan novels. A recent writer has offered two keen insights into this feature of Conrad's early work: that it is the prose counterpart of *fin de siécle* poetry, duplicating its "lazy, measured beat" and languorous tone; and that "inadequate time techniques in Conrad's early novels placed too much responsibility on language itself, which, as a result, became prolix." [2] To these suggestions may be added the one offered in the last chapter, that Conrad needed a meditative internal narrator to extract the full meaning from his imagined experience, and that without such a narrator, he was necessarily thrown back upon sheer redundancy and metaphorical insistence. Early readers' charges of verbosity [3] may have led Conrad to find more econom-

[1] Aubry, *Life and Letters,* II, p. 317.

[2] Frederick Karl, *A Reader's Guide to Joseph Conrad* (New York: Noonday Press, 1960), pp. 91–96, 69; see also *Literary Review,* II (Summer 1959), 565–576, an extended but less easily accessible treatment of the first point. Leo Gurko suggests that these qualities of Conrad's style may also be related to the hothouse quality of late-Victorian writing generally and to Conrad's own love of the grand and baroque aspects of nature (*Joseph Conrad: Giant in Exile* [New York: Macmillan, 1962], pp. 64 ff.).

[3] See Gordan, *Joseph Conrad,* Ch. 6.

ical means to enhance the symbolic value of his descriptive passages; in any case, by the time of *The Nigger of the 'Narcissus'* he had brought his reviewers to see more clearly that he belonged to "a whole school of descriptive writers of a new class, who aspire to make visible . . . the inside of great scenes"; [4] and charges of prolixity were fewer. At the same time, his characteristic image-patterns—tree-and-vegetation images, water images, sun-and-light images, animal images, and the like—had all become sharper and more closely controlled; and with the advent of Marlow, Conrad was able almost wholly to eliminate the needless redundancy of his earlier work.

Beside this continuing attack on the problem of description, which yielded not only sharper image-structures but also the conscious theory of the *Nigger* Preface, there are a rich variety of subthemes, symbols, characters, and scenes which appear early in Conrad's fiction and are brought gradually under esthetic control. There is, for example, a gradually growing awareness that the forces which threaten the dignity and security of Conrad's protagonists arise from within these characters themselves. Almayer and Lingard make themselves vulnerable, but ultimately are victimized by external forces; and Willems lacks the direct symbolic relationship to Aissa that would indicate the ultimate locus of Conrad's moral interest. But gradually Conrad learns that by setting up the external action as heavily symbolic and permitting the narrator to see his own psychology reflected in outward circumstance, he can preserve both the external drama and the inner, presocial source of moral darkness which is central to his vision. Like the principles governing his use of descriptive detail, this technique has by the time of the *Nigger* become more explicit: in his Foreword to the American edition, Conrad tells his readers that Wait is nothing more than the center of the ship's collective psychology. In germinal form, Conrad's contempt for petty commercialism, abstract social theory, and colo-

[4] *Ibid.*, p. 287.

nial idealism is also present from the beginning—the ironic underside of his moral commitments, which is to receive full thematic status in *Nostromo;* and social theorists like Donkin and the colonizers of "Heart of Darkness" gradually achieve a sharper definition. There are even hesitant attempts to formulate something like Stein's paradoxes, as at the end of *Outcast.* And the symbolic motifs of sea and land, light and darkness, form and chaos, terrestrial and infernal, all become more cleanly functional.

In examining this early growth, it is best to take the three novels first; each represents a step toward the Marlow tales, and parallel points may be made about each of them. *Almayer's Folly* and *An Outcast of the Islands,* partly because of their common settings and characters, form something of a unit; and each displays specific analogues to "Heart of Darkness" and *Lord Jim.* In *The Nigger of the 'Narcissus,'* these lines of growth are harder to see, partly because of the unusual circumstance that the whole crew, with the exception of Wait and Donkin, are protagonists, and partly because of Conrad's overriding nostalgia. But the *Nigger* is nonetheless a major advance for Conrad. The early short stories are less interesting. Conrad was essentially a novelist, and his other work is often no more than a technical or commercial bridge to his next novel. But some of the early stories, notably "The Lagoon" and "Karain," suggest exciting technical advances. And finally, the stories written between *Lord Jim* and *Nostromo* must be examined before leaving the first great period of Conrad's career. Whatever their unique pleasures, it is important to see that these stories are chiefly a postlude to *Lord Jim,* a perseveration of themes Conrad could now look back on and place under orderly control, as in "Amy Foster" and "Falk," or a mining of his sea-vein in straightforward realistic terms, as in "The End of the Tether" and "Typhoon." After *Lord Jim* Conrad awaited new inspiration; and the tension and complexity of his work are considerably reduced.

Almayer's Folly is a provocative first novel, but a curiously mixed one. The casual reader may find three different centers of interest—the destruction of Almayer, the romance between his daughter and the native Dain Maroola, and the tangled background of jungle scenery and native intrigue against which these dramas are played out. The novel does have a unity of sorts, however, resting in Almayer's experience, and more particularly in some analogues between Almayer on the one hand and Jim and Kurtz on the other. Like Jim, Almayer is immersed in an ineffably splendid vision: "He saw, as in a flash of dazzling light, great piles of shining guilders, and realized all the possibilities of an opulent existence. The consideration, the indolent ease of life . . . his ships, his warehouses, his merchandise . . . and, crowning all, in the far future gleamed like a fairy palace the big mansion in Amsterdam, that earthly paradise of his dreams, where made king amongst men by old Lingard's money, he would pass the evening of his days in inexpressible splendour" (p. 10). This is, of course, a "foolish dream" (p. 203). The lusts which inspire Almayer to be "king" have none of the strange high seriousness of the principles on which Jim finally does become king of Patusan. Nor is there anything of Jim's exalted dissociation from reality in Almayer's comic madness as the forces of darkness close in: "Was he going mad? Terrified by the thought he turned away and ran towards his house repeating to himself, 'I am not going mad; of course not, no, no, no!' He tried to keep a firm hold of the idea. Not mad, not mad. . . . He saw Nina standing there, and wished to say something to her, but could not remember what, in his extreme anxiety not to forget that he was not going mad, which he still kept repeating mentally as he ran round the table, till he stumbled against one of the arm-chairs and dropped into it exhausted." And his intoxications are comparatively mundane: " 'Give me some gin! Run!' " (p. 100). Almayer is dominated by his environment, and his passivity and clownishness reduce his value as a paradigm of folly.

Yet there are suggestions of a deeper awareness in the book, arising chiefly from the Nina-Dain romance, and from the light-darkness imagery associated with it. If Almayer is in some ways analogous to Jim, in other ways he is analogous to Kurtz; and the dramatic context of his final degradation is much like Kurtz's. Like Kurtz, Almayer is a hollow man, lacking "faith, hope or pride," and even "any sort of sustaining spirit" (*Personal Record*, p. 85). Once this generic relationship between Almayer and Kurtz is recognized, other elements of "Heart of Darkness" become visible: on one side Almayer, white, subject to decadent illusion, moving toward darkness; on the other side Dain Maroola, savage, engaged in discovering romantic illusion, and moving toward light; and in between, as a symbolic middle term for which Almayer and Dain contest, the half-caste Nina, wavering delicately between two worlds. Like Kurtz, Almayer moves along this axis of darkness and light to utter degradation, spending his final days smoking opium with the Chinese Jim-Eng in a "House of heavenly delight" (p. 205). Like Kurtz, Almayer seeks boundless wealth and power at the head of a mysterious tropical river; and he stands between two political structures—the outer shell of Dutch colonialism and the inner core of native and Arab political organization, with its duplicity, savagery, and greed. But Almayer's pettiness and passivity divert the reader's sympathies to Dain Maroola; and Nina herself is bound less by affection for Almayer than by habit and loyalty. The result is that the novel turns into a primitive romance, with Almayer as villain. Only with characters of the stature of Jim and Kurtz—trader Lingards and Rajah Lauts *par excellence*—does Conrad develop figures powerful enough to dominate their jungle settings. Yet the psycho-moral dimensions of the later works are implicit in *Almayer's Folly*.[5]

[5] John H. Hicks, "Conrad's *Almayer's Folly*: Structure, Theme and Critics," *Nineteenth-Century Fiction*, XIX (June 1964), 17–31, offers a perceptive reading, calling attention to the motifs of fidelity, illusion, and destructive passion that help give the novel its unity and relate it to

Correlatively, some of Conrad's most familiar descriptive techniques appear first in *Almayer's Folly*. Dain Maroola, for example, like the natives of "Heart of Darkness," struggles toward
light; he "knew the sunshine of life only in her presence" (p.
72); "she would be his light and his wisdom" (p. 172); and so
on. The lovers emerge finally from jungle darkness into the glare
of civilization. And Nina stands on the symbolic borderline, a
hybrid mixture of form and chaos, light and darkness: "Her firm
mouth, with the lips slightly parted and disclosing a gleam of
white teeth, put a vague suggestion of ferocity into the impatient
expression of her features. And yet her dark and perfect eyes had
all the tender softness common to Malay women, but with a
gleam of superior intelligence. . . . She stood there all in white,
straight, flexible, graceful, unconscious of herself, her low but
broad forehead crowned with a shining mass of long black hair
that . . . made her pale olive complexion look paler still by the
contrast of its coal-black hue" (p. 17). Most of the other characters may be placed somewhere on this axis; at one end Taminah,
the slave girl, in whom "slept all feelings and all passions," and
who "lived like the tall palms . . . seeking the light, desiring the
sunshine, fearing the storm, unconscious of either" (p. 112); at
the other end, the romantic Lingard, whose treatment of Almayer (and later Willems) prefigures Jim's treatment of Gentleman Brown.

Complementing these human struggles are the background
struggles of vegetation, like the parasitic creepers overtaking
higher forms of life "in a sinuous rush upwards into the air and
sunshine" (p. 167); or the plants climbing out of corruption and
chaos, "interlaced in inextricable confusion, climbing madly and
brutally over each other in the terrible silence of a desperate

Conrad's other work. As Hicks points out, Nina seems to achieve a kind
of victory by choosing fulfillment in Dain's native society rather than
remaining in a corrupt white one. Dain's civilized aspects, however, are
otherwise in conflict with his more extensively developed narrative and
symbolic functions.

struggle towards the life-giving sunshine above" (p. 71). Occasionally this lyrical botany is strikingly merged with the human drama, as when the politician Babalatchi discards "the flowers of polite eloquence" in favor of a more savage idiom (p. 78). At the borderline of light and darkness, of form and chaos in *Almayer's Folly,* as in "Heart of Darkness" and in the second half of *Lord Jim,* there is a grotesque conflict of human artifact and formless tropical energy: outside Almayer's house, where "stones, decaying planks, and half-sawn beams" are piled up, like the jungle plants, "in inextricable confusion" (p. 12); at the house of Lakamba, where Babalatchi grinds *Il Trovatore* out of a music box (p. 88); and so on. Nina meets Dain "on the edge of a banana plantation" (p. 63), where formal agriculture meets vegetative chaos. The final destruction of the artifacts of Lingard's office is, of course, a stage in Almayer's attempted regression toward the unconsciousness of Taminah; at the end, he must be cared for by a monkey and brought forcibly into the light: "Whenever it wished for his presence on the verandah it would tug perseveringly at his jacket, till Almayer obediently came out into the sunshine" (p. 203). Babalatchi twists the white man's formal weapon of words to his own savage purposes. And the Malays display occasionally the same inversion of values one finds in Gentleman Brown and later in the villains of *Victory,* as when the women of the village rush off to view a drowned man, "neglecting their domestic duties . . . while groups of children [bring] up the rear, warbling joyously in the delight of unexpected excitement" (p. 93).

Despite his exploration of these symbolic motifs, however, Conrad had barely begun at this point to voice the philosophic attitudes later to be associated with them—his metaphysical skepticism and antirationalism, for example, which are restricted in this novel to a few remarks about the "brutal and unnecessary violence" of the river (p. 4) and the "hidden meaning" of the sea (p. 174); or some gentle irony as Almayer leaves home "speaking English well . . . strong in arithmetic" and ready to "conquer

the world" (p. 5), details which tell the reader very little about
what happens to Almayer up Lingard's river, and are hardly a
satisfactory correlate of Kurtz's colonial idealism. And in most
ways Conrad's narrative techniques, too, are undeveloped here.
Albert Guerard has pointed out an early Marlow-analogue in
Chapters 2–5 of *Almayer's Folly:* the first of Conrad's time shifts,
an impressionistic flashback involving "haphazard and abrupt
transitions of memory," a movement from the "moralizing abstract" to the "highly visualized particular," a tendency to "ac-
tualize the irrelevant through highly visual detail; and to pass
over the absolutely essential in a casual subordinate clause," and
a process of selective dramatization [6] focused on Almayer's moral
history. But compared to Marlow's extended rhetorical structures, all this is rudimentary. And an internal point of view
obviously would have saved Conrad a good deal of awkwardness.
Using nature as a symbolic complement of his characters' emotions, for example, forces the novel's major point of view to yield
too often to the secondary points of view of the characters,
without the stable reference point provided by Marlow. Or
again, since the novel lacks an involved narrator who can speculate meaningfully on Dain Maroola's passion for Nina, it must
somehow be dramatized, and literary proprieties demand that it
reveal itself in words—a device which contradicts Dain's formless savage energy. Nina listens to Dain's words "giving up to her
the whole treasure of love and passion his nature was capable of
with all the unrestrained enthusiasm of a man totally untrammelled by any influence of civilized self-discipline" (p. 64), a
mode of communication distinctly less satisfactory than the "subtle breath of mutual understanding" which had passed "between
their two savage natures" at Dain's first sight of the girl (p. 63).
Too much of Conrad's metaphorical treatment of nature needs
the protection of an inside narrator (e.g., "the sun dipped
sharply, as if ashamed of being detected in a sympathizing atti-

tude"—p. 169); and in many other ways the birth of meaning from sensory fact is a painful process in *Almayer's Folly*.

An Outcast of the Islands, also in Conrad's lush Malayan vein, is generally lumped with the earlier novel as a piece of apprentice work, excessively "literary" and perhaps even a debasement of the legitimate technical experiments of *Almayer*. But criticism of this sort misses Conrad's growth along the axis suggested by the present study. In the stature of its protagonist and the significance of its theme, in its control of symbolic imagery, in its awareness of the moral dimensions of the problem it undertakes to examine, and in its structure and point of view, *Outcast* represents a distinct advance over *Almayer's Folly*.

Like Almayer, Willems bears important resemblances to Kurtz and Jim; and although he never rises to their heroic stature either, his case is an improvement over Almayer's as a paradigm of moral folly. Like Jim, Willems is driven from the society of white men by a fatal "jump" which destroys his public image. At the beginning of the novel, the vectors of his case are defined much as those of Jim's case are later to be defined, even to the near-cosmic significance of his acts—on a lower level, of course, and without the romantic intensity of a Jim or the extraordinary extenuation of the circumstances aboard the *Patna*: "When he stepped off the straight and narrow path of his peculiar honesty, it was with an inward assertion of unflinching resolve to fall back again into the monotonous but safe stride of virtue as soon as his little excursion into the wayside quagmires had produced the desired effect. It was going to be a short episode—a sentence in brackets, so to speak—in the flowing tale of his life: a thing of no moment, to be done unwillingly . . . and to be quickly forgotten. . . . He was unable to conceive that the moral significance of any act of his could interfere with the very nature of things" (p. 3). As Jim is a romantic egoist, so Willems is "ferociously conceited" (p. 6); as Jim must compulsively seek the "new chance" of Patusan, so Willems must "leave this house, leave this island, go far away where he was unknown. To the English Strait-Settlements perhaps. He would find an opening there for his abilities" (p. 26). Just as Jim has breached his faith with "the community of mankind," so Willems feels as if he were "the outcast of all mankind" (p. 30). And just as Jim is inclined to forget his jump from the *Patna* and dream instead of glorious fulfillment, until prodded by Marlow, so Willems "for a short moment . . . [forgets] his downfall in the recollection of his brilliant triumphs," until prodded by Lingard: " 'But whose the fault? Whose the fault?' " (p. 39). Conversely, Jim's successes on Patusan parallel some of the successes of Lingard; and this in turn bears on Willems, since, as will be suggested, Willems and Lingard may be seen implicitly as fragments of a single consciousness, and so prefigure the conscious devices of "doubling" and of Marlow's identification with Kurtz and Jim in the later tales. Once Willems has gone over to the side of the natives, he gains, just as Jim does (or perhaps more exactly as Kurtz does) their obedience and respect. And of course in the most basic thematic sense, Willems is a step toward Kurtz, yielding to unexpected lusts and darknesses within himself. But just as there is a crucial moral distinction between Willems' "unwilling" embezzlement and Jim's paradoxical jump from the *Patna,* so there are crucial differences between Willems and Kurtz: with his pool-hall self-aggrandizement and inability to conceive any other kind of suffering than the physical, Willems lacks the stature that makes Kurtz a significant case. Willems yields too suddenly to Aissa, and his "faint cry" of surrender (p. 81) is a far cry from Kurtz's " 'Exterminate all the brutes!' " or Jim's final proud wordless glance. Even a Lingard lacks the nobility of purpose with which Kurtz approaches his Congo journey or Jim his lordship of Patusan. At the same time, however, Willems has a complexity Almayer had lacked. Clarifying his intentions in a letter, Conrad explains Willems' conflict as one between "thought" and "the senses," [7] a formulation which fails to suggest

⁷ Aubry, *Life and Letters,* I, p. 181.

the symbolic depth of the novel's imagery and characterization, but does say something about both Willems and Kurtz.

Like the relationship between Nina and Dain, that between Willems and Aissa is seen in terms of light and darkness: Willems' first glimpse of Aissa is "a flash of white and colour, a gleam of gold like a sun-ray lost in shadow, and a vision of blackness darker than the deepest shade of the forest" (p. 68); Aissa is likened to "tropical life which wants the sunshine but works in gloom" (p. 70); and in his final submission, Willems falls "back into the darkness" (p. 81). Once again these light-and-darkness images are associated with images of form and chaos: just as what Kurtz sees finally resists specification, so Willems feels himself "lost amongst shapeless things" (p. 80), and the idea of Aissa produces "noise" in his brain (p. 78). Once again the half-caste and half-civilized figures who stand on the borderline between these two worlds are represented in mixed and disrupted forms: Willems' wife, for example, trailing through life in a "red dressing-gown, with its row of dirty blue bows down the front, stained, and hooked on awry; a torn flounce on the bottom following her like a snake" (p. 25); or Willems himself, on his way toward darkness, clothed above the waist in a jacket "soiled and torn," and below the waist "in a worn-out and faded sarong" (p. 87). Again, the tools of civilization lose their function under the impact of savage energy: the neglected office of Lingard and Company, gradually deteriorating under the realities of trade with savages, and exhibiting finally a "hopeless disorder—the senseless and vain decay of all these emblems of civilized commerce" (p. 301); or Almayer's useless watch, which he lets run down in his "apathetic indifference to mere hours" (p. 308). Sometimes this principle is strikingly extended, as when in the novel's climactic scenes Lingard abandons his revolver to choke and strike Willems, and Aissa uses it to kill him—an ironic inversion analogous to Marlow's gradual abandonment of tools and machines, and the Congo natives' gradual accumulation of them. *Outcast* hints at other image-patterns which will appear more fully in the Marlow tales, as when Willems imagines himself peering "into a deep black hole full of decay and of whitened bones" (p. 339), thus anticipating the grove of death in "Heart of Darkness"; or when he sees the darkness "blotchy with ill-defined shapes, as if a new universe was being evolved out of sombre chaos" (p. 236), and senses in the forest around him a "merciless and mysterious purpose, perpetuating strife and death through the march of ages" (p. 337), thus suggesting briefly the historical and evolutionary dimensions of the later story.

Like the highest (or lowest) visions of Jim and Kurtz, Willems' passion for Aissa is ultimately resistant to declarative statement; and *An Outcast of the Islands* offers a variety of evidence to suggest that in struggling with this problem, Conrad was learning the necessity for the enigmatic extremes and "adjectival vagueness" of "Heart of Darkness" and *Lord Jim.* When Willems listens to "the voice of his fate" he hears a "sound inarticulate but full of meaning" (p. 80); he feels the "fear of something unknown that had taken possession of his heart, of something inarticulate and masterful which could not speak and would be obeyed" (p. 72), a phrase significantly related also to the heart-metaphors of the Marlow tales. As Willems regresses along the evolutionary scale, his language habits suffer the same fate as other civilized artifacts and forms: separated from Aissa, he is "heard alone, howling maledictions in Malay, in Dutch, and in English," and calling Aissa's name in "a shout loud, discordant"; Lakamba, staring with "gloomy contempt in the direction of the inhuman sound," observes that " 'his speech is like the raving of a mad dog' " (p. 107). At the same time, Conrad attempts to dramatize these primitive and subverbal passions, which leads to Willems' unfortunate practice of " 'biting myself to forget in that pain the fire that hurts me there!' " and to his striking his own breast so violently with his fist that he "reeled under his own blow, [and] fell into a chair that stood near" (p. 91). If this is an improvement over Dain Maroola's implausible eloquence, it is somehow less persuasive than Kurtz's vague possessiveness, cruelty, and "horror." The lines of development suggested by words such as "inarticulate" and "unknown" and by phrases like "the obscure abominations of Willems' conduct" (p. 239) are more satisfactory, and move *An Outcast of the Islands* closer to "Heart of Darkness." How close Conrad really is in *Outcast* to a conscious control of this device is apparent in its many subtle extensions; the "barbarians" in Lakamba's compound are articulate, for example, but their language lacks the economy and precision of a civilized tongue; their talk is "monotonous," and they "never seem able to thresh a matter out" (p. 95).

By the time of the Marlow tales Conrad had become aware that his early themes ultimately required the highest degree of self-understanding on the part of his protagonists; and although Willems lacks the stature fully to understand his own regression, or even to regress in Kurtz's heroic way, there are hesitant movements toward self-awareness on the part of Willems, Aissa, and Lingard which take Conrad a step at least toward the narrator of the *Nigger*, or Karain, or Marlow. Seeing (like Kurtz) an "image" in "a sudden moment of lucidity—of that cruel lucidity that comes once in life to the most benighted," Willems seems to see what is happening "within him," and is "horrified at the strange sight" (p. 80); and he finds himself drawn irresistibly toward the "degradation" of "those miserable savages" despite "all the hate of his race, of his morality, of his intelligence" (p. 126). Willems wishes consciously, as Kurtz does, to bring form to the formless: to "fashion," "mould," and "soften" Aissa; while she at the other end strives toward light and form and a conceptual grasp of life, feeling "the intense, over-powering desire to see in, to see through, to understand everything: every thought, emotion, purpose . . . inside that white-clad foreign being who looked at her . . . white-haired and mysterious. It was the future clothed in flesh . . . if only first he could be understood! . . . To her the ex-clerk of old Hudig appeared as remote, as brilliant, as terrible, as necessary, as the sun that gives life" (pp. 247–248).

The peculiar combination of desire and resistance to desire that Willems feels in the presence of Aissa ("He was horrified and grateful; drawn irresistibly to her—and ready to run away" —p. 150) leads toward the qualities of paradox in the experience of Jim and Kurtz. Willems' two women are roughly analogous to Kurtz's two "Intendeds" in this respect, although Willems' feeling for either woman is degraded in comparison. It is important to see here that Aissa must not be taken as representative of sexual feeling or "love" per se, but rather of a destructive and regressive passion. After he has yielded to Aissa, Willems sits up suddenly "with the movement and look of a man awakened by the crash of his own falling house" (p. 77); and when late in the novel she clasps Willems passionately, he recoils "in horror" (p. 285), just as Kurtz does late in "Heart of Darkness." Conrad had not at this point fully discriminated the symbolic components that appear later in his treatment of sexual love. In Willems' obsessive illusion, Aissa is sometimes seen as the *source* of light and form; and conflicting ideas of pleasure and pain, life and death, creativity and passivity appear together in the descriptive imagery: "The heat poured down from the sky, clung about the steaming earth, rolled among the trees, and wrapped up Willems in the soft and odorous folds of air heavy with the faint scent of blossoms and with the acrid smell of decaying life. And in that atmosphere of Nature's workshop Willems felt soothed and lulled into forgetfulness of his past, into indifference as to his future. . . . And he lay there, dreamily contented, in the tepid and perfumed shelter, thinking of Aissa's eyes" (pp. 74–75). Conrad's own description of Willems' passion, however— *"l'esclavage physique de l'homme par une femme absolument sauvage"* [8]—as well as the existence of Kurtz's polar Intendeds, suggest that Conrad was capable of further analysis of sexual feeling; and even Willems occasionally sees the difference.

[8] Letter to Mme. Poradowsky dated "Lundi matin" and assigned by Dr. John Archer Gee to Monday, October 29 or November 5, 1894. Quoted by Gordan, *Joseph Conrad*, p. 53.

Yet Willems never develops anything like the self-awareness Conrad's protagonists must have if he is to explore his early themes fully. " 'It wasn't me,' " Willems tells Lingard near the end of the novel; " 'The evil was not in me, Captain Lingard' " (p. 273). It is as if Conrad had split the single consciousness in which Willems' conflict might have been felt fully, so that Willems and Lingard are really two halves of a whole: it is Lingard who idealistically gives Willems a second chance and is victimized by his bad judgment, but Willems who becomes victim and agent of the forces of darkness. Without Lingard's moral stability, Willems yields too easily, and the novel moves away from psychological conflict toward melodrama. The underlying identity of Willems and Lingard is stressed: " 'We are responsible for one another—worse luck. I am almost ashamed of myself, but I can understand your dirty pride. I can!' " says Lingard (p. 40), and Willems' occasional irruptions of conscience and Lingard's descents into darkness tend to bridge the gap between them. It is true, I think, that in Lingard's final confrontation of Willems "one sees a trial edition of the meaning of James Wait to the crew of the 'Narcissus,' Lord Jim's meeting with Gentleman Brown, the betrayal of Haldin (*Under Western Eyes*), the arrival of Mr. Jones at Heyst's Island (*Victory*) —and the secret sharer"; [9] but these later confrontations are technically successful only because the point of view is set so firmly with the higher character, whose consciousness can envelop, and as it were subsume, the lower, thus restoring the unity that is lost in *Outcast*.

More important, *An Outcast of the Islands* gives us "trial editions" of other aspects of structure and point of view in the Marlow tales. The novel hints, for one thing, that Willems' dilemma may be satisfactorily rendered only by an outside observer like Lingard: for reasons that have been suggested, ex-

[9] Vernon Young, "Lingard's Folly: The Lost Subject," *Kenyon Review*, XV (Autumn 1953), 535–536.

tremists like Willems, Kurtz, and Jim do not yield easily to concrete dramatic treatment. In his "long and painful gropings amongst the obscure abominations of Willems' conduct" (p. 239), Lingard begins to identify with Willems; and like Marlow steaming into the Congo or listening to Jim, feels "an emotion unknown, singular, penetrating and sad" in the presence of Aissa (p. 249). Just as Marlow at first supposes that Jim is merely "silly," so Lingard when he first faces the degraded Willems is bitterly scornful of him (significantly, the term "cur" is applied to Willems not long before this meeting), and Lingard is only gradually won to the sense of his own responsibility in Willems' plight and to some degree of identification with him. Lingard's inability to judge Willems may be seen as an early version of Marlow's hesitancy about Jim; but Lingard, unfortunately, is so intimately involved in the action that he must judge—hence the unsatisfactory beating he administers Willems. In any case, the Lingard of *Outcast* suffers moral limitations much like those of a Brierly or a French Lieutenant: "Common sense and experience taught a man the way that was right. The other was for lubbers and fools" (p. 199).

In Conrad's shifting of the secondary point of view in *Outcast* —from Willems to Almayer to Lingard to Aissa to Babalatchi— he produces an early version of the choral structures in *Lord Jim*. Since there is no effective single consciousness to draw all these points of view together and transcend them, the reader may occasionally lose himself; but these narrative experiments are often revealing. Almayer, for example, is the first of the inferior choral reactors in Conrad (if we discount the brief appearance of the Dutch officers in *Almayer's Folly*). The persistent irony at Almayer's expense not only directs the reader beyond Almayer's pompously moralistic view of Willems, but adds, by contrast, to Willems' stature:

"Disgusting exhibition," said Almayer, loftily. "What could father ever see in you? You are as estimable as a heap of garbage."

"You talk like that! You, who sold your soul for a few guilders," muttered Willems, wearily, without opening his eyes.

"Not so few," said Almayer, with instinctive readiness. (p. 91)

In the midst of Almayer's dull and vengeful account of Abdulla's entrance into Sambir, Willems is revealed by contrast as a man of ironic intelligence: " 'Let me congratulate you, Almayer, upon the cleverness of your child. She recognized me at once, and cried "pig" as naturally as you would yourself' " (p. 186). And in Aissa's despairing resentment of Willems' commitments to a mysterious white race, and more specifically to a white woman, Jewel's attitude toward Jim is prefigured.

Some of the other rhetorical and symbolic methods of the Marlow tales are anticipated here as well. Covered with blood after Lingard's assault, Willems seems "an incomprehensible figure marked all over with some awful and symbolic signs of deadly import" (pp. 263–264), thus a precursor of the mysterious Kurtz and a clear step away from the physical details of the narrative toward their meaning in Lingard's consciousness. There is again a time shift, in Part III. There are several "as if" and "it seemed" constructions in the descriptive passages, suggesting a growing tendency on Conrad's part to dissociate himself from the more fanciful uses of physical detail and to assign them to another point of view. And there are occasional long Marlovian paragraphs dropped oddly into the narrative—tart, abstract, ironic, and sometimes so indirectly related to the physical action that they seem merely digressive:

Consciously or unconsciously, men are proud of their firmness, steadfastness of purpose, directness of aim. They go straight towards their desire, to the accomplishment of virtue—sometimes of crime—in an uplifting persuasion of their firmness. They walk the road of life, the road fenced in by their tastes, prejudices, disdains or enthusiasms, generally honest, invariably stupid, and are proud of never losing their way. If they do stop, it is to look for a moment over the hedges that make them safe, to look at the misty valleys, at the distant peaks, at cliffs and morasses, at the dark forests and the hazy plains where other human beings grope their days painfully away, stumbling over the bones of the wise, over the unburied remains of their predecessors who died alone, in gloom or in sunshine, halfway from anywhere. The man of purpose does not understand, and goes on, full of contempt. (p. 197)

In sum, Conrad is beginning to feel the need for Marlow, and to undertake experiments which will lead to his creation.

Stein also is anticipated in *Outcast,* along with some of the ideas and symbolic motifs generated by his domination of *Lord Jim.* The metaphysical framework of the *Patna* voyage, for example—which, as has been suggested, gains significance from Stein's being a "naturalist"—appears also in *Outcast,* couched in descriptive language much like that of *Lord Jim:* "The light and heat fell upon the settlement . . . as if flung down by an angry hand. The land lay silent, still, and brilliant under the avalanche of burning rays that had destroyed all sound and all motion, had buried all shadows, had choked every breath. No living thing dared to affront the serenity of this cloudless sky. . . . Only the frail butterflies, the fearless children of the sun, the capricious tyrants of the flowers, fluttered audaciously in the open" (p. 85). The special position of butterflies in this cosmos reminds the reader of Stein, of course. And it has been remarked that the final message Almayer receives from the dark forests and hills is a primitive form of Stein's affirmation: the single word "hope," repeated, like Stein's enigmatic remarks, in "a whispering echo," and leaving Almayer, like Marlow, with "no other answer" (p. 368). But there are other remarks and figures of speech in *Outcast* equally characteristic of Stein—Lingard's metaphor, for example, as he ponders his own responsibility in the situation created by Willems in Sambir: "Life is foul! Foul like a lee forebrace on a dirty night. And yet. And yet. One must see it clear for running before going below—for good" (p. 191), a moral summation much like Stein's, and with a Stein-like redundancy, or a description of Willems which anticipates Stein's central image: "With a faint cry and an upward throw of his arms he gave up as a tired swimmer gives up: because the swamped craft is gone from under his feet; because the night is dark and the shore is far—because death is better than strife" (p. 81). There is even a Roumanian naturalist at the end of the novel, from whom Almayer demands an explanation of Willems' behavior; and the naturalist's syntactically disorganized response suggests a Stein-like perception of the duality of human nature.

Finally, some important patterns of imagery in the Marlow tales receive their first significant development in *Outcast*. Again, the most striking of these is probably the animal imagery. Encouraged by her howling father, Nina Almayer calls "Pig! Pig! Pig!" after the retreating Willems (p. 94); Almayer likens him to a mad dog, a "sick tiger" (p. 161), and a "snake" (p. 93); like the Chief Engineer of *Lord Jim*, Willems struggles on "wearily with a set, distressed face behind which, in his tired brain, seethed his thoughts: restless, sombre, tangled, chilling, horrible and venomous, like a nestful of snakes" (p. 328). Aissa exhibits "a wild and resentful defiance" (p. 71) and runs with a "startling fleetness" (p. 78), but yields to Willems' "taming" of her (p. 76). Sometimes this metaphor is merged effectively with other strains of imagery: Willems "raged for three days like a black panther that is hungry" (p. 119); Aissa's "delicate nostrils . . . expanded and collapsed quickly, flutteringly, in interrupted beats, like the wings of a snared bird" (p. 247). In addition, there is the motif of a descent into hell that appears in "Heart of Darkness," and again implicitly with Gentleman Brown in *Lord Jim*: Willems feels that his soul is threatened with "damnation," sees Aissa as "sin," and promises to "repent" (p. 278); at other moments he feels himself "without the hope of any redemption" (p. 127); and having fallen "back into the darkness" (p. 81) at the end of Part I, emerges at the beginning of Part II as a "spectre" from "below" (p. 87).

An Outcast of the Islands is thus an important precursor of "Heart of Darkness" and *Lord Jim*. It is easy to find imperfections in the novel, especially in its descriptive technique. Some-

times the imagery simply fails to expand the meaning; sometimes
it is simply inconsistent with the jungle setting, as when Willems tosses "like a grain of dust in a whirlwind" (p. 157).
Sometimes it is too artificially symbolic to be convincing, as
when a giant raindrop is compared to a "superhuman tear" (p.
255). As in *Almayer's Folly*, the use of a house as a symbol of
illusion (not to mention the house of cards that Lingard finds it
impossible to build) may be too obvious. Sometimes the sym-
bolic-descriptive parallels seem too sensitive for the projected
observer, as when Lingard sees a cloud "dragging behind a tail of
tangled and filmy streamers—like the dishevelled hair of a
mourning woman" (p. 241); sometimes the weather and sky, as
in the climactic scene between Willems and Lingard, seem to
follow too obediently the characters' emotions. And sometimes
Conrad's irony seems too heavy and abrupt, as in the discourse
on "men of purpose." But these defects are of a kind which will
be remedied with the entrance of Marlow, and *An Outcast of
the Islands* is much closer to the Marlow tales than has generally
been supposed.

The Nigger of the 'Narcissus' poses special problems. Conrad's shift to a sea setting and his nostalgic wish to celebrate the
entire crew of the *Narcissus* (except the latecomers Wait and
Donkin) tend to obscure the lines of growth lying between
Almayer's Folly and *Lord Jim*. The *Nigger* has always invited
more analytic criticism than the Malayan tales, partly because it
seems resonant with symbolic meanings: while "certainly a tribute to this particular ship on which (for her beauty) Conrad
chose to sail in 1884 . . . it is also a study in collective psychology; and also, frankly, a symbolic comment on man's nature and
destiny; and also, less openly, a prose-poem carrying overtones of
myth." [10] I share Ian Watt's skepticism of too-esoteric readings of

[10] Guerard, *Conrad the Novelist*, p. 100. To gain a sense of the
difficult issues raised by this story, the reader might begin with Guerard's
discussion and Vernon Young, "Trial by Water: Joseph Conrad's *The*

the *Nigger;* Conrad's own simpler description seems more exact: "My effort to present a group of men held together by a common loyalty and a common perplexity in a struggle not with human enemies, but with the hostile conditions testing their faithfulness to the conditions of their own calling . . .—the crew of a merchant ship, brought to the test of what I may venture to call the moral problem of conduct" (*Last Essays,* pp. 94–95). But whether mythic or philosophic or ethical at its center, the *Nigger* shows Conrad's growing control of some of his most characteristic psycho-moral motifs and esthetic devices; a more conscious use of symbolic imagery, and a greater sublety in the projection of psycho-moral forces. The opposition between Donkin and Wait, with their "disdain and hate for the austere servitude of the sea" (p. 11), and Captain Allistoun, with his absolute fidelity to it, needs only to be given greater universality, and the spirit of darkness represented by Wait put into its native context, to provide the symbolic tensions of "Heart of Darkness." In Donkin's alliance with Wait is implicit Conrad's skepticism toward theoretical social reform, which is to appear lightly in the early Marlow tales, and later, in more developed form, in Conrad's political fiction. The inner and outer threats to the *Narcissus,* Wait and the weather, are fused through a highly developed pattern of light-and-darkness imagery and through metaphors of water and night—a strain of imagery which leads Young to speak of the "subaqueous" source of the story's symbolism,[11] and is later to be elevated to near-allegorical status in "The Secret Sharer": like Leggatt, Jimmy bobs up "upon the surface, compelling attention, like a black buoy chained to the bottom of a muddy stream" (p. 138). And what Guerard has called the

Nigger of the 'Narcissus,' " Accent, XII (Spring 1952), 67–81, reprinted in R. W. Stallman, ed., *The Art of Joseph Conrad* (East Lansing: Michigan State University Press, 1960), pp. 108–120; and then turn to Watt, "Conrad Criticism and *The Nigger of the 'Narcissus.' "

[11] Young, "Trial by Water," 80.

"preternatural malevolence" [12] of the storm that threatens the
Narcissus can also be applied to Wait and Donkin, whose malig-
nancy relates them to more obviously preternatural figures like
Gentleman Brown and Mr. Jones.

The Nigger of the 'Narcissus' is, however, a less rigorous test
of Conrad's moral attitudes than the Marlow tales. Despite the
threat posed to the crew's solidarity by Wait and Donkin, the
essential direction of the novel is optimistic and romantic: "Haven't we, together and upon the immortal sea, wrung out a
meaning from our sinful lives? Good-bye, brothers! You were a
good crowd. As good a crowd as ever fisted with wild cries the
beating canvas of a heavy foresail; or tossing aloft, invisible in
the night, gave back yell for yell to a westerly gale" (p. 173).
Just as Willems lacks the stature really to oppose Lingard's will,
and is simply destroyed, so Wait and Donkin are simply repressed. An element of untested melodrama remains in both
novels; and the *Nigger* stays closer to the nostalgic mood of
"Youth" than to the complexly qualified mood of *Lord Jim*, or
the philosophically affirmative mood of *Victory*. Captain Allistoun's command—" 'Mr. Baker, my orders are that this man is
not to be allowed on deck' " (p. 120)—is after all never violated,
despite the dissatisfied murmurings of the crew; and Donkin's
rebellion is quelled by the sheer bitter force of the Captain's
personality. With the sea-burial of Wait a favorable wind arises
for the *Narcissus* (another early analogue to "The Secret
Sharer"), Donkin is returned to the corruptions of the land, and
the crew's solidarity is sustained. An idyllic tone is never very far
from the tale, and inevitably returns to it in dramatically quies-
cent moments, as at the very end.

This essential optimism is reflected in Conrad's most characteristic imagery, as in the profusion of light when the *Narcissus*
enters her berth. The light-and-darkness imagery has been dis-

[12] *Nostromo*, with a General Introduction by Albert J. Guerard, in the
Laurel Conrad series (New York: Dell, 1960), p. 11.

cussed at length elsewhere.[13] It is worth adding, however, that even in this unlikely setting Wait sometimes suggests the oppressive tropical qualities associated with the principle of darkness in Conrad: "a black mist emanated from him; a subtle and dismal influence" (p. 34). This kind of imagery is once again supplemented by other types of symbol and image related to the axis of darkness and light, the primitive and the civilized: most notably the animal imagery which will in *Lord Jim* assume even greater importance in describing the crew of another ship. Jimmy is seen in the presence of Captain Allistoun with "an aspect astounding and animal-like. . . . A thing of instinct . . . a scared brute" (p. 118). Donkin is seen as "some strange creature that looks as though it could sting or bite," a "screechin' poll-parrot," and a "dirty white cockatoo" (p. 110). Like Cornelius, Donkin is "abject"; and at the highest moment of dramatic crisis, when Captain Allistoun is forcing the belaying pin back upon him, he is called a "cur" (p. 136), as Jim mistakenly thinks himself called at an early moment of dramatic crisis in *Lord Jim*. Similarly, the inferno imagery that has been associated with Willems and will later be associated with Kurtz and Gentleman Brown is here associated with Wait: the cook knows that Satan is abroad amongst the crew (p. 38); Jimmy's room has "the brilliance of a silver shrine where a black idol . . . blinked its weary eyes and received our homage" (p. 105); and so on. And surprisingly, even in the ritualized setting of the *Narcissus*, Conrad is able to exploit the symbolic disruption of tools and forms under the pressure of emergent darkness. With the *Narcissus* on her side and Jimmy trapped in his room, the men undertake to reach him through the bulkhead of the carpenter's shop: "The room seemed to have been devastated. . . . The bench, a half-finished meat-safe, saws, chisels, wire rods, axes, crowbars, lay in a heap besprinkled with loose nails. A sharp adze struck up with a

[13] See, e.g., Young, "Trial by Water," 70–73; Cecil Scrimgeour, "Jimmy Wait and the Dance of Death: Conrad's *Nigger of the 'Narcissus,'*" *Critical Quarterly*, VII (Winter 1965), 339–352.

shining edge that gleamed dangerously down there like a wicked smile. . . . He was screaming and knocking below us. . . . We attacked with desperation the abominable heap of things heavy, of things sharp, of things clumsy to handle"; while Wamibo, a Heart-of-Darkness crewman, "[sat] glaring above us—all shining eyes, gleaming fangs, tumbled hair; resembling an amazed and half-witted fiend gloating over the extraordinary agitation of the damned" (pp. 65–66). As in all the early work, this symbolic principle is extended finally to human language itself. The figures of highest dignity and wisdom—Captain Allistoun and old Singleton—are thoroughly reticent, while the depraved Don‧kin is the most loquacious of all. (As "the incarnation of barbar‧ian wisdom" [p. 6], tattooed and reading his *Pelham*, Singleton is also the most consciously symbolic figure so far of Conrad's twilight group, a precursor of Marlow's helmsman in "Heart of Darkness.") After the repression of Donkin, the "problem of life seemed too voluminous for the narrow limits of human speech, and by common consent it was abandoned" (p. 138). And near‧ing his end, Wait, like Kurtz, appears "terrified as though he had been looking at unspeakable horrors" (p. 153). Because of his special artistic purposes, Conrad exploits these devices less than he does in most of his other early work; but they appear in crucial contexts.

The philosophic assumptions which form a context for Con‧rad's early psycho-moral explorations also begin to emerge more clearly in the *Nigger*. As other writers have pointed out, the novel's mythical and metaphysical symbolism helps to universal‧ize its themes, but is so curiously mixed as to imply a final skepticism. These attitudes will be sharpened in "Heart of Dark‧ness" and *Lord Jim* by Marlow's ironic generalities; here, as again in *Lord Jim*, they are reinforced through passages of meta‧phorical description:

The passage had begun, and the ship, a fragment detached from the earth, went on lonely and swift like a small planet. Round her the abysses of sky and sea met in an unattainable frontier. A great

circular solitude moved with her, ever changing and ever the same.
. . . Now and then another wandering white speck, burdened with
life, appeared far off—disappeared. . . . The sun looked upon her all
day, and every morning rose with a burning, round stare of undying
curiosity. She had her own future; she was alive with the lives of
those beings who trod her decks. . . . She drove foaming to the
southward, as if guided by the courage of a high endeavour. The
smiling greatness of the sea dwarfed the extent of time. The days
raced after one another, brilliant and quick like the flashes of a
lighthouse, and the nights, eventful and short, resembled fleeting
dreams. (pp. 29–30)

A point-for-point comparison of this passage with the precisely
parallel description of the *Patna's* voyage in *Lord Jim* (p. 16,
quoted above) will itself demonstrate Conrad's capacity for
growth.

Conrad's skepticism in the *Nigger* is reflected in his treatment
of the cook, who, if he is not precisely an object of levity (as
Conrad himself warned [14]), is certainly an object of satire and a
tool of Conrad's theological skepticism. He is "technically a
seaman, but in reality no sailor" (p. 51), a damning charge in
Conrad's universe. His Christian vision is a "supreme conceit" to
which he sacrifices "the last vestige of his humanity" (p. 116).
Captain Allistoun, at the apex of maritime wisdom, calls the
cook's attempt to convert Wait a "caper" (p. 118) and orders
him out of Wait's cabin. Finally, the cook sinks to the degrading
level of an intimacy with Donkin, a pairing of perverse imagina-
tions which suggests the common denominator of Conrad's skepticism toward all theoretical idealism. As in *The Secret Agent*,
social consciousness here is a grossly comic inversion of prepoliti-

[14] Aubry, *Life and Letters*, I, p. 206. Any notion of conventional
Christian feeling in Conrad, however, can be dispelled by reading his
letters—e.g., "I shall be inexorable like destiny and shall look upon your
sufferings with the idiotic serenity of a benevolent Creator (I don't know
that the ben: Crea: is serene:—but if he is (as they say) then he must be
idiotic) looking at the precious mess he has made of his only job" (I, p.
213).

cal virtues, a resistance to duty rationalized by "labor rights" theory. Donkin "knows all about his rights, but knows nothing of courage, of endurance . . . of the unspoken loyalty that knits together a ship's company" (p. 11). With the *Narcissus* on its side, he leads the cry chop the masts: " 'Cut! Don't mind that murdering fool! Cut, some of you!' " (p. 60); and in this demand he prefigures the grotesque value-inversions of Conrad's later villains.

The emotional immediacy of his materials led Conrad into a strangely shifting point of view in the *Nigger*—from "they" to "we" to "I"—and this yields an important technical advantage which looks ahead to "Heart of Darkness" and *Lord Jim*. Through the narrator's gradual involvement with Wait, the fragmentation of the ship's psychology is made more clearly visible; and Marlow's identifications with Kurtz and Jim are anticipated. In an important passage, in which Wait looks much like the feverish Kurtz in his compound, the narrator defines the crew's reaction to him: "He was becoming immaterial like an apparition; his cheekbones rose, the forehead slanted more; the face was all hollows, patches of shade; and the fleshless head resembled a disinterred black skull, fitted with two restless globes of silver in the sockets of eyes. He was demoralising. Through him we were becoming highly humanised, tender, complex, excessively decadent; we understood the subtlety of his fear, sympathised with all his repulsions, shrinkings, evasions, delusions—as though we had been overcivilised, and rotten, and without any knowledge of the meaning of life" (p. 139). If this is, as the narrator goes on to say, an initiation into "infamous mysteries," it is certainly not the same sort of initiation that Kurtz and Marlow undergo in the Congo, since Kurtz can hardly be said to fall into decadence. But the symbolic mechanisms are closely similar.

Finally, however, the *Nigger* only makes clearer the need for an internal narrator in Conrad's early fiction. By the time of the *Nigger* much of Conrad's symbolism is analogistic, protected by such locutions as "like" and "resembled." With the entrance of

Marlow to take responsibility for these metaphors, Conrad will be able more effectively to preserve both the objectivity and the symbolic fancy of his descriptions. The need for dramatic consistency in Marlow's speech will help to obviate a certain amount of metaphor-mixing—as when the *Narcissus* in the space of a half-dozen lines is shaken "like a toy in the hand of a lunatic," suffers a gust "brutal like the blow of a fist," faces into "the teeth of the screeching squall," receives hail like "a shower of pearls," and finally sees the light extinguished by a "wild night" which "[stamps] out . . . that dismal remnant of a stormy day" (p. 53). If *The Nigger of the 'Narcissus'* justifies the love that Conrad felt for it, it still does not contain his best descriptive writing. Conrad was disturbed, in fact, by Arthur Symons' charge that the *Nigger's* descriptive passages simply lacked thematic coherence: "the whole movement, noise, order, and distraction of a ship and a ship's company during a storm. . . . But what more is there? Where is the idea of which such things as these should be but servants? Ah, there has been an oversight." [15] Whether imperceptive reactions such as these helped drive Conrad toward Marlow cannot be known with any assurance. But it is apparent that he needed some further device to help him "get through the veil of details at the essence of life," [16] as he had felt he was trying to do in *The Nigger of the 'Narcissus.'*

Immediately after finishing *An Outcast of the Islands* Conrad turned to "The Lagoon," his first public venture in short story writing. As Conrad himself observed, "The Lagoon" retains the mood of *Outcast;* and an extraordinary intensification of symbolic overtones in its descriptive passages, along with a cloying naïveté introduced by the internal narrator Arsat, have made it an easy target for parody. Even Conrad jokingly viewed the style

[15] *Saturday Review*, LXXXV (1898), 145–146; quoted by Gordan, *Joseph Conrad*, p. 289.
[16] Aubry, *Life and Letters*, I, p. 200.

as "second-hand Conradese." [17] But "The Lagoon" does represent
a radical step toward Marlow: except for Almayer's account of
indignities suffered at the hands of Willems and his native allies,
this is the first example in Conrad of an extended narration
within a narration. With just one more step away from the
immediacy of Arsat's experience—so that the white man, little
more than a listener in the tale as it stands, might tell Arsat's
story to still a further audience, Conrad would have created a
point of view closely analogous to that of the Marlow tales, and
would have been relieved both of the story's too-active *décor* and
of its odd spiritual simplicity.

Even more interesting is "Karain: A Memory." Written after
the *Nigger*, and therefore significantly closer to the Marlow
tales, "Karain" displays a variety of analogues to both "Heart of
Darkness" and *Lord Jim*. Here Conrad makes his first attempt to
"justify" a narrator—the native chieftain Karain himself—and
to create a figure of high symbolic stature. The first section
consists solely of such background exposition and characterization of Karain as will tend to elevate him appropriately. His
significance is universal: "It was almost impossible to remember
who he was," the frame narrator says, ". . . he summed up his
race, his country, the elemental force of ardent life, of tropical
nature" (p. 7). A man superior both in "wisdom" and in physical
skills to the rest of his people (p. 8), Karain has the power "to
awaken an absurd expectation of something heroic going to take
place" (p. 6); and when he sweeps his arm toward his domain,
the movement seems "to drive back its limits, augmenting it
suddenly into something . . . immense and vague" (pp. 4–5).
On the other hand, Karain bears surprising resemblances to
Marlow: he tells his story at night, aboard a ship, to a spectrum
of moral types seated around the ship's table; speaks with "an
ironic and melancholy shrewdness"; smokes a "cheroot"; and
pauses in pensive silence (pp. 13–14). And like the Marlow

[17] *Ibid.*, I, p. 194.

both of "Heart of Darkness" and *Lord Jim*, Karain is seen in a curiously trancelike state just before he takes over the narrative: "upright and motionless . . . gleaming and still as if cast in metal. Only his lips moved" (p. 27).

Since Karain is both narrator and hero of his story, there are generic similarities also between Karain and Jim, and Karain and Kurtz. But again the closeness of these parallels is striking. Karain adjudicating disputes among his people might easily be Tuan Jim on Patusan: "He dispensed justice in the shade; from a high seat he gave orders, advice, reproof. . . . To no man had been given the shelter of so much respect, confidence, and awe. Yet at times he would lean forward and appear to listen . . . as if expecting to hear some faint voice, the sound of light footsteps" (p. 16). Or preparing for war (one of his weapons, like Jim's, is a "six-pounder brass-gun"—p. 20): "He was plotting . . . with patience, with foresight. . . . Our attempts to make clear the irresistible nature of the forces which he desired to arrest failed to discourage his eagerness. . . . He did not understand us, and replied by arguments that almost drove one to desperation by their childish shrewdness. He was absurd and unanswerable" (p. 18). Like Jim, Karain has a faithful bodyguard, leaps out of a stockade, is pursued by the phantom of his betrayal, gets a second chance through the agency of an older and wiser man, and becomes through military conquest the lord of a grateful and awe-struck people. And his listeners feel much as Marlow does in the presence of Kurtz: "We did not know what to do with that problem from the outer darkness" (the significant difference beween "outer darkness" and Kurtz's "Inner Station" suggesting the direction of Conrad's own growth); ". . . We felt as though we three had been called to the very gate of Infernal Regions to judge, to decide the fate of a wanderer coming suddenly from a world of sunshine and illusions" (p. 45).[18] The device of the

[18] Bruce M. Johnson, "Conrad's 'Karain' and *Lord Jim*," *Modern Language Quarterly*, XXIV (March 1963), 13–20, confirms some of these observations and suggests a variety of other parallels.

native narrator is less successful than Conrad apparently had hoped. Despite Arsat's reminder that he had merely behaved "like you whites" (p. 196) and the frame narrator's effort to universalize "Karain," neither story succeeds in establishing the *identification* between the native speaker and his audience that Marlow so crucially feels with Kurtz and Jim. Only if the first auditor of the tale—e.g., Marlow—can *retell* it, can the gradual spiritual involvement and self-discovery essential to Conrad's themes be satisfactorily dramatized; and only with a second narrator like Marlow can the primitive dilemmas of an Arsat or Karain or Jim be satisfactorily universalized and extended meditatively to other contexts. But Conrad made significant progress in these two early tales.

The remaining three stories in *Tales of Unrest* are of less interest. "The Idiots" is more in Maupassant's idiom than Conrad's, and may be set respectfully aside. "An Outpost of Progress" has achieved a certain notoriety, as Conrad's first experiment with the Congo setting, and thus an obvious forerunner of "Heart of Darkness." But it is closer both in time and spirit to the early Malayan tales, and shows the same defects. A semicomic depiction of low illusion and its destruction by the emergent madness of the station-keepers Kayerts and Carlier, the story is reminiscent of *Outcast*. As in the earlier work, there are passages of a disturbing abstractness, which lack the protection of Marlow's personality and seem just as intrusive as comparable passages in *Almayer* or *Outcast*: for example, "The contact with pure unmitigated savagery . . . brings sudden and profound trouble into the heart. To the sentiment of being alone of one's kind . . . to the negation of the habitual, which is safe, there is added the affirmation of the unusual, which is dangerous; a suggestion of things vague, uncontrollable, and repulsive, whose discomposing intrusion excites the imagination and tries the civilized nerves of the foolish and the wise alike" (p. 89). And just as Conrad's technical methods have not progressed far enough to yield the profounder meanings of his Congo experience, so Kayerts and Carlier simply lack the stature of Conrad's later protagonists, and like Willems and Almayer, are easy marks for irony. In some details, the story throws light on "Heart of Darkness": the "incomprehensible" native chief is called an "old image" by Kayerts (p. 95), a clue to the epistemological paradox of Kurtz's death scene; the whites are addressed by an emissary of darkness in speech which is "like a reminiscence . . . like one of those impossible languages which sometimes we hear in our dreams" (p. 97); and so on. But Kayerts' final debility and madness are not much more convincing than Almayer's, and his death scene not much more dramatically persuasive than Willems'.

Finally, there is "The Return," which even Conrad felt was a "left-handed production" (p. viii). Standing apart from his central line of development, imitative rather than inspired by his own experience, "The Return" at first seems wholly uncharacteristic of Conrad. Its chief interest, perhaps, is its position as the first of his exercises in extended irony at the expense of social convention, and hence an early indicator of his political attitudes. Yet in its account of the destruction of Alvan Hervey's illusions, the story does fit also into the psycho-moral framework Conrad had been developing in his early fiction: in its abstract phrasing, "The Return" seems as close to *Lord Jim* in idea as in time. Hervey has ignored "the hidden stream, the stream restless and dark" (p. 123); in the face of his wife's apparent infidelity he feels a "loathsome rush of emotion breaking through all the reserves that guarded his manhood" (p. 130); and like Jim, he would like to "Forget! Forget!" (p. 138). In Conrad's commentary on Hervey's misfortune and self-delusion, he approaches the later Marlovian commentary on Jim's persistent idealism: "There are in life events, contacts, glimpses, that seem brutally to bring all the past to a close. There is a shock and a crash as of a gate flung to behind one. . . . Go and seek another paradise, fool or sage. There is a moment of dumb dismay, and the wanderings must begin again; the painful explaining away of facts, the feverish raking up of illusions" (p. 134). Finally, the story's close attention to psychological process—Hervey's attention to his own feelings, and, with slight ironic differences reminiscent of James, the author's study of Hervey's stream of consciousness—is only one step removed from the interplay of Jim's self-analysis and Marlow's ironic counterpoint.

In none of the stories lying between *Lord Jim* and *Nostromo*, except perhaps "Falk," does Conrad make a genuine thematic or technical advance. He was to do nothing really new until he introduced his readers to the Golfo Placido and the Silver of the San Tomé mine. But it is important to see just how directly these stories do extend the interests that had finally come to full expression in "Heart of Darkness" and *Lord Jim*—to bring further illumination to individual works, if possible, and to demonstrate how sharply Conrad's major periods do divide themselves off from one another.

The contingent subjects of these post-*Lord Jim* stories are so diverse that there is no point considering them in chronological order.[19] One may turn first, perhaps, to "The End of the Tether," whose protagonist, Captain Whalley, Conrad felt he could readily part with "in affectionate silence" (*Youth*, p. viii) when he reviewed his work for the Author's Note. Although published together with "Youth" and "Heart of Darkness," "The End of the Tether" lacks the profundity and technical concentration of the Marlow tales. In its broadest moral dimension, however, Captain Whalley's experience duplicates that of the young Marlow of "Youth" and the older Marlow of "Heart of Darkness"; and in this sense the three stories of the *Youth* volume form a unit. If in "Youth" the young sailor is brought up against the substratum of hard fact beneath his dream of the "East," and if in "Heart of Darkness" the mature mariner discovers the black chaotic sources of his own being, the over-ripe Captain Whalley

[19] Baines, *Joseph Conrad*, gives dates of composition, first publication, and first book publication of Conrad's works.

of the third story discovers that even the tolerant, pragmatic idealism of old age is subject to sharp revision in the face of destructive forces. Captain Whalley lacks the psychological or moral stature of a Marlow or Jim or Kurtz; the darkness that creeps upon him in his blindness is more physical than psycho-moral. But it clouds his judgment of his fellow mariners as well; and he is forced, in his final self-immolation aboard the *Sofala,* to resort to the same ironic victory over his own darkness that Jim had refused aboard the *Patna* and achieved finally in his confrontation of Doramin:

"Captain Whalley! Leap! . . . pull up a little . . . leap! You can swim."
  In that old heart, in that vigorous body, there was, that nothing should be wanting, a horror of death that apparently could not be overcome by the horror of blindness. . . . The light had finished ebbing out of the world; not a glimmer. . . .
  "Leap as far as you can sir; we will pick you up." (p. 333)

Unlike Jim, Whalley does not leap; and despite its comparative lack of technical complexity and tension, his story thus touches gently upon the same paradoxes of moral idealism that had been explored in the earlier Marlow tales.

  More needs to be said of "Typhoon," which has often been praised as a descriptive *tour de force,* and which helped create the reputation as a writer of sea yarns which irritated Conrad so intensely. "Typhoon" does have a rare pictorial charm; but its documentary qualities have distracted readers from the conflict of human motive and value Conrad set at the heart of the tale. As he insists in his Author's Note, the interest of "Typhoon" is "not the bad weather but the extraordinary complication brought into the ship's life at a moment of exceptional stress by the human element below her deck" (p. v). And to see this "complication" clearly, it is useful to return momentarily to the closely analogous *Nigger of the 'Narcissus,'* a companion piece in more than setting.

In "Typhoon," as in the *Nigger*, the protagonist of the tale is confronted simultaneously by two forces which threaten to disrupt a rationally ordered situation—in the *Nigger*, the extraordinary gale which tips the *Narcissus* on her side and calls for the most heroic fidelity from her crew, coupled with the inner force of rebellion inspired by Wait and Donkin; in the case of "Typhoon," the impressive storm which jumbles normal routine and provides MacWhirr with a new standard of "dirty weather," coupled with the subcivilized rioting of the Chinese below deck. Conrad stresses the moral effect of the typhoon at the beginning of his famous description: "It seemed to explode all round the ship with an overpowering concussion and a rush of great waters. . . . In an instant the men lost touch of each other. This is the disintegrating power of a great wind: it isolates one from one's kind. An earthquake, a landslip, an avalanche, overtake a man incidentally, as it were—without passion. A furious gale attacks him like a personal enemy, tries to grasp his limbs, fastens upon his mind, seeks to rout his very spirit out of him" (p. 40). When Jukes's heart rebels against "the tyranny of training and command" (p. 53) and the crew begin to "grumble and complain" (p. 54), they are yielding naturally to the storm's power of shaking a moral frame of reference by threatening its metaphysical substructure.

And just as in the *Nigger*, a second threat is posed from below by a human element superficially exterior to the crew (Wait and Donkin are technically crewmen, but their refusal of duty sets them apart), and one capable of inspiring mutinous feelings in normally loyal breasts. Like Wait, the Chinese aboard Mac-Whirr's ship have the appearance of "bilious invalids" (p. 21) and introduce a principle of disorder associated with chaos and the lower regions (although Wait emerges finally to be housed guiltily above deck, the reader can hardly forget the powerfully symbolic scene in the chaotic carpenter's shop). The external and internal threats to the *Nan-Shan* are tied together through a disruption of order: the storm in its shattering of the *Nan-Shan's* structure and routine, the coolies in their rejection of civilized judicial procedure. On his way below to find a lamp for the grumbling crew, Captain MacWhirr's boatswain is at first trapped in an "impenetrably black" coal-bunker in the threatening company of a wildly clattering iron slice. And then he opens the hold and is confronted with a "tempest" of rioting over the coolies' loose dollars: a "gust of hoarse yelling," a man "sliding over, open-eyed, on his back, straining with uplifted arms for nothing," another "bounding like a detached stone," and finally "an inextricable confusion of heads and shoulders, naked soles kicking upwards, fists raised, tumbling backs, legs, pigtails, faces" (pp. 57–58). When Jukes reports this outburst of formless possessiveness through the speaking tube, his words mount "as if into a silence of an enlightened comprehension dwelling alone up there"—recalling the taciturn elevation of Singleton and Captain Allistoun in the *Nigger*.

"Typhoon" remains an essentially comic story, however, closer to "Youth" in mood and tone; and much of its irony is directed at MacWhirr. His approach to the typhoon—" 'We must trust her to go through it and come out on the other side' " (p. 88)—has a simple strength, and Conrad's irony is mixed with affection for the Captain's dogged seamanship. There is even a hint of the romantic tone of the *Nigger*: questioning MacWhirr in the face of the storm, Jukes hears a "frail and resisting voice in his ear, the dwarf sound, unconquered in the giant tumult" (p. 47). But MacWhirr lacks the complexity of Conrad's major protagonists; his solution to the coolie problem—keep the whole matter quiet, and divide the contested money up equally—has all the sub-Solomonian wisdom of a too simple man. And the story as a whole lacks creative intensity; Conrad had merely remembered the ill-fated coolies, according to his own account, while "casting about for some subject which could be developed in a shorter form than the tales in the volume of 'Youth' " (p. v). Nevertheless, "Typhoon" is built upon the same conceptions of value and of the threats to human dignity and human solidarity as the earlier works, and its plot closely duplicates some of the dramatic elements Conrad had already used to record and examine those threats.

Conrad's persistence in his familiar conceptual and symbolic patterns is even more striking in "Amy Foster" and "Falk," two stories which have received considerable critical attention, but have not yet been related satisfactorily to Conrad's earlier work. This persistence of theme and motif is particularly surprising in "Amy Foster," which is based on an anecdote in Ford's *The Cinque Ports*, and seems at first glance to offer an unlikely setting for a characteristically Conradian problem. But Conrad adds elements to the story to warp it violently into the framework of his early interests and commitments. Yanko Goorall, the hero, is in Ford's account one of the crew of a German merchant vessel shipwrecked off the coast of England,[20] and therefore presumably an articulate man of some civilized skills; in Conrad's story he has become an inverted Kurtz, a civilizable savage emerging *from* darkness to join himself with a white Intended and suffer the same destruction of self that Conrad's extremists along this axis usually suffer. Like all Conrad's emissaries of darkness, Yanko is seen in animal metaphors—a "woodland creature" (p. 111) who in his captivity reminds the narrator of "an animal under a net" (p. 112), "a bear in a cage" (p. 120), and, like Aissa, "a wild bird caught in a snare" (p. 126). Yanko behaves like the natives of "Heart of Darkness": "striving upwards" (p. 111); learning to use the tools of civilization; "parting with his black hands the long matted locks that hung before his face, as you part the two halves of a curtain," and staring out "with glistening, wild, black-and-white eyes" (p. 120), just as the natives peep at Marlow through the foliage; and even, in his homeland, "bargaining away . . . the paternal cow for the mirage of true gold far away" (p. 117), just as the natives bargain away their ivory for the mirage of colonial improvement. Yanko's dialect remains a wild

[20] Ford Madox Hueffer, *The Cinque Ports* (London, 1900), p. 163.

babble, even under the scrutiny of a team of parochial linguists (p. 126); the terms in which he finally does communicate (e.g., "steam-machines" for railroad engines—p. 115) are childlike; and even his Catholicism is seen as primitive superstition and ritual.

Yanko's first overtures after coming ashore are rejected. He is lashed with a whip, stoned, struck with an umbrella, and in general viewed with "intense terror" (p. 119), as if he were indeed the "Jack-in-the-box" (p. 137) that the narrator calls him ("Yanko," the reader is twice told, means "Little John"). But in Amy Foster, Yanko finds his contact with this hostile civilization. In the midst of the general terror, Amy displays a "stolid conviction . . . that the man 'meant no harm' " (p. 119), and appears to Yanko "with the aureole of an angel of light" as she offers him his first food—white bread (p. 124). Passive, inert, all but illegitimate in the eyes of her society, and as a kitchen-maid occupying its lowest rung, Amy is the ideal romance for the upward-striving Yanko. Amy's sympathy for Yanko is the same for all distressed animals—"dogs, cats, canaries," "a poor mouse in a trap," "a toad in difficulties"; and appropriately, her feeling for these creatures is more savage than sentimental, since on one occasion she has refused to rescue a parrot under attack from the cat, even though the bird had "shrieked for help in human accents" (p. 109). Like Aissa, Amy falls in love "silently, obstinately" (p. 110). And standing as she does at the borderline between the primitive and the civilized, she exhibits the mixed and uncertain forms that are characteristic of Conrad's half-castes: her face a "vague shape" with a "curious want of definiteness" (p. 108); her brain a "white screen" (p. 142); her speech characterized by "a sort of preliminary stammer" (p. 108); and even her costume, with its "stout boots," "absurdly slender parasol" (p. 110), and "white cotton gloves" (p. 135), displaying the inconsistency of a Willems' or a Babalatchi's half-civilized dress. In marrying Amy, Yanko thus takes only a small formal step into the society into which he has been thrust. But even Amy finally abandons Yanko, as she feels creeping over her "the terror, the unreasonable terror, of that man she could not understand" (p. 139).

Like Kurtz, Yanko dies feverishly, summing up his experiences at the last in a single enigmatic word: "Merciful!" (p. 141). And like both Kurtz and Jim, Yanko has the benefit of a sympathetic narrator distinguished for the "penetrating power of his mind" and "an inexhaustible patience in listening" (p. 106). Only he and Amy "alone in all the land, I fancy," the narrator says in a peculiarly Marlovian tone, "could see his very real beauty" (p. 134). As protagonist, however, Yanko is something less than satisfactory. An initial difficulty—analogous to the difficulty Conrad discovered in trying to dramatize the passion of Dain Maroola and Willems—lies in the very attempt to use the civilized vehicle of prose narrative to record the progress of darkness into light. Seen from the outside, through Kennedy's eyes, Yanko Goorall is an incredible creature to emerge in the English countryside, belonging perhaps instead to a W. H. Hudson novel; when he speaks, it is in an unintentionally comic pidgin English. And none of this is much in accord with the usual idea of a central European emigrant, coming from a land with its own peasant dignities and social traditions. Despite its subtleties of technique and curiously appealing eeriness, "Amy Foster" is finally a semigrotesque.[21]

The same is true of "Falk." In "Falk," however, the grotesque quality arises not so much from Conrad's attempt to introduce his psycho-moral notions into an unpromising context, as from his attempt to dramatize a single motif of his earlier work—the cannibalism that appears in Gentleman Brown and faintly in other characters—in isolation from the others. An incongruity arises between this subject and Conrad's realistic method; for

[21] Richard Herndon, "The Genesis of Conrad's 'Amy Foster,'" *Studies in Philology*, LVII (July 1960), 549–566, gives biographical and textual evidence to confirm the relationship between "Amy Foster" and Conrad's Congo experience, one of the story's scenes had even been intended originally for "Heart of Darkness."

while some civilized behavior no doubt is sublimated cannibalism, or is motivated by kindred instincts, the very process of
sublimation renders it unrecognizable in the direct form of Falk's
frighteningly appetitive love affair. Conrad does adopt some
semiallegorical devices which move the story away from the
strict realism of "Typhoon" toward the more calculated symbolic
effects of "The Secret Sharer" and *Victory;* but this allegorizing
process has not gone far enough in "Falk," so that what Conrad
obviously intended to appear as a presocial psychic force
emerges instead as a grotesque abnormality. Falk is driven back
toward cannibalism as he drifts south on a disabled ship, away
from the normal moral framework of civilized man, and is placed
under the immense pressure of overwhelming animal need. But
without a correspondingly gradual initiation and sympathetic
regression—of the kind Marlow provides in "Heart of Darkness"
—the reader is faced too abruptly and too realistically with Falk's
hungers; and Falk's story yields the same sense of unintentional
comedy the reader feels with Yanko Goorall.

These incongruities aside, however, the story is a minor-key
masterpiece. Conrad is at pains to extend his theme sharply into
narrative and descriptive details—perhaps because he realizes
the difficulty of developing it at all in the peculiar domestic
setting he has chosen—and the result is an interesting study in
ironic allusion. Falk himself is a commercial predator whose
captaincy of the only tugboat on the river has earned him the
half-respectful enmity of the other mariners: "He extracted his
pound and a half of flesh from each of us," says the narrator (p.
161). The cannibalism implicit in the narrator's metaphor is
associated in turn with Falk's romantic leanings toward Captain
Hermann's niece: "I could not have believed," the narrator
observes as he recalls Falk's servicing of Hermann's ship, "that a
simple towing operation could suggest so plainly the idea of
abduction, of rape" (p. 170). Falk is a man of the senses, subject
chiefly to the laws of self-preservation and sexual instinct: a man
of "hard, straight masculinity" (p. 210). In his catlike eyes, with

irises like "two narrow yellow rings" (p. 202), Falk anticipates Ricardo, the sexual predator of *Victory;* and in one of the most surprising of all Conrad's animal images—in which Falk's passion is seen lurking "like a wary old carp in a pond" (p. 167)—Conrad pushes sexuality far back along the evolutionary scale and associates it with the hunger of an ancient subterranean scavenger.

The object of Falk's affections, Hermann's inarticulate niece, can best be described as having the single quality of immense succulence: "She was built on a magnificent scale. Built is the only word. She was constructed, she was erected, as it were, with regal lavishness. . . . Such shoulders! Such round arms! Such a shadowing forth of mighty limbs . . . it's perfectly indescribable!" (p. 151). Hermann himself—in what seems like too broadly grotesque a joke, but may be only a good example of the difficulty of rendering Conrad's theme realistically—is described as a "sedentary grocer" (p. 168); and his ship, the *Diana,* is "like any grocer's shop" (p. 208), a civilized, even decadent, derivative of the need that originally created the goddess of the hunt. The *Diana's* antiseptic German purity is of course an ironic context for the emergence of Falk's passion; and Mrs. Hermann's remote consciousness of the danger is horribly hinted at: "It was as if . . . that ship had been arduously explored with—with tooth-brushes" (p. 157). And in the bestial appetitiveness of the hotelkeeper Schomberg, Conrad's old friend, who is to be threatened by another Falk-like character in *Victory,* is one more extension of this motif: " 'A white man should eat like a white man, dash it all. . . . Ought to eat meat, must eat meat' " (p. 174).

Other commentators have remarked on the similarities between Marlow and the narrator of "Falk"; the privileged insolence, for example, as he explicates his own story: "He wanted that girl. . . . He was hungry for the girl, terribly hungry, as he had been terribly hungry for food. Don't be shocked if I declare that in my belief it was the same need, the same pain, the same torture. We are in his case allowed to contemplate the foundation of all the emotions—that one joy which is to live, and the one sadness at the root of the innumerable torments" (p. 224). The narrator warns his audience of the difficulty of grasping Falk's experience (an indication, probably, of Conrad's own sense of the incongruity of what he had set out to do): "So difficult is it for our minds, remembering so much, instructed so much, informed of so much, to get in touch with the real actuality at our elbow" (p. 226). The story's frame, an obvious technical extension from the Marlow stories, is brilliantly done, gently "justifying" the narrator and hinting with grotesque economy at what is to follow: the unsatisfactory dinner which brings to mind an image of "primeval man" scorching "lumps of flesh" at his fire and talking of the "hunt—and of women, perhaps!"; or the passing of the ship *Arcadia,* manned by a German skipper, which raises visions of "jolly good dinners" (pp. 145–146).

More interesting for the student of Conrad's growth, however, are certain allegorical and symbolic devices he uses to universalize his theme. There are classical overtones, mixed in such a way as to suggest a fusion of hunting and cannibalism and seduction: Diana, huntress and patroness of maidens; a scattering of islets which looks like a "cyclopean ruin" (p. 209); Hermann's niece with her hair unplaited and covering her "all round as low as the hips, like the hair of a siren" (p. 236). There are references to early-evolutionary creatures like centipedes, scorpions, and lizards, which, like the classical allusions, tend to distance the events of the story and give them archetypal status, and which remind the reader of the serpent-imagery on the underside of Jim's experience. Symbolic devices like these will be central in the fiction of Conrad's third period, in which they will be required both for esthetic distancing and for thematic scope. "Falk" is thus a significant technical experiment for Conrad. But in spite of its technical subtleties and horrific pleasures, the story's depiction of brutal instinct operating on the plane of domestic romance is not wholly successful; like "Amy Foster," "Falk" is too forced to be convincing.

"Tomorrow," the last story in the *Typhoon* volume, is a trifle. Conrad will say nothing about it in his Author's Note, except that he was persuaded to turn it into a play. And perhaps the most interesting thing about this story is that Conrad later remembered it as the end of his early period, the last story before *Nostromo*—when in fact it was written before he had begun "The End of the Tether." Abstract, artificial, and faintly allegorical, reminiscent of Hawthorne in its style and in the primitive quality of its irony, "Tomorrow" is at best a weak experiment, foreshadowing the more conscious symbolism, the shore settings, and the greater use of dialogue in Conrad's work from this point forward. Some of the symbolic structure of the early fiction is extended, even here—the story's heroine, Bessie Carvil, is caught between the conflicting demands of her blind, appetitive father and the ascetic, deluded Captain Hagberd; and in this schematic opposition Bessie bears a faint generic resemblance to Conrad's other early protagonists. But what "Tomorrow" shows most clearly is Conrad's need for fresh inspiration, for a new field of moral interest, a different characteristic tone and a new sort of technical growth. The well of *Almayer's Folly* had run dry.

3

Anarchists and Revolutionaries
—The Political Phase

By temper and discipline Joseph Conrad was hostile to the life of politics. He could not identify with a cause or idea, in the manner of Dostoevsky; he did not live by the glow of an exalted historical moment, as did Stendhal; he would have shuddered at Disraeli's fondness for the mechanics of intrigue; and it is difficult to imagine him trapped, as was Turgenev, in a barrage of polemic. . . . Yet, by some curious paradox of his creative life, he repeatedly abandoned his established subjects and turned, with a visible shudder of distaste, to the world of London anarchists, Russian émigrés, Latin revolutionaries.

—Irving Howe, in *Politics and the Novel*

Of all Joseph Conrad's works, *Nostromo* is most difficult to judge. Ever since its first readers wrote letters "complaining of so much space being taken by utterly unreadable stuff," [1] critics have been of two minds about the novel. Conrad himself had mixed feelings toward it, confessing to H. G. Wells that he felt

[1] Attributed to Conrad by Richard Curle in his Introduction to *Nostromo* in the 1958 reprinting of the Dent Collected Edition, p. viii.

as if he were cycling "over a precipice along a 14-inch plank" [2] while writing it; and he never quite decided where to rank it among his works. A great deal can be learned about *Nostromo*, and about Conrad's political fiction generally, by examining the sources of this critical ambivalence. But again it will be best to interrupt chronology, and look first at *The Secret Agent* and *Under Western Eyes*. After seeing what the ironies of Conrad's political vision really require for their successful expression, the reader can return to the complex vistas of *Nostromo* with a freshened critical sense, just as he can return to the early Malayan novels with clearer insight after studying the Marlow tales. And before even the later political novels can be approached directly, it will be necessary to identify the fundamental concerns that motivated Conrad's fiction in the period immediately following the *Typhoon* volume: the change of stance and theme that yielded first *Nostromo* and then a series of other political novels and stories, ending finally with *Under Western Eyes* and marking off the second major stage of Conrad's growth.

This change is recorded in Conrad's letters and his Author's Notes: "I don't mean to say that I became then conscious of any impending change in my mentality and in my attitude towards the tasks of my writing life. And perhaps there was never any change, except in that mysterious, extraneous thing which has nothing to do with the theories of art; a subtle change in the nature of the inspiration. . . . After finishing the last story of the 'Typhoon' volume it seemed somehow that there was nothing more in the world to write about. This so strangely negative but disturbing mood lasted some little time; and then . . . the first hint for 'Nostromo' came to me" (*Nostromo*, p. xvii). As the preceding chapter has suggested, there *was*, in the basic thematic sense, "nothing more in the world" for Conrad to write about after he had finished *Lord Jim* and the *Typhoon* volume, if he were to stick to the familiar psycho-moral dilemmas that had

---

[2] Aubry, *Life and Letters*, I, p. 311.

motivated his fiction from the first and had culminated finally in the paradoxes of Stein. *Lord Jim* and "Heart of Darkness" were end products of a profound artistic growth and an advancing self-clarification; what followed had been at best the partially successful hybrids and grafts of the *Typhoon* stories. Conrad did need a new source of inspiration—and he found it by moving one step away from these positive, presocial spiritual commitments to their essentially negative and satirical implications when applied to an examination of society's relation to the individual: he turned, in other words, to the strain of social criticism which had been only secondary in the earlier work, and made it his major subject for the next decade. His famous remark that "silver is the pivot of the moral and material events" in *Nostromo*, "affecting the lives of everybody in the tale," [3] catches the shift of focus perfectly.

No one can say why Conrad's interests should have taken this particular turn after the *Typhoon* volume. The South African war seems to have revived his interest in statecraft just about the time he was finishing *Lord Jim;* [4] his essay "Autocracy and War" appeared in 1905; and his essay on Anatole France, which had appeared a year earlier, had applauded France's perception that "political institutions, whether contrived by the wisdom of the few or the ignorance of the many, are incapable of securing the happiness of mankind" (*Notes on Life and Letters,* p. 33). In any case, the transition outward, from an exploration of the individual's psycho-moral condition to a study of his relations to society, is wholly natural, and can be found in other writers. And as with other writers whose primary commitments are to the individual and to those presocial values which define the notion of individual responsibility, Conrad's attitude toward group idealism must necessarily be predominantly satirical. *The Secret Agent,* that "Simple Tale" of multiple deaths and multiple betrayals and multiplied misunderstandings, is the most nearly

[3] *Ibid.,* II, p. 296.   [4] See *Ibid.,* I, pp. 285–286 ff.

complete and exact of Conrad's political expressions; like *Lord Jim* in his first period, it may be seen as the artistic pole toward which all the fiction of his second period tends. It has often been argued that *Nostromo* is more comprehensive and more complex. But Conrad simply did not descend into the abyss over which he was cycling in *Nostromo;* and if he felt a "humbug" and a "fraud" over it, and was able to observe that it was "something, —but not *the* thing I tried for," [5] it is because *Nostromo* is hollow at the core, dissipating its central subject through inappropriate narrative techniques, some of them the result of trial and error with new materials, and some of them carried over uncritically from the Marlow tales. There is an analogy here between *Nostromo* and *Almayer's Folly:* in *Almayer's Folly* a certain amount of personal experience had interfered with the book's artistic unity; in *Nostromo* interference arises from the only partially relevant artistic experience Conrad had gained in working his way toward *Lord Jim.*

The second phase of Conrad's career thus duplicates the lines of its first phase—the adumbration of a characteristic fictional subject, its gradual clarification and subtilization as Conrad finds the techniques and symbolic economies adequately to deal with it, and finally its concentrated expression in a novel which effectively ends the period and turns Conrad once again to new interests and new subjects. *Under Western Eyes,* like "Falk" and "Amy Foster," can best be seen as a perseveration of these thematic interests into a new and unlikely context, and thus somewhat anticlimactic. And finally, the political tales in *A Set of Six* display some of the stages of Conrad's growth toward *The Secret Agent,* just as his earliest short stories had shown his growth toward "Heart of Darkness" and *Lord Jim.*

Conrad has sometimes been called a "conservative" in politics. As Albert Guerard has observed, however, his political novels reflect not so much political conservatism as "a deep skepticism

[5] *Ibid.,* I, pp. 337, 336.

concerning all political motive and intention, be it conservative, radical, or liberal." [6] And what needs to be stressed, if their full satirical power is to be felt, is the derivation of this skepticism from other, morally prior, spiritual commitments. When Conrad remarked late in his career that *"The Mirror of the Sea* is my book—the soul of my life," [7] he was expressing more than simple nostalgia. Embedded in *The Mirror of the Sea* is a highly developed personal ethics that controls the value structures of almost everything Conrad wrote: the seaman's virtues of courage, fidelity, simplicity, and self-trust (even to occasional "audacity" [p. 34], recalling the Captain of "The Secret Sharer"), coupled with a prudent sense of human insecurity ("For what is the array of the strongest ropes, the tallest spars, and the stoutest canvas against the mighty breath of the infinite, but thistle stalks, cobwebs, and gossamer?"—p. 37). Conversely, the vices of the sea are all perversions of individual dignity and force—self-delusion, over-confidence, betrayal of trust, willful exercise of power or willful self-indulgence, greed, egotism, excessive passion —and the early villains of Conrad can be arranged along this spectrum in such a way that each has his peculiar niche. The transgression of an Almayer or a Jim or a Willems has a "social" bearing only in the broadest, prepolitical sense, as "a breach of faith with the community of mankind" (*Lord Jim*, p. 157). As both Jim and Marlow observe, Jim's failure lies beyond the competence of a legally oriented board of inquiry: when Marlow first meets Jim, he feels that he is in a "wood" (p. 70); Jim's situation on Patusan is "Arcadian" (p. 175); and so on. Similarly, the Malayan locale of *Outcast* is "beyond the pale of civilized laws" (p. 235). And even the labor agitator Donkin is treated in a way that subsumes the sociopolitical issues he might have raised to the immediately felt needs of individuals. As Gordan has pointed out, "When Donkin promoted insurrection

[6] Guerard, Introduction to *Nostromo*, p. 17.

[7] R. L. Mégroz, *Joseph Conrad's Mind and Method: A Study of Personality in Art* (London: Faber and Faber, 1931), p. 41.

among the sailors, their interest was at first in ' "the same wages as the mates." ' This was afterwards changed to ' "the same grub." ' Conrad avoided the larger social aspect." [8] Conrad's interest in isolated individuals is revealed even in his way of referring to his novels-in-progress: "Almayer" is almost finished, "Willems" is coming along, and so on. Even *Nostromo*, with its panoramic scope and social implications, is named after an individual; this is, in fact, one symptom of the mixed character of the book itself.[9]

It is this prepolitical ethical focus that makes the primitive and maritime settings of Conrad's early work so powerfully appropriate. The "plights" Conrad imposes on his early protagonists stand at the very threshold of barbarism, as Kurtz's and Willems' do, or are in some other way anterior to the problems another novelist might pose in a social setting. They must be faced in isolation, frequently of a primitive-regressive kind, simply because no external point of view, no communal opinion or custom or mere factual information, can bear upon them; they arise from the recesses of consciousness, and most sharply when the protagonist is farthest from his own kind: as with Jim, aboard the *Patna*; or Kurtz, in the heart of the Congo; or the Captain of "The Secret Sharer," on his lonely deck watch. The clarity and rigidity of the seaman's code furnish a counterbalance to these subterranean threats, and for this reason Conrad's sea stories have sometimes seemed to create more dramatic tension than his other work. The presocial focus of Conrad's moral interests is suggested by his treatment of time in the early stories. Physical chronology is rarely stressed; the reader is taught instead the symbolic universality of Conrad's moral cases. Marlow's rhetorical impressionism negates the normal cause-and-effect patterns

---

[8] Gordan, *Joseph Conrad*, p. 147.

[9] Adam Gillon, in his modest but useful book *The Eternal Solitary* (New York: Bookman Associates, 1960), has traced this well-known ethical root of Conrad through a variety of biographical and literary materials.

between individuals in a social setting, and substitutes for it a different sort of cause and effect, perhaps epitomized in the historical parallels and evolutionary allusions of "Heart of Darkness." Both the *Narcissus* and the *Patna*, in passages quoted earlier, are described in terms which evoke man in his metaphysical, rather than his social setting; and the "unshaken monotony" (p. 7) and sense of timelessness Conrad describes in *The Mirror of the Sea* create the same effect. It is the present moral moment and the redemption of the individual that attract Conrad's interest; and the instrumentalism that would propose silver or social revolution, working themselves out through temporal causes and effects, as an answer to the human condition, incites only his scorn. "The grave of individual temperaments is being dug by G. B. S. and H. G. W. with hopeful industry," [10] Conrad once remarked, identifying at once the moral root of his objection to collective idealism, and, in an unconscious pun, the economic guise such idealism had taken in his own time.

The social successes which are occasionally held up in a positive light in the earlier works are merely extensions of prepolitical virtues into a social context. Jim reforms the social structure of Patusan, eliminating divisiveness and hostility, introducing economic fair play, and so on; but these reforms are only the result of his insisting upon such elementary virtues as cleanliness, honesty, and industry, and require no social ideal for their justification. In settling a conflict over the ownership of three brass pots which had engaged the interest of an entire village and threatened to erupt into divorce and civil war, Jim's chief concern is to get at "the truth" and be "fair to all parties," and ultimately to send the villagers back to "attending to their bally crops" (p. 269). And his discourse on theft has the simplicity and directness of a commandment: "Resolutely, coolly, and for some time he enlarged upon the text that no man should be prevented from getting his food and his children's food honestly.

[10] Aubry, *Life and Letters*, II, p. 12.

. . . When Jim had done there was a great stillness. . . . No one made a sound till the old Rajah sighed faintly . . . 'You hear, my people! No more of these little games' " (pp. 249–250). Marlow makes the distinction in his final letter to the frame narrator: "You contended that 'that kind of thing' was only endurable and enduring when based on a firm conviction in the truth of ideas racially our own, in whose name are established the order, the morality of an ethical progress. . . . The point, however, is that of all mankind Jim had no dealings but with himself, and the question is whether at the last he had not confessed to a faith mightier than the laws of order and progress" (pp. 338–339). Figures so diverse as Captain Whalley, Captain Lingard, and the native chieftain Karain, in the earlier fiction, can be found acting upon similar conceptions of social value.

Conrad's political skepticism is thus rooted deeply in beliefs about the individual's responsibility to save himself and in psychological and metaphysical beliefs about the extraordinary difficulty—perhaps ultimately the impossibility—of doing so. The impenetrability of men to each other is one source of the Marlovian irony which so irritates his listeners, and results in even sharper irony in other contexts: in the scenes between Winnie and Verloc, for example. Perhaps the closest any of Conrad's characters come to full communication (if we except the unusual case of "The Secret Sharer") is in the silent mutuality of old Singleton and Captain Allistoun, or the belated recognition of Lena by Heyst. Even self-understanding is a final wordless vision granted only to heroic figures. To attempt to save others, under these conditions, is little short of folly. As Robert Penn Warren has pointed out, even the revolutionist's claim to create the "conditions" of human self-improvement externalizes an evil which for Conrad is an internal responsibility.[11]

If political involvement distracts the moral agent from his private responsibility, this would be enough by itself to generate

[11] Warren, Introduction to *Nostromo,* p. xxxiii.

the irony of Conrad's political novels. Equally important, how-ever, is his awareness that political idealism and economic instru-mentalism are essentially divisive, setting one group or individual against another in violation of their greater ties to the "human community." Political idealism may be used as a justification for abandoning these broader rights and obligations, since it de-mands a radical allegiance to some group less than the total human or Western community. Conrad's political villains and political idealists are not simply inversions of his earlier heroes —as Gentleman Brown, say, might be construed. They are com-mitted to some course of action (or talk) which claims to super-sede self-interest and masquerades as a higher good than the more fundamental values it violates or ignores—Dr. Monyg-ham's moral dignity, for example, or Winnie Verloc's filial ties. As Dr. Monygham remarks in *Nostromo*, "material interests . . . have their law, and their justice. But it is founded on expe-diency, and is inhuman . . . without the continuity and the force that can be found only in a moral principle" (p. 511). The conflict between political and individual values had been visible in Conrad from the first: with Babalatchi, who in his "contempt for early principles so necessary to a true statesman . . . [had] equalled the most successful politicians of any age" (*Outcast*, p. 56); or Donkin, "who never did a decent day's work in his life," but doubtlessly went on after the *Narcissus* voyage "discoursing with filthy eloquence upon the right of labour to live" (*Nigger*, p. 172). These inversions reach their extremes in the anarchist "Professor" of *The Secret Agent*, who would cure the ills of society by the simple process of random extermination, and whose own loss of identity is shown in his remaining nameless and thinking of himself merely as a "force." Of all the sources of Conrad's political irony, none is more important than this re-structuring of values at the expense of the individual. When Father Romàn sees the "working of the usual public institutions . . . as a series of calamities overtaking private individuals and flowing logically from each other through hate, revenge, folly, and rapacity" (p. 399), he voices Conrad's own pessimistic view.

Still another root of Conrad's political irony, of course, is his skepticism toward the self-announced altruism of social idealists. This strain too had been present in his fiction from the first, most notably in the greedy "pilgrims" of "Heart of Darkness." "The way of even the most justifiable revolutions is prepared by personal impulses disguised into creeds," the author remarks in *The Secret Agent* (p. 81): impulses like the love of "a delicious and humanitarian idleness" and a "dislike of all kinds of recognized labour" (p. 53). Even the genuine idealist or selfless reformer will be corrupted by the exigencies of political action. The end may appear to justify the means; but as Mrs. Gould observes, looking up near the end of *Nostromo* at the "soulless" and "autocratic" San Tomé mountain, "there was something inherent in the necessities of successful action which carried with it the moral degradation of the idea" (p. 521).

These three observations about social idealism and public institutions—their tendency to distract the individual from his private responsibilities, their corruption or inversion of primary values, and their ultimate hypocrisy—are the most important sources of Conrad's political skepticism. Still another is his epistemological and metaphysical skepticism. It is the human intellect which makes dogma, and the human intellect is an unreliable tool; the planned human drama dictated by social theory must play itself out against an enigmatic universe, and Conrad's universe is notably uncooperative with human schemes. Conrad's most intense idealists and reformers are associated with words, words, words—treatises, pronunciamentos, chatter in "revolutionary parlors"—and his most stable and pragmatic figures, like Singleton and Captain Whalley, and his most heroic, like Jim and Kurtz, with verbal reticence. This aspect of Conrad's political irony emerges pithily in his letters: "We, old Europeans, with a long and bitter experience behind us of realities and illusions," he writes, "can't help wondering as to the exact value of words expressing these great [political] intentions"; and as for postwar reconstruction, "It is like people laying out a tennis court on a ground that is already moving under their feet." [12] One consequence of this epistemological skepticism is Conrad's disbelief in social remedies predicated on the workings of cause-and-effect relations in time—as for example "science," or "progress"; and his political attitudes are sufficiently clear and conscious in *The Secret Agent* so that "time" as an abstraction, or as a condition of significant social or moral perception, receives specific ironic treatment.

Conrad's political position, then, can best be described as a radical commitment to the individualism of a democratic system and a gentle skepticism toward the correlated idea of majority rule, a skepticism increasing in intensity as the tyranny of the majority moves toward autocracy, and increasing in satirical tone as the rights and responsibilities of individuals are violated by revolutionary folly and false idealism. "Everyone must walk in the light of his own heart's gospel. No man's light is good to any of his fellows. That's my creed from beginning to end," Conrad says in an early letter.[13] Whatever doing-for-others he does approve is corrective, compensating for the effects of more destructive social action, like Natalia Haldin's helping to relieve conditions in crowded jails. At the same time, it must be stressed that Conrad's political position is in no sense anarchical or nihilistic. Social morality for him is roughly equivalent to English law [14] (to be sharply distinguished, of course, from English lawyers or English law-enforcement officers or English public opinion); and radical departures in any direction from this freedom-granting norm, whether "the ferocity and imbecility of an autocratic rule rejecting all legality" or "the no less imbecile and atrocious answer of a purely Utopian revolutionism," evoke the same degree of scorn, since neither can effect "a fundamental

[12] Aubry, *Life and Letters,* II, pp. 210, 217.

[13] *Ibid.,* I, p. 184.

[14] E.g., "liberty . . . can only be found under the English flag all over the world . . ." (Aubry, *Life and Letters,* I, p. 288).

change of hearts" (*Under Western Eyes,* p. x). Conrad's commitment to democratic law is plain throughout *The Secret Agent,* by
a kind of reverse irony. The Machiavellian Mr. Vladimir, for
example, deplores the "sentimental regard for individual liberty"
(p. 29); and the dedicated anarchist Professor equates a "worship
of legality" with the "old morality" (p. 73), a phrase recalling the
"early principles" Conrad had used in *Outcast* to denote the
timeless presocial morality that is always his central commitment.
If this seems somewhat too vague and reflexive a political ideal,
one need only recall Thaddeus Bobrowski's words about Conrad's father: "I could never establish the real composition of his
political and social ideas, apart from a hazy inclination towards a
republican form of state incorporating some equally hazy ag-
glomeration of human rights." [15] Like his father's, Conrad's political commitments were firm and exact, but they did not require
the fine intellectual distinctions of political theory.[16]

As remarked earlier, "The Return" provides the first extended
indication of Conrad's attitudes toward urban civilization and its

[15] Thaddeus Bobrowski, *Pamiętniki* (Lwów, 1900), I, p. 362; quoted
in Baines, *Joseph Conrad,* p. 8.

[16] Eloise Knapp Hay's *The Political Novels of Joseph Conrad* (Chicago: University of Chicago Press, 1963) is a thorough work of scholarship, detailing the immediate biographical and historical influences on
Conrad's political fiction, and defining as exactly as possible his views on
topical questions, particularly as they relate to his homeland. Where
intellectual content is a major source of unity, as in *Nostromo,* Mrs. Hay's
book is extremely useful; and even where her study tends to slip into the
genetic fallacy, or to read Conrad's fiction in terms too topical to find
support in the text, it continually reminds the reader that Conrad did
have active political commitments of the kind described here. A former
student of Guerard, Mrs. Hay to some extent shares the achievement-
and-decline theory, but she has a guarded view of *Nostromo.* Avrom
Fleishman's *Conrad's Politics: Community and Anarchy in the Fiction of
Joseph Conrad* (Baltimore: Johns Hopkins Press, 1967), and Claire
Rosenfield's *Paradise of Snakes: An Archetypal Analysis of Conrad's
Political Novels* (Chicago: University of Chicago Press, 1967) appeared
too late to be consulted here.

effects on the individual. The story's central focus, as in the other works of his early period, is not precisely in this social irony, which furnishes merely a background and partial explanation for the Jamesian psycho-moral difficulties of its protagonist. But some of its descriptive passages do illustrate, better even than comparable passages in *The Secret Agent*, the terrible opposition Conrad sees between the life of the city and the moral health of its inhabitants. The story opens on a characteristic urban scene: the commuter train rushing out of a "black hole" and pulling up with "a discordant, grinding racket in the smirched twilight of a West-End station"; the "little woman" and the "tottering old man" disregarded by the other passengers; and the regimented commuters themselves, with their "indifferent faces" and hollow eyes, "concentrated and empty, satisfied and unthinking" (pp. 118–119). Alvan Hervey, who emerges from this throng, is distinguished by urban standards—handsome, healthy, good at games and at the difficult art of making money, with just the right "tinge of overbearing brutality" in his "mastery over animals and over needy men" (p. 119). In Hervey's world, dominated by custom and by a paralyzing inhumanity toward the special case, only the "commonest thoughts" can be tolerated (p. 120). Human habitations are "flimsy and inscrutable graves of the living, with their doors numbered like the doors of prison-cells, and as impenetrable as the granite of tombstones" (p. 156). And morality is a matter entirely closed to individual conscience: " 'Nothing that outrages the received beliefs can be right. . . . They are the received beliefs because they are the best, the noblest, the only possible. . . . You must respect the moral foundations of a society that has made you what you are. . . . That's duty—that's honour—that's honesty' " (pp. 157–158). Mrs. Hervey's attempt to break out of her own prison-cell ought to have shaken Hervey in these convictions, of course; but to him the problem is merely one of appearances: " 'The ideal must—must be preserved—for others, at least. It's clear as daylight. If I've a—a loathsome sore, to gratuitously display it would be abominable—abominable!' " (p. 165). "The Return" thus depicts, on the comparatively simple level of sexual relations, the hazards in society's control of the individual—its denial of individual personality, its inversion of primary values, and its hypocrisy—and suggests a context of basic attitudes against which Conrad's political fiction may usefully be viewed.

The urban setting of *The Secret Agent*—with significant additions of detail to be examined later—is much the same as that of "The Return." Marching to the Embassy at the beginning of the novel, Verloc enters a side street haunted with the lifelessness of urban existence, "a street which could with every propriety be described as private. In its breadth, emptiness, and extent it had the majesty of inorganic nature, of matter that never dies. The only reminder of mortality was a doctor's brougham arrested in august solitude close to the curbstone. . . . And all was still" (pp. 13–14). The Assistant Commissioner in his turn, stalking Verloc, enters a street which gives the impression of "an immensity of greasy slime and damp plaster interspersed with lamps, and enveloped, oppressed, penetrated, choked, and suffocated by the blackness of a wet London night" (p. 150). In this environment children run and squabble with a "joyless, rowdy clamour" (p. 62); and even the gaiety of public houses is "harshly festive" (p. 151), with "lonely" mechanical pianos playing "Blue Bells of Scotland" in "painfully detached notes" (p. 79). The intimacy of urban friendships is suggested by the Assistant Commissioner's daily whist party at his club, whose members seem to approach the game "in the spirit of co-sufferers, as if it were indeed a drug against the secret ills of existence" (p. 103). And as for the press, that great common heart of any city's life: "A dismal row of newspaper sellers standing clear of the pavement dealt out their wares from the gutter. . . . The grimy sky, the mud of the streets, the rags of the dirty men harmonized excellently with the eruption of the damp, rubbishy sheets of paper soiled with printers' ink. . . . The effect was of indifference, of a disregarded distribution" (p. 79).

Several critics have shown how thoroughly Conrad's dark irony permeates the narrative background of *The Secret Agent,* defining the forces that deaden the individual moral sensibility and help spawn the Verlocs and Vladimirs and Ossipons.[17] It is precisely this pervasive irony—the product partly of Conrad's growing clarity as to his own social and political attitudes, and partly of his having chosen, as in *Lord Jim,* the crucial case of a moral phenomenon he wished to place under fictional study— that makes *The Secret Agent* the purest and most powerful of his political novels. Conrad's remark that "ironic treatment alone would enable me to say all I felt I would have to say in scorn as well as in pity" (p. xiii) identifies his central esthetic tactic. The meditative and dramatic tensions of Conrad's earlier work are largely absent, since the novel's values are firmly established from the beginning. *The Secret Agent* is built instead on the characteristic esthetic tensions of satirical fiction—misunderstandings, dramatic ironies, revealing symbolic parallels and contrasts, and the like. And just as a recognition of Conrad's ironic method and its sources in prior values is the key to understanding his tone and point of view in *The Secret Agent,* so a recognition of the intended scope of his irony is one important key to understanding the novel's narrative materials and structure. Anarchism per se is not Conrad's subject. His attention focuses upon any group idealism, or material interest, or self-aggrandizement posing as revolutionary principle, or socially de-

[17] Elliott B. Gose, Jr., " 'Cruel Devourer of the World's Light': *The Secret Agent," Nineteenth-Century Fiction,* XV (June 1960), 39–51; Wilfred S. Dowden, "The 'Illuminating Quality': Imagery and Theme in *The Secret Agent," Rice Institute Pamphlets,* XLVII (October 1960), 17–33; Avrom Fleishman, "The Symbolic World of *The Secret Agent," ELH,* XXXII (June 1965), 196–219; and Miller, *Poets of Reality,* pp. 39–67, are all excellent.

fined role (like that of the police) which tends to operate at the expense of the free individual; and this means, in *The Secret Agent,* a pervasive satire which extends all the way from Verloc and his spectrum of "revolutionary" acquaintances to the diplomatic and official figures who appear at the apex of the social scale, and finally to urban society itself.

Not all readers have been aware of this symbolic scope. It is generally allowed, for example, that the Embassy Verloc visits is Russian. But it is not generally seen that Conrad adopts symbolic and expository devices to universalize both the Embassy and its "Secret Agent." Mr. Vladimir's name and his "guttural Central Asian tones" (p. 36) are clearly Russian. But State Councillor Wurmt and the previous ambassador Baron Stott-Wartenheim suggest something more Teutonic; a variety of languages are spoken during Verloc's visit; Wurmt, having first been titled "State Councillor," is referred to thereafter as the "Chancelier d'Ambassade"; Mr. Vladimir alludes both to Chinese and to Latin and observes the view from the French windows; and so on. Verloc himself is French-English, with the German given name of "Adolf." Like Kurtz, like the *Patna,* like Sulaco, Mr. Vladimir's Embassy is politically synthetic.

Viewed in this light—as the focal point of an ironic attitude and an effort at symbolic generalization which permeate the whole novel—Verloc's role becomes clear. His is the paradigm case of antivalue, hypocrisy, and passivity, simply because he is *the* secret agent—or rather, the most secret, in conception at least, of all the political agencies in the book. He is a betrayer of betrayers, a secret agent within secret agents: "The practice of his life . . . had consisted precisely in betraying the secret and unlawful proceedings of his fellow-men" (p. 245). But at the same time, his ultimate loyalty is not to his employers at the Embassy, since in the last analysis he too is "a member of a revolutionary proletariat" and nourishes "a rather inimical sentiment against social distinction" (p. 245). The political house of mirrors inhabited by Verloc—whose perspectives reveal only a regression to deeper and deeper levels of false appearance and duplicitous political motive—reduces social instrumentalism and revolutionary scheming to the level of absurdity. Verloc furnishes the most extraordinary example of contrast between social idealism and the emotional contradictions that may lie behind it: the deadening passivity, for example. With commitments in several quarters, and the pressure of Mr. Vladimir's threats weighing heavily on him, Verloc still delays an anxious month before mustering the "demonstration" at Greenwich. He is a perfected Donkin: "His idleness . . . suited him very well. . . . He was too lazy even for a mere demagogue, for a workman orator, for a leader of labour. It was too much trouble" (p. 12). And Conrad underscores Verloc's passivity with animal-imagery of the kind he had developed earlier, notably in *Lord Jim,* to suggest the dark underside of man's nature. The descriptions of Verloc's swinishness recall the beastly Captain of the *Patna,* who stands as low on the moral scale of *Lord Jim* as any character (excepting the artificially symbolic Gentleman Brown). "Undemonstrative and burly in a fat-pig style" (p. 13), Verloc enjoys "wallowing" in bed till noon, his "thick lips" closed and his "heavy-lidded eyes" rolling amorously (pp. 6–7); and when Wurmt tells Verloc "you are very corpulent," Conrad remarks that "this observation [was] really of a psychological nature" (p. 18). This sort of imagery, employed unobtrusively but consistently throughout *The Secret Agent* (culminating in the last sentence, where the Professor is seen as a "deadly . . . pest in the street full of men"—p. 311) is an excellent indicator of the sources of Conrad's political irony, suggesting as it does the regressive self-interest Conrad finds in most political behavior.[18] In Verloc's case—and again, his is the typical, if extreme, case— this spiritual darkness is further compounded by the contagion of the urban setting, where men prey upon men. In purveying his pornography, Verloc turns his young customers into skulking

[18] Fleishman, "The Symbolic World of *The Secret Agent,*" offers a perceptive study of the animal-imagery.

Willemses, and thus contributes to what Conrad's Edwardian audience would have regarded as a fundamental form of degeneracy: even in his public role, Verloc is a secret agent. As Conrad observes, there is about him "the air common to men who live on the vices, the follies, or the baser fears of mankind; the air of moral nihilism common to keepers of gambling hells and disorderly houses; to private detectives and inquiry agents; to drink sellers and, I should say, to the sellers of invigorating electric belts and to the inventors of patent medicines" (p. 13). Here, too, Verloc is the special case only in degree, and merges with a general range of social phenomena.

Branching upward and outward from Verloc's parlor (some of them collected there early in the novel for the reader's edification) appear various specimens of the revolutionary and official parasitism which Verloc epitomizes. Sham revolutionaries, police officials whose chief weapon of detection is a liaison with the underworld, statesmen whose vanity and sadism pose as wit; all share the moral nihilism and hypocrisy and misuse of reason which can (naturally enough) be seen most radically in the novel's self-announced radicals, and all bear some responsibility in the pitiful history of Winnie Verloc, which is the central narrative thread of the novel. To see these types, especially the other "anarchists," as diversifications and subtilizations of Verloc's essential character, is important to an understanding of the symbolic method of *The Secret Agent.*

All of Verloc's friends, for example, share his passivity, a quality which in itself, for a doctrinaire revolutionary, amounts to hypocrisy. The great catchword for the apostolic Michaelis is "Patience." It is Michaelis's view that the rightful inheritance of the proletariat will come to it by the inexorable workings of a historical law, and that revolutionary propaganda must "advance its tenets cautiously, even timidly, in our ignorance of the effect that may be produced" (pp. 49, 50); a conviction enforced by fifteen years of silent meditation in a prison cell, and thus one of Conrad's cruelest ironies. Comrade Ossipon, with his faith in

Lombroso and his conviction that "the only thing that matters to us is the emotional state of the masses" (p. 50), is an even less promising activist. And Karl Yundt, the internationally famed "terrorist" who had "never in his life raised personally as much as his little finger against the social edifice" has proven his own political impotence over a lifetime of wholly vicarious agitation, serving, like the serpent in the garden, as a "venomous evoker of sinister impulses" in others (p. 48). The most superficially active of the revolutionaries is the Professor, but even he relies on someone else to use his explosives, and misconstrues the events that follow. When Verloc closes the door and, "with the insight of a kindred temperament," pronounces his verdict—"a lazy lot" (p. 52)—the reader must agree. Equally obvious are the nihilistic inversions of the anarchist temperament. Michaelis professes an ethical relativism and a disbelief in self-determination; and Yundt shares the Professor's faith in the therapeutic powers of destruction: "'I have always dreamed . . . of a band of men absolute in their resolve to discard all scruples in the choice of means, strong enough to give themselves frankly the name of destroyers, and free from the taint of that resigned pessimism which rots the world. No pity for anything on earth, including themselves, and death enlisted for good and all in the service of humanity—that's what I would have liked to see'" (p. 42). All the revolutionaries are associated in some way with Verloc's animal underside (Michaelis through his corpulence, for example, and Yundt through the serpent-imagery) and even with his pornography-peddling (e.g., Yundt's "worn-out passion" resembles in its "impotent fierceness the excitement of a senile sensualist"—p. 43; Ossipon's eyes "leered languidly" at his comrades—p. 44).

The *reductio ad absurdum* of all this is to propose, as a political tactic, "an act of destructive ferocity so absurd as to be incomprehensible, inexplicable, almost unthinkable; in fact, mad" (p. 33). The phrasing is Mr. Vladimir's; but the principle (underscoring once again the continuity of types in Conrad's political universe) is that of the Professor, who is the extreme case of the fatuous "reasoning" of the other revolutionaries and of the accidental destructive power implicit in the revolutionary mind. The Professor's moral assurance, as he himself realizes, is less a product of his actual power than of other people's conception of it: " 'I have the means to make myself deadly, but that by itself, you understand, is absolutely nothing in the way of protection. What is effective is the belief those people have in my will to use the means. That's their impression. It is absolute. Therefore I am deadly' " (p. 68). And his philosophical assurance emanates less from the hollow jargon he utters than from his "supremely self-confident bearing" and "a particularly impressive manner of keeping silent" (p. 62). The Professor, in whom the moral contradictions and hypocrisies of the other characters rise to genuine paradox and insanity, rightly dominates the last paragraph of the novel—walking the streets, "averting his eyes from the odious multitude of mankind . . . frail, insignificant, shabby, miserable—and terrible in the simplicity of his idea calling madness and despair to the regeneration of the world" (p. 311).

Conrad's irony lightens gradually as he moves up the social scale, Sir Ethelred and the Assistant Commissioner appearing sometimes to escape it entirely. These figures are by definition more closely committed to the legal and public bases of society than his "lower" characters, and their thinking is more rational and pragmatic. As a consequence, Conrad's satire of them tends to be gentler and more subtly intellectualized. But they never do quite escape it, especially where, in fulfilling and protecting their public roles, they rely too vainly on their own powers of reason or too grossly lose sight of the human feelings behind the "case" of the Greenwich explosion. Chief Inspector Heat, the "eminent specialist" on anarchist activity, who had declared the impossibility of any such demonstration shortly before the explosion and imprudently continued to declare it even after the fact (p. 85), is of course Conrad's easiest mark. ("The mind and the instincts of

a burglar are of the same kind as the mind and the instincts of a
police officer," Conrad says in his famous characterization of the
Chief Inspector—p. 92). When Heat callously leaves Winnie
Verloc to learn of her brother's death from a sporting sheet, he is
implicated along with the Vladimirs and Verlocs in her fate. But
it would be possible to demonstrate at length also Conrad's ironic
treatment of the Assistant Commissioner and Sir Ethelred. Both
are victims of the passivity, hypocrisy, and insensitivity displayed
so grotesquely by Verloc; and both sacrifice primary values to
their social roles. One example is the willful evasion of evidence
and the dissociation from emotional particulars implicit in Sir
Ethelred's demand for "lucidity" and conciseness: " 'Don't go
into details. I have no time for that. . . . Spare me the details' "
(pp. 136–137). Here at the bureaucratic apex, the human facts
necessarily get lost; and the Assistant Commissioner's statement
of recommended policy is a masterpiece of pompous polysyllabic
remoteness: " 'In principle, I should lay it down that the existence of secret agents should not be tolerated, as tending to
augment the positive dangers of the evil against which they are
used. . . . The professional spy has every facility to fabricate the
very facts themselves, and will spread the double evil of emula-
tion in one direction, and of panic, hasty legislation, unreflecting
hate, on the other' " (p. 139). Even when told the truth of the
Greenwich affair, the Assistant Commissioner and the "great
personage" (a phrase Conrad reiterates with Arnoldian wicked-
ness) fail to grasp it, viewing Mr. Vladimir's orders to Verloc as
"a ferocious joke" (p. 219) which Verloc has unfortunately
taken seriously; and Conrad generates a good deal of dramatic
irony at their expense (as when the Assistant Commissioner,
unaware of Stevie's complicity in the Greenwich affair, defines it
as "barefaced audacity amounting to childishness of a peculiar
sort," and the "great and expanded personage" replies that "we
can't put up with the innocence of nasty little children"—pp.
138–139).

This breadth of satirical purpose helps determine the novel's structure: the narrative progresses upward, from the opening scenes with Verloc and the diplomatic sadist Mr. Vladimir, through the social and economic scales, to Sir Ethelred at the apex (actually even Sir Ethelred is not quite the apex, as will presently appear), and then turns downward again, moving through the scene of Verloc's murder and terminating finally in a vision of the mad Professor. Mr. Vladimir, whose ultimate loyalty (or hypocrisy) is just one step less hidden than Verloc's, is the second major male character to be introduced; then we find the relatively more sincere and open (if socially disreputable) anarchists and revolutionaries, culminating in the purist Professor; then Inspector Heat, who serves in the twilight world between these revolutionaries and the public arena of recorded police work; then the Assistant Commissioner, who occupies a more distinctly public role but delights in the occasional opportunity to don a disguise and go snooping; and finally Sir Ethelred, the titled and thoroughly public figure. The continuity between these types is reinforced by some crucial details: the "Bill for the Nationalization of Fisheries" Sir Ethelred has sponsored, for example, is "a revolutionary measure" and is called by its opponents "the beginning of social revolution" (p. 145); and the charitable foundation which finally houses Winnie's mother— and is the true apex of the series—is not far from Michaelis's dream of an " 'immense charity for the healing of the weak' " (p. 305). Significantly, as the novel moves away from the Adolf Verlocs and Karl Yundts toward the more and more socially committed and socially active figures, each new character tends to be denoted by a less and less personal term: "Chief Inspector" Heat, the "Assistant Commissioner," the "great lady" who observes Michaelis in her parlor and the "great personage" Sir Ethelred, and finally the abstract "foundation" with which Winnie's mother is forced to deal and which ends the series of truncated personalities with the substitution of a wholly abstract personality.

There is another kind of rhetorical structure in the plotting of

The Secret Agent, as well. Its first half establishes a set of
sociopsychological conditions which work themselves out fully,
at the expense of the novel's central characters, only in the
second half; and each of these halves proceeds along a scale from
the most private concerns of a central character to the most
public—and hence most abstract and artificial—concerns of pe-
ripheral characters. The first half rises from the excessively secret
and compounded anxieties of Verloc to the open and impersonal
social "protection" of an official charity; the second descends
from the spiritualized public suffering of Winnie's mother to the
despairing suicide of Winnie herself. Winnie's mother leaves
Winnie and Stevie "as an act of devotion and as a move of deep
policy" (p. 162); and this strange inversion makes her sufferings
seem remotest of all from the direct human experience of pain
and deprivation: the structural equivalents of Sir Ethelred's
abstract efforts to grasp the human facts of the Greenwich affair,
which appear just on the other side of the apex and physical
center of the novel. In general, the same principle of balance
holds true as the novel works its way back down toward the final
sufferings of Winnie, through the collapse of Mr. Vladimir's
theoretical structure, the murder of Verloc, and so on; and these
structural analogues are reinforced by mirror-scenes, like those in
the Verlocs' bedroom. In his Author's Note Conrad insists that
The Secret Agent is "Mrs. Verloc's story" (p. xiii), but it does
after all derive its title from Verloc's activities. This apparent
contradiction can be resolved by considering the novel's structure, and by remembering the sources of Conrad's political irony.
The ironic subject of the book is Verloc (in all his Protean
transformations and minor reflections), but what makes that
subject significant and generates its irony is the fate of Winnie
Verloc and the other innocents—not excluding Verloc himself
and even Ossipon and the Professor, in their capacities as human
individuals. Thus Verloc dominates the first half of the book,
and Winnie the second.

Readers have sometimes objected to the length of the second

part, particularly to the amount of time Winnie takes to absorb the fact of her brother's death, fix the blame where it belongs, and murder Verloc. But the points to be made here are almost the same as in considering *Lord Jim*. The second half must necessarily be drawn out to equal the first, if only to maintain the structural and moral balance between the two spiritual poles of the book: the irony and the irony's source, the "scorn" and the "pity" of Conrad's Author's Note (p. xiii). The destructive emotional blindness of Verloc, a condition, or perhaps a consequence, of his multilayered political allegiances, can be developed dramatically only through this final interaction with Winnie; and his outrageous attempts at self-justification require an extended, even redundant, development, if they are to create the grotesque emotional tension that finally drives Winnie to free herself by the one irrevocable act of murder.

Conrad's own intellectual remoteness during these long scenes is itself a fine ironic instrument, and is at the same time proof against sentimentality ("By the position of the body the face of Mr. Verloc was not visible to Mrs. Verloc, his widow," the author observes with crushing remoteness just after Winnie has killed her husband—p. 264). This tone, along with the grotesque comic elements of the novel and Winnie's limitations, makes "tragedy" an inappropriate term here. But the power of Conrad's own feeling (implied, of course, by the high satirical tone itself) is revealed clearly in a pungent thickening of dramatic and verbal ironies as the novel progresses and Winnie's fate becomes clearer. When Verloc, having already accidentally brought about Stevie's death and the subsequent collapse of the whole static system of secret agentry he had been involved in, proposes a foreign sojourn, it is Winnie's thought that Stevie is "sufficiently 'peculiar'" so that he ought not "to be taken rashly abroad" (p. 195); when she persists in the "deaf-and-dumb sulks" (p. 258) which are to culminate in his murder, Verloc begins to long "for a few hours of delicious forgetfulness" (p. 259); and so on. What had begun chiefly as a mild irony of

statement at the expense of Verloc in Chapter I, and then
gathered force with the "revolutionary" and official dialogue of
the other characters and with the dramatic ironies generated by
the reader's early knowledge of Stevie's death, draws itself together finally in these hundred pages to create a genuine climax
on the novel's most important axis. Verloc's grotesque inversions
of domestic emotion ("It was an occasion when a man wants to
be fortified and strengthened by open proofs of sympathy and
affection"—p. 252) may be seen as the climax of Conrad's satire;
what follows, in the dénouement, merely brings Winnie's fate
under the scrutiny of figures even less likely than Verloc to
comprehend it—the fantastic "scientist" Ossipon and, indirectly,
the sardonically bloodthirsty Professor. Ossipon, the low exemp-
lar of theoretical remoteness, is fittingly Winnie's last resource:
"terrified scientifically" by his analysis of her as a "degenerate"
(p. 290), he sends her alone toward France, minus the money
she had entrusted to him, and then provides the saving explanation of his own overwhelming guilt: " 'I am seriously ill,' he
muttered to himself with scientific insight" (p. 311). This is the
final and most outlandish of the misconceptions of human feeling and of the evasions of guilt which had begun with Sir
Ethelred at the top of the scale and descended with ever-sharper
irony toward Ossipon, whom the reader sees finally at the end of
the novel "marching in the gutter as if in training for the task of
an inevitable future" (p. 311), and haunted by the newspaper
summation of Winnie's death: " *'An impenetrable mystery
seems destined to hang for ever over this act of madness or
despair'* " (p. 307). After Ossipon, there can be nothing more for
Conrad's reader but a final reminder of the wholly dissociated
Professor, quietly strolling the streets of society with a suicidal
detonator in his hand.

Conrad's skeptical scrutiny of political motive seems to raise a
doubt as to the very possibility of charitable or revolutionary
doing-for-others, at least in the forms he examines here. Any
reader of Conrad's Marlow tales might have anticipated the

problem: the difficulty, if not impossibility, of sympathizing enough with another human being to know what his welfare requires, or what obstacles he might encounter in realizing it. Again, Verloc's is the paradigm case; to him, the situation created by Stevie's destruction seems to require "calmness, decision, and other qualities incompatible with the mental disorder of passionate sorrow. Mr. Verloc was a humane man; he had come home prepared to allow every latitude to his wife's affection for her brother. Only he did not understand either the nature or the whole extent of that sentiment. And in this he was excusable, since it was impossible for him to understand it without ceasing to be himself" (p. 233). In less highly charged contexts, this fundamental emotional privacy appears as simple selfishness, or insensitivity, or at best an unconscious hypocrisy of motive. Among the "anarchists" and "revolutionists," for example, runs a current of mutual contempt and a hoarding of private social solutions that sharply contradict their self-professed proletarian solidarity; the Professor, whose double capacity for hollow boasting and inadvertent truth-speaking is one of the delights of the book, even articulates his independence: " 'Ossipon, my feeling for you is amicable contempt. You couldn't kill a fly' " (p. 305). The Professor's own vengeful commitment to explosives is of course a product of the "revolting injustice" he had suffered personally at the hands of society; and more generally, "the most ardent of revolutionaries are perhaps doing no more but seeking for peace . . . the peace of soothed vanity, of satisfied appetites, or perhaps of appeased conscience" (p. 81).

Nor do the official and public figures escape this strain of Conrad's irony; it is, if anything, more visible among them, if only because private motive and hidden response are more shocking in characters so explicitly committed to public service. Again Chief Inspector Heat is Conrad's easiest game. Through an association of the Assistant Commissioner's which can have its full force only for the reader familiar with Conrad's earlier fiction, the Chief Inspector's moral insides are brought out for examination: his "memory evoked a certain old fat and wealthy native chief . . . whom it was a tradition for the successive Colonial Governors to trust and make much of . . . whereas, when examined sceptically, he was found out to be principally his own good friend, and nobody else's . . . a man of many dangerous reservations in his fidelity, caused by a due regard for his own advantage, comfort, and safety . . . (allowing for the difference of colour, of course) Chief Inspector Heat's appearance recalled him to the memory of his superior" (p. 118). It is Chief Inspector Heat who would arrest the innocent Michaelis on the grounds that it would be "expedient" and would moreover help to solve a "little personal difficulty" having to do with the Inspector's public reputation (pp. 121–122); but the Assistant Commissioner, mulling the probable reactions of the "great lady" who had patronized Michaelis, sees an even more authoritative reason for not arresting him: " 'If the fellow is laid hold of again . . . she will never forgive me' " (p. 112). Both characters suggest the futility of institutionalized compassion. The Inspector is properly horrified at the sight of Stevie's remains ("an accumulation of raw material for a cannibal feast"—p. 86), but manages to convert even this problem in demolition of identity into the prospect of personal advantage: "He would have liked to vindicate the efficiency of his department by establishing the identity of that man" (p. 89). And the Assistant Commissioner, having just received a description of Stevie's remains from the Inspector, finds a greater spiritual burden in the weather: " 'Horrible, horrible!' thought the Assistant Commissioner to himself, with his face near the window-pane. 'We have been having this sort of thing now for ten days; no, a fortnight—a fortnight' " (p. 100).

Correlated with this merciless skepticism toward "public service" is Conrad's skepticism toward the control of social and political events by any means other than the open, legal, and democratic machinery which grants the individual a maximum of self-determination. Underlying this attitude, and more consciously emphasized in *The Secret Agent* than it had been before, is an awareness both of the role of chance in human affairs and of the general unreliability of theories based on temporal cause and effect. As usual, Verloc's is the prime case, his disrupted scheme to blow up the Greenwich observatory radiating through the novel like cracks in broken glass and producing faulty vision in every quarter; and the epitome of useless calculation is no doubt his elaboration of a "plan of defence" in the second or two he sees Winnie's knife descending on him (p. 262). But Conrad's contempt for rational calculation and theoretical pomposity is plain throughout: from the bickering of the revolutionists in Verloc's parlor, to the "lucid" summaries of events given Sir Ethelred by the Assistant Commissioner (so absurdly abstract they are nearly impenetrable), to the hollow utterances of the Professor (no sense, but "the sound of a general proposition"—p. 61). Even the street markings of the city (like Conrad's hypothetical tennis court) shift about under the impact of actuality, so that No. 1 Chesham Square is a full sixty yards from the Square itself, and No. 10 Chesham Square appears between No. 9 Chesham Square and No. 37 Porthill Street (p. 14). Temporal expectations and temporal criteria themselves become objects of satire. Chief Inspector Heat finds his theoretical confidence shaken by "sudden holes in space and time" (p. 85). The Assistant Commissioner's polished summaries are played off against the movement of a domineering clock: "While he was speaking the hands on the face of the clock behind the great man's back—a heavy, glistening affair . . . with a ghostly, evanescent tick—had moved through the space of seven minutes. He spoke with a studious fidelity to a parenthetical manner . . . and at the end of the time mentioned above he broke off with a sudden conclusion, which, reproducing the opening statement, pleasantly surprised Sir Ethelred by its apparent swiftness and force" (pp. 137–138). One need only contrast this with Marlow's disrespect for rhetorical time and rhetorical form to sense the strength of Conrad's irony. And the

Professor—that pervasive final term of revolutionary illusion—establishes "time" as the most important precondition of social progress: " 'The time! The time! Give me time!' " (p. 304). Mr. Vladimir's diabolical intention to blow up the first meridian thus strikes symbolically at the very core of socioscientific idealism; and one of the novel's basic ironies, paralleling the ironies generated by Verloc's multilayered intriguing, is that the dynamite attempt must rely on temporal calculation and infirm human nature, and is disrupted by the chance intrusion of the root of a tree, itself perhaps an elementary symbol of uncalculated organic growth.[19]

Morally, however, Conrad's deepest interest lies with Winnie and Stevie, the norms of male and female innocence, and Verloc's essential victims. Conrad speaks in his Author's Note of establishing Winnie's "humanity" and the "reality" of her story (p. xiii); and the reader finds a continual, if gentle, effort to make hers the representative case: she is "provided with a fund of unconscious resignation sufficient to meet the normal manifestation of human destiny" (p. 241), and so on. At the same time, her virtues are those of Conrad's superior figures, even if qualified by her enforced domestic passivity: she is a woman of "singularly few words" and of a "philosophical reserve" (p. 241); and her "maternal passion" (p. xii) for Stevie, her "straight, unfathomable glance" (p. 8), her singleness of purpose, her physical neatness, even perhaps her "full, rounded form," are all qualities that suggest the prepolitical moral fiber Conrad respects. Winnie's maternal love of Stevie—the "noble unity of inspiration" Conrad sees in her life—renders it morally archety-

---

[19] The esthetic compression and close metaphorical control of *The Secret Agent* have invited many studies of textual detail. Fleishman's article is especially perceptive and complete; Dowden, Gose, Gurko (*Joseph Conrad,* pp. 191–197), Miller, and others offer stimulating suggestions on individual points. It is one sign of the finished quality of *The Secret Agent* that its fundamental meanings can be approached in this way—the only one of Conrad's political fictions with enough esthetic coherence to permit that.

pal, "like those rare lives that have left their mark on the thoughts and feelings of mankind" (p. 242). And the stages of her destruction are likewise fundamental. There are, to begin with, the passivity and denial of personality implied by the very conditions of urban existence (the "obscurity" of her life "in that immense town," as Conrad says—p. xiii) and by her obedience to the dissociated Verloc. Then there is the abolition of her *raison d'être* with the death of Stevie, and the consequent abolition of her marital tie to Verloc (not to be underestimated, although Conrad may not have succeeded in establishing its strength, even with Winnie's powerfully symbolic final relinquishment of her wedding ring). Winnie's murder of Verloc; her conniving with Ossipon to escape the threat of execution ("that last argument of men's justice"—p. 267); and finally her self-destruction in the face of social forces too powerful to cope with; all are the inevitable consequents of Verloc's moral disorientation. In a sense Winnie suffers the worst possible fate: to "hang for ever" (an ironically reiterated phrase from the newspaper account of her death which haunts Ossipon) without the redemption even of civil punishment or any human understanding.

From an artistic standpoint, however, the case of Stevie— "blown to fragments in a state of innocence and in the conviction of being engaged in a humanitarian enterprise" (p. 266)—is even more interesting. Like that of Faulkner's Benjamin Compson, Stevie's radical masculine innocence is destroyed by a sophistication and duplicity that are far beyond his powers of recognition; in the special context of *The Secret Agent* this makes him the male complement of Winnie, drawn into "humanitarian" action by his own good will and emotional susceptibility, and undone in the process. Stevie is only a little revolutionist, but he is a full-scale one; and in Conrad's development of his fatal commitment to Verloc is a full analysis of revolutionary psychology. Stevie is a perfect mark for the atrocity stories of incendiaries like Yundt ("He was out of his mind with something he overheard about eating people's flesh and drinking blood," Winnie tells Verloc—p. 59). His own experience of evil yields the "symbolic longing" to take the decrepit horse and greasy cabman to bed with him (p. 167); and he struggles with the problem of theoretical articulation, "muttering half words, and even words that would have been whole if they had not been made up of halves that did not belong to each other. It was as though he had been trying to fit all the words he could remember to his sentiments in order to get some sort of corresponding idea" (p. 171). Finally he achieves the true revolutionary ambivalence: "In the face of anything which affected directly or indirectly his morbid dread of pain, Stevie ended by turning vicious. . . . The tenderness of his universal charity had two phases. . . . The anguish of immoderate compassion was succeeded by the pain of an innocent but pitiless rage" (p. 169). Stevie is thus a miniature humanitarian and idealist, sitting quietly at his table "drawing circles, circles, circles; innumerable circles, concentric, eccentric; a coruscating whirl of circles" whose "confusion of intersecting lines" (p. 45) duplicates the "Squares, Places, Ovals, Commons" (p. 300) imposed on the city's humanity in an effort to create topographical form. And his fate demonstrates, in miniature, what happens when the search for form and moral balance becomes instead the incendiary destruction of form. From the fireworks demonstration he had earlier set off on his employer's staircase to protest the injustices dealt out to his fellow employees, Stevie progresses to the accidentally premature fireworks of the Greenwich demonstration, and finally to Winnie's terrifying vision: "A park—smashed branches, torn leaves, gravel, bits of brotherly flesh and bone, all spouting up together in the manner of a firework. . . . After a rainlike fall of mangled limbs the decapitated head of Stevie lingered suspended alone, and fading out slowly like the last star of a pyrotechnic display" (p. 260). The denial of identity implicit in revolutionary idealism and public service, which for the other revolutionists and figures of officialdom is only partial, here reaches its most bitterly satiric form.

Before beginning serial publication of *The Secret Agent* in 1906, Conrad tried two preliminary experiments with the novel's psychological analyses and esthetic devices: "An Anarchist" and "The Informer," both to appear in *A Set of Six* in 1908. "An Anarchist" is perhaps the weakest of Conrad's political stories, but it is the first to have seized upon the true radical term in political revolutionism. Like Kurtz and Jim, the protagonist Paul is a paradigm case, symbolically exaggerated, but "real" enough to engage the reader's sensibilities and force his recognition that the character is, after all, only an absurd extension of forces implicit in his own political behavior. Like Stevie, Paul is led into revolutionary activity by the misguided impulses of a warm humanitarianism. Having celebrated his birthday with wine, liqueurs, cognac, and beer, and then more liqueurs and cognac, he has the misfortune to fall into conversation with anarchists: "Gloomy ideas—*des idées noires*—rushed into his head. All the world outside the café appeared to him as a dismal evil place where a multitude of poor wretches had to work and slave to the sole end that a few individuals should ride in carriages and live riotously. . . . The pity of mankind's cruel lot wrung his heart" (pp. 146–147). Stevie's susceptibility is constitutional, and Paul's is the product of a drunken bonhomie; but the feeling is the same, and their inarticulate agitation shows the same ambivalence of pity and rage. As a gesture of protest, Stevie sets off a fireworks display; Paul's fireworks are oratorical: "With a howl of rage he leaped suddenly upon the table. Kicking over the bottles and glasses, he yelled: '*Vive l'anarchie!* Death to the capitalists!' " (p. 147). Released from prison, Paul is driven back to the anarchists by social persecution; and in a robbery-and-bombing plot, Paul (like Stevie) is assigned the "beginner's part": "to keep watch in a street at the back and to take care of a black bag with the bomb inside" (pp. 149–150). From his inevitable fate—deportation to a prison island—to the more spectacular fate of Stevie is only a short imaginative step. And the frame narrator of the tale, using a phrase offered by the "anarchist" himself, is able to formulate the psychological principle which is to be dramatized so forcefully in *The Secret Agent*: "Warm heart and weak head—that is the word of the riddle" (p. 161). In its sometimes harsh comic irony, and in the tension between this comedy and Conrad's wry compassion for his protagonist, "An Anarchist" also anticipates some of the novel's complex emotional tone.

"The Informer" is closer to *The Secret Agent* both in tone and descriptive language, and almost exactly congruent in some of its characterization. Looking back on the story to select the subtitle required by the format of *A Set of Six*, Conrad acknowledged this similarity of tone and method, choosing to call the story "An Ironic Tale." The first title, "The Informer," refers to Sevrin, a police spy and counterrevolutionary threat to the story's anarchists, and thus a character not unlike Verloc; in trapping the informer by bringing in still more anarchists to don police uniforms and conduct a false raid, the trouble-shooter Mr. X extends the principle of conspiracy to still another level. In his "conspiracy within a conspiracy" (p. 87), Mr. X almost outdoes Verloc; but it remains for Verloc to be the genuinely rootless political agent, since Mr. X, despite his loss of identity, is at least perfectly consistent. The explosive Professor, on the other hand, appears without much change in "The Informer"—divided into parts and assigned to different characters, but otherwise intact. During his account of the fake police raid, Mr. X explains that "a comrade, nick-named the Professor (he was an ex-science student) was engaged in perfecting some new detonators. He was an abstracted, self-confident, sallow little man. . . . He perished a couple of years afterwards in a secret laboratory through the premature explosion of one of his improved detonators" (p. 88). This description of the Professor contains elements of both

Stevie and Ossipon; conversely, other parts of *The Secret Agent*'s Professor are distributed among other characters: the engraver Horne, for example, who is "strung up to the verge of insanity" (p. 83); or Mr. X himself, who asserts that " 'there's no amendment to be got out of mankind except by terror and violence' " (p. 77), and looks like the Professor chatting over his beer with Ossipon, his "meagre brown hands" pouring wine with "quiet mechanical precision" and his voice "rasping, cold, and monotonous" (pp. 75–76). The superiority of *The Secret Agent* lies partly in its sorting out of revolutionary characters into consistent types, so that the mechanisms of destructive political action gain their clearest definition.

Most important, perhaps, "The Informer" helps Conrad clarify some of the novel's psychological and ethical motifs. The frame narrator suggests a conflict between revolutionary commitments and domestic ties: "Organization into families . . . is based on law, and therefore must be something odious and impossible to an anarchist. . . . If such a faith (or such a fanaticism) once mastered my thoughts I would never be able to compose myself sufficiently to sleep or eat or perform any of the routine acts of daily life. I would want no wife, no children; I could have no friends" (p. 75). That Mr. X eats at good restaurants and suffers none of the agitated dissociation imagined by the frame narrator helps make a different point; but it is significant that Conrad questions the domestic status of the nihilist so early in his story. Conrad's awareness of hypocritical motive is suggested in Mr. X's allusion to " 'the fund of secret malice which lurks at the bottom of our sympathies' " (p. 89); and animal imagery reappears strongly for the first time since *Lord Jim*, indicating the imminent synthesis, in *The Secret Agent*, of the moral insights of Conrad's first and second periods (Mr. X's pamphlets are "a plague of crimson gadflies"—p. 74; he is a "rare monster" capable of "venomous pen-stabs"—p. 76; and so on.) There is even an effort to extend the satire to the upper classes, in the person of the anarchists' patroness, who had been drawn into contact with revolutionists through " 'the gesture of charity and personal service which was so fashionable some years ago' " (p. 81) and who subsequently " 'felt it necessary to round and complete her assumption of advanced ideas, of revolutionary lawlessness, by making believe to be in love with an anarchist' " (p. 85). The anarchist sympathies of the upper classes are not quite a proper analogue of the anarchist's nihilistic revolutionism; Sir Ethelred's demand for lucid generalization and his concern with nationalizing the Fisheries are subtler forms of the multivalent political impulse which invites Conrad's irony. Here, as in other respects, "The Informer" falls short of *The Secret Agent*. But the value to Conrad of having written this story, along with "An Anarchist," before finishing *The Secret Agent*, can hardly be overestimated.

Despite its lines of continuity with *The Secret Agent*, and its acknowledged political prescience, *Under Western Eyes* is finally less successful than the earlier work—an analogue to the *Typhoon* stories in Conrad's first period. To see how this is so, and more particularly how some of Conrad's peculiar technical experiments in *Under Western Eyes* succeed or fail, will help both to clarify the novel's themes and to suggest some of the ways in which Conrad's political fiction had begun to be a preparation for his final major period.

The best place to begin is with Conrad's own somewhat defensive Author's Note, where he feels compelled not only to specify the book's thematic centers, but also to account for an unusual choice of narrator. The novel is, according to Conrad, "an attempt to render not so much the political state as the psychology of Russia . . . together with my honest convictions as to the moral complexion of certain facts more or less known to the whole world" (p. vii). *Under Western Eyes* extends the interests of *The Secret Agent* by examining a still more radical case of political behavior, not this time in England, where autocracy and revolutionism were checked by the root ideals of a liberal culture, but rather in a country where both autocracy and revolutionism seemed recognized social forces. The "senseless desperation provoked by senseless tyranny" that Conrad offers as a "formula" (p. viii) for interpreting *Under Western Eyes* catches this extension of subject precisely. And Conrad's awareness of the difference is partly responsible for his use of an elderly Western language teacher as narrator and mediator. "To us Europeans of the West," the narrator assures the reader, "all ideas of political plots and conspiracies seem childish, crude inventions for the theatre or a novel" (p. 109); and both he and the novel's other major characters insist repeatedly on the difference between Western and Russian politics. The sense of mystery, of something "inconceivable" in the " '*mouvements d'âme*' " (p. 105) of the Russian people (the reader is reminded of Kurtz when Conrad indulges in diction of this sort) is intruded repeatedly between the reader and the novel's apparent subject, and is enforced by the old narrator's self-deprecatory tone.

So far as these mysteries are accessible at all to the Western understanding, however, this particular narrator is well qualified to perceive them. As a teacher of languages, he has both an immediate grasp of the Russian mind and the cosmopolitanism to distinguish it from other national minds; and his friendship with the Haldin ladies makes him an especially privileged outsider, since it gives him "a standing in the Russian colony which otherwise I could not have had" (p. 103). *Under Western Eyes* is full of epistemological machinery of this sort, and some of it sets up an extended clatter: "These sentiments stand confessed in Mr. Razumov's memorandum. . . . The very words I use in my narrative are written where their sincerity cannot be suspected. The record, which could not have been meant for any one's eyes but his own, was not, I think, the outcome of that strange impulse of indiscretion common to men who lead secret lives. . . . Mr. Razumov looked at it, I suppose, as a man looks at himself in a mirror" (p. 214). Such devices as these tend also, of course, to preserve the claim of realism Conrad feels essential in

dealing with his Russian mysteries. The narrator presses this
claim repeatedly: "This is not a work of imagination; I have no
talent; my excuse for this undertaking lies not in its art, but in its
artlessness. Aware of my limitations and strong in the sincerity of
my purpose, I would not try (were I able) to invent anything. I
push my scruples so far that I would not even invent a transition" (p. 100). Even Razumov joins the narrator in this insistence: "I am not a young man in a novel," he exclaims (pp.
185–186). Why Conrad should have thought that the reader
would doubt the veracity of *Under Western Eyes* is at best
speculative; but he did his best to counter such a reaction,
strange and artificial as his devices may sometimes seem.

Like Marlow, then, the narrator of *Under Western Eyes*
serves to interpret the experience of the novel to the reader, to
give him access to mysteries otherwise difficult of approach, and
to stipulate general propositions which will help limit and define
the reader's response. It is probable that Conrad's anxious concern for "scrupulous impartiality" (p. viii) also had something to
do with the creation of the old language teacher. But as will
presently be suggested, all this is not enough to account for the
pedantic excess and epistemological self-analysis of the novel; to
really understand this aspect of *Under Western Eyes* one must
turn to the more general question of Conrad's artistic development, and recognize that the narrator's attitudes represent a
phase of Conrad's own growth.

Aside from the special problems raised by the narrator and by
Conrad's intellectualizing impulses generally, *Under Western
Eyes* is in many ways the best of Conrad's political stories.
Whether by intuition or by bitter personal experience, Conrad
grasps certain kinds of revolutionary character with excruciating
clarity. The political giant Peter Ivanovitch, with his "overpowering bass" and impassive mechanical tea-drinking, and Madame
de S——, with her "unexpected clamour, which had in it something of wailing and croaking, and more than a suspicion of
hysteria" (pp. 216–217), are etched in deft detail. Razumov

himself is one of Conrad's best-developed characters. The mechanisms of paranoia and guilt that lead him finally to confess his betrayal of Haldin emerge with satisfying concreteness; and his extended reflections on autocracy and revolution at the beginning of the novel, after Haldin has raised the problem for him in practical form (pp. 33–36), are intellectually and dramatically persuasive, especially flavored as they are with the wry sympathy Conrad directs toward Razumov. In Razumov's encounters with such figures as General T—— and Councillor Mikulin, Conrad produces perhaps his best dialogue, with some pricelessly ironic lines. (" 'We live in difficult times,' " Councillor Mikulin remarks innocently to Razumov, " 'in times of monstrous chimeras and evil dreams and criminal follies. We shall certainly meet once more' "—p. 297.) Razumov's subtle interchanges with such figures are made inherently absurd, of course, by the fact that he is in the process of rendering a self-destructive service to an autocratic state; and Conrad exploits this irony with a delicate humor. There are fine psychological touches throughout (like the "professional jealousy" of the executioner Nikita toward Razumov—p. 267); and good epigrammatic touches as well (" 'Remember, Razumov,' " says the revolutionist Sophia Antonovna, " 'that women, children, and revolutionists hate irony' " —p. 279). In Conrad's descriptions of political atrocities there is a near-Swiftian control of syntax and diction: after Haldin had thrown his bomb, "the crowd broke up and fled in all directions, except for those who fell dead or dying where they stood nearest to the Minister-President, and one or two others who did not fall till they had run a little way. The first explosion had brought together a crowd as if by enchantment, the second made as swiftly a solitude" (pp. 9–10). But *Under Western Eyes* is irredeemably marred by the presence of the old language teacher and by Conrad's overdone mystique about Russia. In his effort to push beyond *The Secret Agent* to an even more radically revolutionary setting, Conrad involves his novel in burdensome tactics of rhetorical and symbolic exaggeration. The political processes dramatized in *Under Western Eyes* do not really seem generically new, nor any less accessible to the Western understanding than those of the earlier novel. If Conrad's own deeply bred feelings led him to assert the difference implied in the elaborate mechanics of *Under Western Eyes,* the reader need not accept the distinction as final.

Irving Howe, among others, has trenchantly identified some significant differences among Conrad's political novels.[20] It is important to discriminate one political subject from another, and to perceive the exact emotional shades Conrad brings to each one, since the pleasures of one literary work are never identical with those of another. Nevertheless, the basic values and motifs of Conrad's political stories are the same; and in this most important sense, he made no advance in *Under Western Eyes* sufficient to justify the book's technical peculiarities. One finds, for example, the same crushing paradoxes of political misunderstanding and misinformation, proceeding in part from the secrecy and vagueness of revolutionary communication, but also in part from willful irrationality. The most obvious instance is perhaps the revolutionists' automatic assumption of Razumov's complicity in Haldin's "heroic" assassination of de P——; or their romantic restructuring of Ziemianitch's suicide so that it becomes a gesture of remorse on the part of one who (like Nostromo) is a "Man of the People." The "mystically bad-tempered, declamatory, and frightfully disconnected piece of writing" (p. 163) penned by Madame de S—— after her flight from Russia is merely an absurd extension of the Professor's insane dogmatism; and her fantastic plan for a Balkan intrigue to inflame Russian public opinion and inspire a military revolt is Vladimirism raised to a national scale. (Both Razumov and the police-spy Nikita, of course, duplicate the principle of secret agentry in their multilayered political characters.) The ironies of political instrumentalism which had been developed in both *Nostromo*

[20] Irving Howe, *Politics and the Novel* (New York: Horizon Press and Meridian Books, 1957), pp. 76–113.

and *The Secret Agent* appear also in *Under Western Eyes:*
" 'The Russian soul that lives in all of us . . . has a mission, I tell
you,' " Haldin exclaims to Razumov, " 'or else why should I have
been moved to do this—reckless—like a butcher—in the middle
of all these innocent people—scattering death—I! I! . . . I
wouldn't hurt a fly' " (p. 22); the destruction of "Tekla's" identity and personality, and even of Sophia Antonovna's romantic
love for Yaklovitch, in the service of a remote ideal, are variations
of the same point. There is in Madame de S—— and in Peter
Ivanovitch the familiar animal greed (even, in the brilliant tea-
drinking and cake-eating scene at Madame de S——'s château, a
suggestion of Verloc's cannibalism). And finally—though by no
means can the common elements of *Under Western Eyes* and
The Secret Agent be exhausted by any such brief list as this—
one finds in the later novel, in a more pronounced and sometimes
incredible form, the full inversions of value characteristic of
Conrad's political figures: from the hapless Tekla's "envious
ecstasy" when she learns of a successful assassination attempt (p.
158); to the fantastic slogans of Madame de S——
(" 'spiritualize the discontent' "—p. 221); to the universal inversion of the Russian character, "where virtues themselves fester
into crimes in the cynicism of oppression and revolt" (p. 356).
National differences between the anarchists and revolutionaries
of the two novels may help to explain the degrees and shades of
political cynicism in each case; but otherwise, Conrad seems to
have developed the same sort of moral and psychological subject.

In one important sense, however, Conrad's attitude does differ
in *Under Western Eyes*. For the first time he appears to have
recognized a dilemma which necessarily removes some of the
point from any political satire: for the strong individual in an
active society, a nonpolitical existence is impossible. The humanist critic who finds Conrad's loathing of revolutionaries too intense may prefer the later novel for this reason alone.[21] As

[21] Michael Wilding, "The Politics of *Nostromo*," *Essays in Criticism*,
XVI (October 1966), 441–456, asks whether a different kind of techni-

Razumov discovers, his very reserve inspires a trust which in turn leads to irresistible political solicitation from all sides. Once Haldin has come to him, Razumov cannot escape; even to do nothing would be decisive. From this point forward the truth will destroy Razumov, and his own integrity will be an obstacle to his survival. Razumov's tragedy is not that he breaks a moral bond, but that there exists in his society no proper and deserving object of political attachment, whether autocrat or revolutionary. Moreover, choosing either side will raise further dilemmas: if he chooses the revolutionists, for example, he will be caught "between the drunkenness of the peasant incapable of action and the dream-intoxication of the idealist incapable of perceiving the true reason of things" (p. 31). And simply to run is impossible; "it would have been a fatal admission, an act of moral suicide" (p. 204). Razumov's, moreover, is the typical case. As Conrad insists in his Author's Note, "If he is slightly abnormal it is only in his sensitiveness to his position. Being nobody's child he feels rather more keenly than another would that he is a Russian—or he is nothing. He is perfectly right in looking on all Russia as his heritage" (p. ix). As a political neuter, Razumov is not unlike Stevie (he is even given to drawing geometrical figures—p. 57); and he is inevitably placed at the violent intersection of autocracy and revolution.

On the whole, however, too little of *Under Western Eyes* is new or mysterious to justify the novel's rhetorical exaggerations. The old language teacher is perhaps an exaggerated gesture of

---

cal development might not have led Conrad into a more complex awareness: "If Conrad had dealt with more complex characters, with something other than fable figures, could he have argued his case? It is possible that the attitude toward politics is arguable only in the simplicity and simplified characters that he has used. If he had created a sense of society, filled in the continuities of social living, wouldn't his conclusions necessarily have been different?" (p. 455). An excellent question, and one which might be raised about any of Conrad's political fictions. But the aspects of political truth Conrad does see are best revealed, it seems to me, through the tight and polished satirical techniques of *The Secret Agent*.

compensation for Conrad's own hatred of Russia. But this sort of emotional withdrawal yields a narrator who is full of theory instead of feeling, and whose pompous abstractions often hide the book's subject, instead of bringing it closer. Sometimes these abstractions rise to levels of paradox and rhetorical balance that are all but impenetrable: "A train of thought is never false. The falsehood lies deep in the necessities of existence, in secret fears and half-formed ambitions, in the secret confidence combined with a secret mistrust of ourselves in the love of hope and the dread of uncertain days" (pp. 33–34). Such statements tell us little about Razumov; and without the dramatic check provided by Marlow's audiences, they are practically insupportable. Similarly, the book's epistemological machinery is over-geared; so that locutions such as "I am in a position to say that, as a matter of fact" (p. 167) repeatedly stall the reader and send him looking for nonexistent mysteries. From time to time the narrator complains of a lump under his mental mattress, but discovers only a rhetorical pea:

Approaching this part of Mr. Razumov's story, my mind, the decent mind of an old teacher of languages, feels more and more the difficulty of the task.

The task is not in truth the writing in the narrative form a *precisé* [*sic*] of a strange human document, but the rendering—I perceive it now clearly—of the moral conditions ruling over a large portion of this earth's surface; conditions not easily to be understood, much less discovered in the limits of a story, till some key-word is found; a word that could stand at the back of all the words covering the pages, a word which, if not truth itself, may perchance hold truth enough to help the moral discovery which should be the object of every tale.

I turn over for the hundredth time the leaves of Mr. Razumov's record, I lay it aside, I take up the pen—and the pen being ready for its office of setting down black on white I hesitate. For the word that persists in creeping under its point is no other word than "cynicism." (pp. 66–67)

At least until it has been demonstrated in the dramatic development of the novel (which eventually, to some extent, it is) this revelation will hardly strike the reader with the force Conrad intends; and after it has been demonstrated, the narrator's elegant locution will seem by the way.

The whole question of concrete development is puzzling with respect to *Under Western Eyes,* in fact. Though the novel contains some of Conrad's best scenes, in many important areas it is left undeveloped (as in *Nostromo,* where there is the same paradox of superficial concreteness and actual underdevelopment). Razumov's dilemma would have more force, for example, if the misery of a populace under autocratic rule were presented in significant detail. There are occasional vignettes of suffering —some of them designed to connect Razumov's fate symbolically with even more extremely harsh destinies—but for the most part the reader is left with the narrator's abstract assurances: "The house was an enormous slum, a hive of human vermin, a monumental abode of misery towering on the verge of starvation and despair" (p. 28). Occasionally a character will assure the narrator (and hence the reader) that the omitted dramatic detail is in any case " 'something you have no conception of' " (p. 166); and at one point even the narrator renounces the quest: "It's no use to go into details" (p. 162). But the reader does often miss a more specific style. How much of Conrad's total vision of revolutionaries is left untouched by any of the detail of *Under Western Eyes* may be judged from the narrator's abstract description of revolutionary processes: "A violent revolution falls into the hands of narrow-minded fanatics and of tyrannical hypocrites at first. Afterwards comes the turn of all the pretentious intellectual failures. . . . You will notice that I have left out the mere rogues. The scrupulous and the just . . . may begin a movement —but it passes away from them. They are not the leaders of a revolution. They are its victims" (p. 134). Not all of this is relevant to *Under Western Eyes,* of course, with its focus on the unfortunate Razumov; but it suggests an empirical awareness to which the novel does not do justice. Even the dialogue, wonderful as it sometimes is, too often tends to consist of thumbnail autobiography and self-analysis. If the real differences between the Russian revolutionaries of *Under Western Eyes* and Conrad's earlier anarchists are matters of philosophical premise and temperament, then the failure of dramatic development is serious, since it is only through finely analyzed and concretely presented emotional states, along with the carefully done philosophic exchanges which would establish the "Russian" frame of intellectual reference, that Conrad might have defined these differences.

But the most troublesome feature of *Under Western Eyes* is its dramatic and symbolic exaggeration. When the reader learns that Razumov "had set his teeth so hard that his whole face ached [and] it was impossible for him to make a sound" (p. 62), or that "he shrugged his shoulders so violently that he tottered" (p. 184), he is likely to feel a gratuitous dramatic force reminiscent of the early Malayan tales. The analogy is not incidental: just as when Willems bit himself to forget the pain in his heart or struck himself so hard that he reeled under his own blow, Conrad is here trying to work out a symbolic method that will indicate an extreme of moral conviction while at the same time preserving the superficial reality of his subject. The direction of Conrad's growth is not, at this point, as it was in the earlier instance, toward the presocial and "inner" dilemmas of a Marlow or Kurtz; it is toward the allegorical firmness of *Victory*; but the creative impulse is much the same.

This exaggeration takes a variety of forms in *Under Western Eyes*. After a mere six weeks of wandering in the Siberian forest, for example, Peter Ivanovitch has lost the faculty of speech, an important event in Conrad's symbolic universe, but surely overdone here. Conversely, the speech of more sympathetic characters is sometimes tangled in a Jamesian complexity that has little point:

. . . Miss Haldin was unwilling to enter into the details. . . . But I was not hurt. . . .

"Very well. But on that high ground which I will not dispute, you, like any one else in such circumstances, you must have made for yourself a representation of that exceptional friend, a mental image of him, and—please tell me—you were not disappointed?"

"What do you mean? His personal appearance?"

"I don't mean precisely his good looks, or otherwise." We turned at the end of the alley and made a few steps without looking at each other.

"His appearance is not ordinary," said Miss Haldin at last.

"No, I should have thought not—from the little you've said of your first impression. After all, one has to fall back on that word. Impression! What I mean is that something indescribable which is likely to make a 'not ordinary' person." (p. 170)

The same reaching for effect yields ironies which are too broadly incredible, as when Razumov risks discovery by using the events of his own visit to Ziemianitch and to General T—— to illustrate a philosophical point for Haldin, (p. 59), or when he assures Sophia Antonovna that " 'I can't speak for the dead' " (p. 261). With its remoter point of view, *The Secret Agent* can indulge in ironies equally pungent with no danger of esthetic conflict; but *Under Western Eyes* makes a repeated claim of documentary accuracy. Finally—and this is no doubt the most bothersome sort of stretching in the novel—everything Russian seems to take on superhuman dimensions. A drunkard is "a proper Russian man" (p. 28), a devil-may-care sledge driver "a proper Russian driver" (p. 29). To Razumov, Russia is "this Immensity . . . this unhappy Immensity!" (p. 61); and even his nightmares (mere Western depth psychology to the contrary) are couched in metaphors of Russian politics: "Several times that night he woke up shivering from a dream of walking through drifts of snow in a Russia where he was as completely alone as any betrayed autocrat could be; an immense, wintry Russia" (p. 66). Russians are stronger than the inhabitants of other countries: the stress Miss Haldin feels after the death of her brother "would have undermined the health of an Occidental girl; but Russian natures have a singular power of resistance" (p. 177).

Russians are precocious: "The young begin to think early" (p. 102). Russians are subject to the greatest extremes of misery: "I mean the people who have nowhere to go and nothing to look forward to in this life. . . . Sometimes I think that it is only in Russia that there are such people and such a depth of misery can be reached" (p. 150). Hardened Russian revolutionaries melt at the notion of their common political motherhood:

". . . Don't you think, Sophia Antonovna [Razumov asks], that you and I come from the same cradle?"
   The woman, whose name he had forced himself at last to pronounce (he had experienced a strong repugnance in letting it pass his lips), the woman revolutionist murmured, after a pause—
   "You mean—Russia?"
   He disdained even to nod. She seemed softened. (p. 253)

Proverbs which are true everywhere else suddenly lose their validity: " 'No news—good news,' I said cheerfully. . . . 'Not in Russia,' she breathed" (p. 108). Even Russian handwriting seems "cabalistic, incomprehensible" (p. 133). And Razumov's internal monologues are hothouses of exotic political metaphor: " 'Better that thousands should suffer than that a people should become a disintegrated mass, helpless like dust in the wind. Obscurantism is better than the light of incendiary torches. The seed germinates in the night. Out of the dark soil springs the perfect plant. But a volcanic eruption is sterile, the ruin of the fertile ground" (p. 34). Passages like these lead the reader to suspect that Conrad's anti-Russianism—which emerges obversely in these passages as a kind of exaggerated respect—has simply interfered too thoroughly with his artistic judgment to permit *Under Western Eyes* to approach the controlled success of *The Secret Agent*.
   When *Under Western Eyes* is put into the context of Conrad's total artistic growth, however, it is possible to see a further reason for the novel's peculiarities, and to account for that margin of rhetorical and symbolic exaggeration left untouched by

other explanations. *Under Western Eyes* is a transitional book
—in its subject and central attitudes belonging to Conrad's political period, but exhibiting also certain technical devices which
will be of major importance in Conrad's third phase: the intellectually remote narrator or protagonist, the self-conscious episte-
mology, and the use of near-allegorical characters, all of which
are essential to *Chance* and *Victory,* and reflect the growing
firmness of Conrad's philosophical beliefs. The pedantic narrator
of *Under Western Eyes* is much like the Marlow of *Chance*—a
sophisticated, condescending interpreter of mysteries too deep for
the unaided reader to grasp. These later narrators are eager to
supply paragraphs of exposition—philosophical and psychological theory and the like—to help the reader interpret the events
of the tale. The early Marlow had more often let such matters
rest in asides and in the symbolic imagery; the later Marlow digs
them out and expands them, often to the point of a wearisome
digressiveness. The later narrators are more dogmatic, and perhaps more cynical; and they are less emotionally involved: the
Marlow of *Chance* finds something farcical in the most pathetic
and even tragic events, and the old language teacher finds Mrs.
Haldin "a sight at once cruel and absurd" (p. 335). Both *Under
Western Eyes* and *Chance* are analyzed into parts (*Chance* even
into titled chapters), and the reader is likely to be reminded
sharply of the controlling function of the narrator at the beginning of each of these parts—something too tiresomely true of
Under Western Eyes. The old language teacher is more the
empiricist and less the analyst than Marlow; he is charged principally with translating a strange setting and a cabalistic document
into terms the Western mind can understand. Moreover, the
political subject carries itself best through concrete detail and
dialogue, and the narrator's chief reflective function is more
likely to rest on matters of psychology and philosophical clarification. But with these differences taken into account, both these
narrators represent the self-conscious theoretical intellect that
was beginning to emerge more strongly in Conrad's fiction.

Under Western Eyes also uses allegorically tinged detail in a more persistent way than any of Conrad's earlier novels. He had experimented with such figures as Gentleman Brown and Kurtz's black Intended, of course; but not until *Under Western Eyes* had he used allegorical detail so markedly and repeatedly in a novel (it is significant that he had written "The Secret Sharer" not long before). In this respect *Under Western Eyes* foreshadows the "Damsel" and the "Knight" of *Chance* and the Mr. Jones gang of *Victory*. Razumov, to take the central instance, is an "individual case" with "general meaning" (p. 293); his bastardy means that "his closest parentage" is all Russia (p. 10); and if the vague and generalized "Prince K——," a characteristically declining aristocrat with moderately heavy autocratic loyalties, admits siring Razumov, that merely confirms the allegory. " 'I've never known any kind of love,' " Razumov tells Natalia Haldin (p. 360). In this dissociation from normal emotional ties, he becomes almost purely a conceptual character, moved only by aspirations of national service and personal survival and torn between conflicting political claims. In a remarkable piece of artifice, Razumov even undergoes a change of physiognomy as he is drawn from his state of political passivity and projected into action. At the beginning of the novel, he is characterized by "a peculiar lack of fineness in the features. It was as if a face modelled vigorously in wax (with some approach even to a classical correctness of type) had been held close to a fire till all sharpness of line had been lost in the softening of the material"; and this softness of feature in turn reflects a mental and moral softness: "In discussion he was easily swayed by argument and authority" (p. 5). But seen later in Geneva, after he has been hardened in the cold blasts of political reality, Razumov is almost craggy: "His features were more decided than in the generality of Russian faces; he had a line of the jaw, a clean-shaven, sallow cheek; his nose was a ridge, and not a mere protuberance" (p. 179). Many of the other characters similarly have physical features which stand in parallel with their mental characteristics:

Haldin has a "supple figure" with a "white forehead above which the fair hair stood straight up" to give him "an aspect of lofty daring" (p. 18); Madame de S—— is seen as "a wooden or plaster figure of a repulsive kind," with "artificial" eyes and teeth (p. 225); Nikita, the revolutionary executioner, has "lifeless, hanging hands" and an "enormous bloodless cheek" (p. 266); and so on. And this sort of symbolic detail is extended by other kinds of paralleling. Haldin, for example, about to flee from Razumov's room, appears to Razumov to be "posed for the statue of a daring youth listening to an inner voice" (p. 63); shortly before, Razumov has been forced to admire Spontini's "Flight of Youth" in the office of General T——. Later, still another statue adds to the dimensions of Razumov's political dilemma, as he sits writing his own confessions: "the people crossing over in the distance seemed unwilling even to look at the islet where the exiled effigy of the author of the *Social Contract* sat enthroned above the bowed head of Razumov in the sombre immobility of bronze" (p. 291). This kind of device can be seen more fully in the fiction of Conrad's third period, as he begins to examine the philosophic context of his early psycho-moral themes. But first it will be necessary to return to the protean *Nostromo,* and assess its place in the Conrad canon.

4

Nostromo

Conrad's material in "Nostromo" . . . is perhaps richer than that of any of his other books. In fact, it is much too rich even for a book of this size. . . . The result is that only the most resolute lovers of Conrad can push their way through the tangled underbrush of this well-nigh pathless forest. . . . Priceless things are buried there under a complication of tropical growth. . . . But no one should undertake such an expedition without being warned of its perils and ardors.
>   —Joseph Warren Beach, in *The Twentieth Century Novel: Studies in Technique*

Nostromo has always been a favorite among writers on Conrad. His first biographer spoke of it as "his vastest, most powerful, most minutely thought-out novel," creating "the authentic atmosphere of a South American republic"; [1] and one of his earliest critics thought it his "most elaborate and weightiest," a fictional creation of "convincing concreteness" and "vivid light and shade." [2] Such recent authorities as Guerard, Leavis, and Warren have continued to view *Nostromo* as a major achievement, Leavis, in particular, echoing the earlier judgment: "It is Conrad's supreme triumph in the evocation of exotic life and

[1] Aubry, *The Sea Dreamer*, p. 242.
[2] Mégroz, *Joseph Conrad's Mind and Method*, p. 127.

colour. . . . Sulaco . . . is brought before us in irresistible reality, along with the picturesque and murderous public drama of a South American State": an accomplishment made possible by the novel's "serious and severe . . . conception of the art of fiction" and by the "rich economy" of a structural pattern that plays representative attitudes and motives off against one another.[3] *Nostromo* has been praised variously as a philosophical novel, as the best novel in English on South American politics, and as an "ambitious and daring" technical experiment in which "time is all-inclusive and partakes fully of the historical sense," so that "the novel is unfolded as history in the making."[4]

There is, however, a persistent ambivalence in *Nostromo* criticism, a feeling that while it is "incomparably rich among English

[3] F. R. Leavis, *The Great Tradition: George Eliot, Henry James, Joseph Conrad* (New York: George W. Stewart; London: Chatto and Windus, 1948), pp. 190–191, 195.

[4] Karl, *Reader's Guide*, pp. 77, 87. The most comprehensive interpretation may belong to Leo Gurko: "*Nostromo* deals with the cycle of life and death in the mythical republic of Costaguana, but it also summons almost every other theme encompassable in fiction. It is a full-scale account of politics, society, the historical process, geography, economics, morality, love, revenge, primitivism, civilisation and imperialism. . . .

"To transform the story into a microcosm of earth and man, Conrad equips his scene with multiple ramifications. The landscape includes the ocean, a gulf, islands, an extended seacoast, a plain, foothills, the snow-capped peak Higuerota, a rampart of mountains virtually cutting off the province of Sulaco from the rest of Costaguana, a city, villages, hamlets and every kind of weather including a peculiarly windless, cloud-banked darkness that settles over the coast at night. . . . A maze of nationalities, races and religions appears: Englishmen, Americans, Latin Americans, Italians, Frenchmen, Spaniards, Indians, Caucasians, Negroes, Catholics, Protestants and Jews. Five languages are heard, not alone in their formal but in their dialect versions as well. Extensive reading had supplied Conrad with a mass of authentic information about South America. . . . He proceeded to transfuse it into the intensely visualised and extraordinarily mapped state of Costaguana, which becomes not simply his 'broadest canvas' as a writer but his most nearly universal frame of reference as a psychologist, moralist and philosopher" (*Joseph Conrad*, pp. 141–142).

novels in conception and material" it is "equally incomparable in dramatic impenetrability." [5] Even Leavis finds that the "reverberation of *Nostromo* has something hollow about it . . . a suggestion of a certain emptiness." [6] Sometimes this response reaches the level of paradox: one writer holds simultaneously that *Nostromo* is Conrad's "broadest and most profound" novel, the "high point" of his "literary maturity," and "one of the most spoiled, one of the most imperfect" of his works, with "numerous moments of failure." [7] Such critical ambivalence is, I think, perfectly appropriate and understandable here. For despite its scope and energy, *Nostromo* can most usefully be viewed as an ambitious experiment with new material (in the most basic thematic sense), marking the beginning of a new phase of Conrad's career, and in its only partial success moving him toward the more impressive *Secret Agent* and *Under Western Eyes*. In sheer weight and complexity, *Nostromo* may outrank *The Secret Agent* (so does the *Encyclopaedia Britannica*); but in terms of the special truths and pleasures prose fiction can yield, *The Secret Agent* is better. If this judgment is sound, some downward revaluation of *Nostromo* is in order; and more generally, the notion of a near-linear growth and decline in Conrad's art must be abandoned.

As suggested in his famous stricture about the symbolic importance of the silver,[8] the thematic center of *Nostromo* lies in Conrad's critical attitude toward economic instrumentalism. Don Carlos Gould, "The King of Sulaco" by virtue of his control of the San Tomé mine, is charged with defining an idealistic conception of the silver: " 'What is wanted here is law, good faith, order, security. . . . I pin my faith to material interests. Only let the material interests once get a firm footing, and they are bound

[5] Zabel, ed., *The Portable Conrad*, p. 42.
[6] Leavis, *The Great Tradition*, p. 200.
[7] Karl, *Reader's Guide*, p. 154.
[8] Aubry, *Life and Letters*, II, p. 296.

to impose the conditions on which alone they can continue to exist. That's how your money-making is justified here. . . . It is justified because the security which it demands must be shared with an oppressed people. A better justice will come afterwards' " (p. 84). And to the casual observer—the European or North American visitor to Sulaco after the defeat of the Monterists and the success of Martin Decoud's plan to create an Occidental Republic—the silver will surely seem to have served Gould's purpose. Order, uniformity, civic pride, a commonsense justice, all spread gradually outward from the mining villages as the treasure pours down the mountain and creates the conditions of its own survival. Even Captain Mitchell, who has witnessed and participated in the "historical events" leading to these ends, can exhibit Sulaco with pride, and no sense of the ironies implicit in its growth. In Gould's formulation, however, is an ominous warning: money-making will bring an enforced stability at once, but a "better justice" will come only "afterwards." The ethical difficulties inherent in such an instrumentalism are sufficiently developed in *Nostromo* so that Gould is able to reflect finally that it is "impossible to disentangle one's activity from its debasing contacts" (p. 360), and Mrs. Gould sees "something inherent in the necessities of successful action" which carries with it "the degradation of the idea" (p. 521). When Dr. Monygham warns that " 'all that the Gould Concession stands for shall weigh as heavily upon the people as the barbarism, cruelty, and misrule of a few years back' " (p. 511), he points up the same paradox, and reminds the reader of Conrad's deepest moral concerns. *Nostromo,* like *The Secret Agent,* is founded on a persistent critical irony toward social idealism; and it is no accident that Conrad's first association, when he sets out years later to explain the inception of *The Secret Agent,* is to the creative labor of writing "that remote novel, 'Nostromo' " (*The Secret Agent,* pp. viii–ix).[9]

[9] Baines and others have suggested that Conrad identified the moral root of *Nostromo* in two articles written shortly after the novel, in which

Once this underlying similarity between the two novels is
seen, the reader begins to recognize other thematic and technical
parallels, and more particularly, to see in *Nostromo* the experimental versions of ideas and devices which are fully realized only
in *The Secret Agent*. Like the later novel, for example, *Nostromo* is placed in a setting which is universalized through the
use of synthetic descriptions, so that Costaguana becomes not
merely a generalized South American state, but, in miniature
and on a primitive level, a generalized European state also. The
English Captain Mitchell and the Italian Nostromo supervise an
"outcast" crew "of very mixed blood" (p. 14); the English railroad engineers direct a crew of Italian and Basque workmen (p.
14); the Italian Mrs. Viola is served by "squat, thick-legged
China girls" and "a cinnamon-coloured mulatto" with "languish-
ing almond eyes" (pp. 17–18). Among the representatives of the
material interests in Sulaco are "a Dane, a couple of Frenchmen,
a discreet fat German" (p. 192). And Holroyd, the North American Protestant financier whose influence appropriately enough
is the true wellspring of Sulaco's "progress," is "German and
Scotch and English, with remote strains of Danish and French
blood" and bears the profile of "a Caesar's head on an old Roman
coin" (p. 76). By synthetic devices such as these the drama of
Nostromo is projected beyond the merely historical or local scale.
At the same time, the primitive setting is excellent for Conrad's
purposes. Its comparative simplicity—due partly to Sulaco's geographical isolation and partly to its backwardness—along with
the normal rhetorical exaggerations of the Latin temperament,
help to reveal clearly the political follies and evils that interest
Conrad. The "cynicism of motives" implicit in social instrumentalism, for example, which proliferates in *The Secret Agent* in a
variety of subtle forms, is in *Nostromo* by contrast "very outspo-
ken" (p. 115) or covered with the faintest veneer of idealistic

---

he condemns the notion that political institutions, however wisely conceived (and particularly those resting on "material interests") can secure
the happiness of mankind (*Joseph Conrad*, pp. 311–312).

protestation. The simple, active, and direct public surface of Ribierism can stand in sharp ironic tension with the brutality and greed of figures like Guzman Bento. And having created his own isolated setting, Conrad can shift its political and economic character as rapidly as he wishes and on as grand a scale as he wishes.

Like that of *The Secret Agent,* the tone of *Nostromo* is predominantly ironic (though this remark will need qualification later). Conrad's irony is especially sharp and successful when he is dealing with political primitives like Sotillo and General Montero; or with instances of outright barbarity, like the drumhead executions of Guzman Bento's prisoners:

A lucky one or two of that spectral company of prisoners would perhaps be led tottering behind a bush to be shot by a file of soldiers. Always an army chaplain—some unshaven, dirty man, girt with a sword and with a tiny cross embroidered in white cotton on the left breast of a lieutenant's uniform—would follow, cigarette in the corner of the mouth, wooden stool in hand, to hear the confession and give absolution; for the Citizen Saviour of the Country (Guzman Bento was called thus officially in petitions) was not averse from the exercise of rational clemency. The irregular report of the firing squad would be heard, followed sometimes by a single finishing shot; a little bluish cloud of smoke would float up above the green bushes, and the Army of Pacification would move on over the savannas. (p. 138)

Guzman Bento's savage inversions of value; Sotillo's blustering fear ("a flash of craven inspiration suggested to him an expedient not unknown to European statesmen when they wish to delay. . . . Booted and spurred, he scrambled into the hammock with undignified haste"—p. 442); Pedro Montero's oratory ("The mouth of the orator went on opening and shutting, and detached phrases . . . reached even the packed steps of the cathedral with a feeble clear ring, thin as the buzzing of a mosquito"—p. 390); all contribute to Conrad's pervasive irony at the expense of Costaguana's politician-soldiers. As in *The Secret Agent,* the irony directed at figures higher on the social scale is lighter, but effective: the sheets of Don José Avellanos' "Fifty Years of Misrule" " 'littering the Plaza, floating in the gutters, fired out as wads for trabucos loaded with handfuls of type, blown in the wind, trampled in the mud' " (p. 235); or Captain Mitchell's misconceptions of Costaguanan history (not the least of which is his hearty conviction, after Nostromo's theft of the silver, that Nostromo is " 'a man worth his weight in gold' "—p. 530); or Giorgio Viola's nostalgic reminiscences of Garibaldi, which suggest the ultimate futility of even the most ethereal revolutionism. Conrad's irony extends finally to Charles Gould, nominally the highest figure in this spectrum of idealists: "For all the uprightness of his character, he had something of an adventurer's easy morality which takes count of personal risk in the ethical appraising of his action" (p. 365).

What *Nostromo* dramatizes, then, centrally, is the inevitable corruption of political and economic idealism, in a world where figures like old Viola, who sees political action as something to be undertaken "for the sake of universal love and brotherhood" (p. 313), are mere anachronisms. Conrad sees all the varieties of political thought and action in the novel, from the tyranny of Guzman Bento up to the beneficent materialism of Charles Gould, as members of the same family, differing only in degree, rather than kind; just as in *The Secret Agent* he will see even high public officials as remote variants of Verloc. Gould forecloses his wife's appalled attempt to discuss the Costaguanans' atrocious political methods with the gentle admonition, " 'My dear, you seem to forget that I was born here' " (p. 49); conversely, Sir John, the English railway-builder and one of the "high" links between Costaguana and modern European states, is already well-versed in the ideas of bribery, force, and invasion of private rights which are basic principles of Costaguanan politics (p. 37). The brilliant flexibility with which Conrad shifts the secondary point of view in *Nostromo*—sometimes two or three times on a single page—serves admirably to help record the effects of progress and of "The Silver of the Mine" on the minds and motives of a whole spectrum of major and minor characters; and the use of flashbacks gives this spectrum a third dimension, as the reader is given vignettes of past exploitation: "Worked in the early days mostly by means of lashes on the backs of slaves, [the Mine's] yield had been paid for in its own weight of human bones. Whole tribes of Indians had perished in the exploitation; and then the mine was abandoned, since with this primitive method it had ceased to make a profitable return, no matter how many corpses were thrown into its maw" (p. 52). Decoud's allusion to the " 'old times . . . when the persistent barbarism of our native continent did not wear the black coats of politicians, but went about yelling, half-naked, with bows and arrows in its hands' " (p. 231) expresses perfectly the principle of moral continuity which controls Conrad's use of the associative flashback in *Nostromo,* just as it controls the extension of his irony in *The Secret Agent.*

As Conrad's camera eye moves across and through this social and historical spectrum, it progresses gradually from an outer periphery of myth, legend, and minor and primitive figures toward an inner core of major figures, tending to focus more, toward the end, on characters like Emilia and Charles Gould and Dr. Monygham; and coming to rest finally on the destruction of Nostromo, the "incorruptible" Capataz de Cargadores, in the final section of the book. Nostromo is the crucial test case of the power of the silver: the broad-based popular hero who emerges gradually from the welter of conflict and revolution to dominate the narrative in Part Third. The Italian word which denotes his social role and becomes his name (until, significantly enough, he becomes a successful thief), is derived from the Spanish *nostramo* (our master, a person of trust), and ultimately perhaps from the Latin *nostro uomo* (our man, servant).[10] As Conrad explains in his Author's Note, Nostromo is "a man of the People.

[10] Roger L. Cox, "Conrad's Nostromo as Boatswain," *Modern Language Notes,* LXXIV (April 1959), 303–306.

. . . Nostromo does not aspire to be a leader in a personal game. He does not want to raise himself above the mass. He is content to feel himself a power—within the People" (pp. xxi–xxii). If this is so, Conrad apparently wanted Nostromo to suggest the hopelessness of the proletariat (that last argument of romantic revolutionism) as an agent of social growth. Nostromo is the most deeply radical term in Conrad's political series—"a revolutionist at heart," but at the same time a man "subjective almost to insanity" (p. 525). And in these abstract statements, at least, if not in the concrete development of the novel, Conrad approaches the paradoxes of revolutionary motivation more fully examined in the unfortunate Stevie and the other anarchists of *The Secret Agent.*

It is in the mode of abstract statement, in fact, that Conrad deals with most of the complexities of his subject in *Nostromo.* Martin Decoud, who is something of a choral figure in the novel, and who like Marlow has strong affinities with Conrad, is called upon to describe aspects of the Costaguanan political temperament which Conrad cannot adequately dramatize: "There is a curse of futility upon our character: Don Quixote and Sancho Panza, chivalry and materialism, high-sounding sentiments and a supine morality, violent efforts for an idea and a sullen acquiescence in every form of corruption" (p. 171). It is Decoud who invents the epithet *"Gran bestia!"* to be applied to General Montero, and in thus supplying the " 'last word on a great question' " (p. 191) points to the animal substratum of political scoundrelism which appears so strongly in *The Secret Agent;* and it is Decoud who defines a "conviction" as " 'a particular view of our personal advantage either practical or emotional' " (p. 189), and thus forecasts the hypocrisy of that novel's idealists. The correlated idea of psycho-moral privacy (exploited so mercilessly in the scenes between Verloc and Winnie) appears occasionally in *Nostromo:* the view Gould takes of his father's outrageous fortunes in Costaguana is "calm and reflective," since "it is difficult to resent with proper and durable indignation the physical or mental anguish of another organism, even if that other organism is one's own father" (pp. 58–59); Decoud discovers in the Gulf that there is "no bond of conviction, of common idea" between him and Nostromo (p. 295); and so on. Conrad's antirationalism appears occasionally: it is no good attaching "too much importance to form" (p. 56) in Costaguana; "everything merely rational fails in this country" (p. 315). Most importantly, perhaps, there is a clear awareness of the conflict between social instrumentalism and the legitimate needs of individuals. Mrs. Gould reflects on her marriage: "It was as if the inspiration of their early years had left her heart to turn into a wall of silver-bricks . . . between her and her husband. He seemed to dwell alone within a circumvallation of precious metal, leaving her outside with her school, her hospital, the sick mothers and the feeble old men, mere insignificant vestiges of the initial inspiration" (pp. 221–222). Deprived of "all the intimate felicities of daily affection which her tenderness needed as the human body needs air to breathe" (p. 512), Mrs. Gould sees finally a vision of the San Tomé mine "possessing, consuming, burning up the life of the last of the Costaguana Goulds. . . . The last! She had hoped for a long, long time, that perhaps—— But no! There were to be no more. An immense desolation, the dread of her own continued life, descended upon the first lady of Sulaco" (p. 522). Her fate thus prefigures Winnie Verloc's. The successful merchant Nostromo suffers the same loss of identity, with "the vigour and symmetry of his powerful limbs lost in the vulgarity of a brown tweed suit" (p. 527); and so ultimately does Sulaco itself: "The material apparatus of perfected civilization . . . obliterates the individuality of old towns under the stereotyped conveniences of modern life" (p. 96). Finally, in a significant moment of awareness, Emilia Gould formulates the objection to rigid idealism which is dramatized with such shocking impact in *The Secret Agent*: "Charles Gould's fits of abstraction depicted the energetic concentration of a will haunted by a fixed idea. A man haunted by a fixed idea is insane. He is dangerous even if that idea is an idea of justice; for may he not bring the heaven down pitilessly upon a loved head?" (p. 379). Unfortunately, however, these motifs remain largely undeveloped.

It is possible to argue a superior magnitude in *Nostromo*—a richness of historical concept and social analytic that the later work seems to lack. Irving Howe does this brilliantly, in *Politics and the Novel*. But this difference is less than has been thought, when *The Secret Agent* is closely read; and in any case, the extra increment of meaning, if any, exists in *Nostromo* almost exclusively as exposition. The humanist may of course prefer *Nostromo* on these grounds, as a superior exhibit of political insights and suggestions. The novel's greater superficial scope automatically invites variants of Conrad's basic ideas, and the peculiar setting invites a more conscious historical orientation. But the fundamental vectors of value and political concept are the same. And viewed in relation to these basic sources of artistic unity, *Nostromo* is inconsistent and underdeveloped. Despite its intermittently brilliant irony and occasional strong scene, and its extraordinarily flexible structure, the novel fails repeatedly to dramatize the issues with which it is centrally concerned, and its irony is mingled too frequently with romance and nostalgia. *Nostromo* is devoid of story where it ought to have it; the reader is told repeatedly that greed and selfishness have corrupted what looked like a selfless social ideal; but he is rarely shown the workings of that corruption, except with easy marks like Sotillo; and except for the brief interior monologues of Mrs. Gould and Dr. Monygham, he is never shown the destruction of individuality implicit in the power of the Mine. In contrast, *The Secret Agent* shows the reader exact modes of corruption and self-delusion, and, in the long interchanges between major characters which *Nostromo* largely lacks, dramatizes some of the moral contradictions inherent in revolutionary social action.

The uncertain development of *Nostromo* can be seen in the uneasy quality of Conrad's irony, which is strong and controlled in the treatment of the novel's political primitives, but tends to flicker out when approaching figures higher on the moral scale. For more than half the novel it is impossible to tell, for example, what Conrad's attitude is toward Giorgio Viola—whether he is to be exempted from the novel's dominant tone and held out as the sole representative of a valid political idealism (even if a powerless and anachronistic one), or presented merely as a high and gently pathetic figure, self-delusive like the novel's other idealists, but less crudely so. Early in the novel, Conrad defines Viola's character as it had been developed in service under Garibaldi: "The spirit of self-forgetfulness, the simple devotion to a vast humanitarian idea which inspired the thought and stress of that revolutionary time, had left its mark upon Giorgio in a sort of austere contempt for all personal advantage" (p. 31). At the same time, and for all his concern with "the wrongs of down-trodden nations" (p. 32), Giorgio is clannish in his idealism, declaiming to his audience of Italians in the Casa Viola, and excluding English engineers and even native Costaguanans from the benefits of his oratory (pp. 32–33). By the end of the novel, after the author and a variety of more-or-less choral figures have supplied an analysis of political motives, and after Giorgio has unwittingly killed Nostromo and escaped into an entire delusion, Conrad seems finally to have made up his mind; but meanwhile the reader has been vexed with an apparent contradiction. There even appear to be some accidental notes of comedy at Viola's expense, growing from Conrad's uncertainty of intention. The attempt to romanticize Viola through his memories of Garibaldi and the use of such words as "immortal" and "invincible" is potentially dangerous, for example, since Viola is now enmeshed in domestic duties, keeping a hotel and raising children. When the ideal and the domestic are accidentally juxtaposed, the effect is disastrous: "He had been one of the immortal and invincible band of liberators who had made the mercenaries of tyranny fly like chaff before a hurricane, 'un uragano terrible.' But that was before he was married and had children" (p. 25). The same conflict is felt in the case of Nostromo, who is the chief object of

Conrad's irony by the end of the novel, but who begins with a fund of sympathy and respect, and dissipates it almost without reason. (The initial elevation of Nostromo may be explained partly by his origin in Conrad's old friend Dominic of the *Tremolino*.) Charles Gould is perhaps the crucial case, since as "King of Sulaco" and the most powerful idealist in the novel he certainly ought to be brought firmly under the light of Conrad's critical vision. But in the end even Mrs. Gould finds it impossible to blame him: "Incorrigible in his devotion to the great silver mine was the Señor Administrador! Incorrigible in his hard, determined service of the material interests to which he had pinned his faith in the triumph of order and justice. Poor boy! . . . He was perfect—perfect. What more could she have expected? It was a colossal and lasting success; and love was only a short moment of forgetfulness" (p. 521).

The secret of these ambivalent attitudes toward his own characters may be simply that Conrad had not yet realized the implications of his own ethical commitments and of his personal brand of political skepticism. Still exploring his own political intuitions, and essentially conservative, in the sense that he valued dignity and law and a hierarchy of merit, he was inclined to limit his irony until its proper extent became clear, or until he had found the proper devices for lightening and subtilizing it, as in *The Secret Agent*. The case of Charles Gould, however, raises the whole question of concrete dramatic development in *Nostromo*, since Gould appears so infrequently, and then so reticently, that it is hard to see in any case how Conrad might have dramatized his corruption by the silver of the mine. To see the superiority of *The Secret Agent* in this respect, it is only necessary to compare the passage quoted earlier, in which Emilia Gould realizes that "a man haunted by a fixed idea is insane . . . even if that idea is an idea of justice," to the scenes between the anarchist Professor and Ossipon in *The Secret Agent*, where the reader is led through dialogue and ironic description to the same sort of awareness. All *Nostromo* can bring forth to demonstrate the corruption and the disillusionment of Gould is a series of abstract reflections in the minds of Gould, Mrs. Gould, and Dr. Monygham; and those infrequently. The narrative juxtaposes various points of view but rarely brings them into dramatic competition to draw out their implications, strengths and weaknesses—instead of conflict, problems of choice, mutual misunderstandings, and the like, working themselves out in significant situations, *Nostromo* describes an almost frictionless counterpointing of private reflections, as if a dozen Marlows at once were trying to comprehend Costaguanan politics.[11]

Nostromo's fall from grace in Part Third probably reveals most clearly Conrad's uncertainty of intention and his difficulty in giving his themes concrete form. As the previous remarks on the novel's structure have suggested, it is quite to the point that Nostromo, who carries with him the emergent spirit of the "People," should dominate the final part of the book. But Conrad apparently could not see how to relate Nostromo's corruption to his political themes. For the first two-thirds of the novel, the reader sees Nostromo from the outside, in gradually closer and more intimate perspectives (a relic of the Marlovian method of studying Kurtz and Jim); when Conrad finally moves into Nostromo's consciousness, the reader finds at least three distinct motives offered for his stealing the silver, none of them adequately developed, and the most important of them irrelevant to the politico-economic ideas of the book. At first the reader is led to suppose that Nostromo's theft is an act of cynicism—that having penetrated the hypocrisy and self-interest of the novel's "high" figures, Nostromo imagines his desire for the silver to be somehow justified: "He understood well that the doctor was anxious to save the San Tomé mine from annihilation. He would be nothing without it. It was his interest. Just as it had been the interest of Señor Decoud, of the Blancos, and of the Europeans to get his Cargadores on their side. . . . 'What are

---

[11] Wilding, "The Politics of *Nostromo*," makes some related points.

your politics and your mines to me—your silver and your consti-
tutions—your Don Carlos this, and Don José that——' " (pp.
455–456). On his deathbed, however, Nostromo is able to formulate something more like conventional proletarian revolutionism:

"You are all alike, you fine people. The silver has killed me. It has
held me. It holds me yet. Nobody knows where it is. But you are the
wife of Don Carlos, who put it into my hands and said, 'Save it on
your life.' . . ."
    "Nostromo!" Mrs. Gould whispered, bending very low. "I, too,
have hated the idea of that silver from the bottom of my heart."
    "Marvellous!—that one of you should hate the wealth that you
know so well how to take from the hands of the poor. The world
rests upon the poor." (pp. 559–560)

And meanwhile, having fallen in love with Giselle Viola, Nostromo has found still another reason: "He would put her beauty
in a palace on a hill. . . . He would keep her there like a jewel
in a casket. He would get land for her—her own land fertile
with vines and corn—to set her little feet upon. . . . He flung
the mastered treasure superbly at her feet in the impenetrable
darkness of the gulf" (p. 541). Some of Conrad's best writing in
Nostromo is in Part Third, in the scenes between Nostromo and
the Viola family, but the fog of motives lying behind Nostromo's
behavior simply obscures the novel's themes.
    Conrad himself, looking back on *Nostromo* after some fifteen
years, recalls his uncertainties: "It took the best part of the years
1903–4 to do; with many intervals of renewed hesitation, lest I
should lose myself in the ever-enlarging vistas opening before me
as I progressed deeper in my knowledge of the country. Often,
also, when I had thought myself to a standstill over the tangled-
up affairs of the Republic, I would . . . rush away from Sulaco
for a change of air" (p. xx). The result is a fragmented, kaleidos-
copic narrative movement that draws *Nostromo* perilously close
to an essay with illustrations rather than a work of prose fiction.
At the same time, the exploratory quality of the first part yields

almost a random selection of historical and geographical detail. The first chapter, particularly, which has sometimes been admired as a descriptive *tour de force,* imposes a mass of vegetation, topography, and weather on the reader—details which appear in a position of such extraordinary emphasis that they seem portentously symbolic and force the reader to stock his memory, but turn out to be of relatively little importance in the course of the novel. *Nostromo* is full of irrelevant information (e.g., Mrs. Gould hears of Charles's father's death "at the bottom of the hill, where three poplars stand near the wall of a vineyard"—p. 61), and its style is hampered generally by adjectival excess (e.g., Don Pépé rides "an ewe-necked silver-bitted black brute with a hammer head"—p. 114). Conrad's experiments with redundancy and incremental repetition as a form of irony, which are reasonably successful with such key phrases as "the Capataz de Cargadores" and such adjectives as "incorruptible," occasionally underscore details which have too little importance to merit it—as in the reiterated description of Don Pépé's horse, or of Viola's head as "leonine." In each case, the reader is forced to ponder what seems to be an elusive significance, but is often no significance at all. And the same redundancy extends into the interior monologues of Conrad's many characters, and even into dialogue, so that a spurious feeling of emotional and rhetorical pressure is built up without any substance underlying it. For a single example among many, one may take a portion of a scene between Decoud and Mrs. Gould:

"And also let me tell you something more. I have been making friends with this man called Nostromo, the Capataz. We had a conversation this very evening, I walking by the side of his horse as he rode slowly out of the town just now. He promised me that if a riot took place for any reason—even for the most political of reasons, you understand—his Cargadores, an important part of the populace, you will admit, should be found on the side of the Europeans."

"He has promised you that?" Mrs. Gould inquired, with interest. "What made him make that promise to you?"

"Upon my word, I don't know," declared Decoud, in a slightly surprised tone. "He certainly promised me that, but now you ask me why I certainly could not tell you his reasons." (p. 220)

Part of *Nostromo*'s unusual length can be traced to padding of this sort, and length in this case clearly does not imply weight. Finally, Conrad relies too heavily on style for dramatic and ironic effect in *Nostromo*. Some sentences are so thornily abstract they must be studied rather than read: at the beginning of his career in Sulaco, for example, Charles Gould "had had to accommodate himself to existing circumstances of corruption so naively brazen as to disarm the hatred of a man courageous enough not to be afraid of its irresponsible potency to ruin everything it touched" (pp. 142–143)—an analysis of feeling lacking either the subtle polish of a Henry James sentence or the colloquial clarity of a Marlow sentence. Others are syntactically distracting ("This was what said his Excellency, the popular Pedrito"—p. 391), or unsuccessful attempts to rejuvenate clichés ("the still watches of the night"—p. 54; "pacing to and fro like a tiger in a cage"—p. 333). Even here, *Nostromo* is an experimental and exploratory novel.

One indication of Conrad's anxiety over *Nostromo*'s lack of dramatic development is the tendency of his associative flash-backs to slip out of the conditional or past perfect tense into the straightforward past, as if he wished nervously to get out of the flashback somehow, and into the novel's action. A single example will suffice to give the idea of these distracting shifts:

Señor Avellanos was in the habit of crossing the patio at five o'clock almost every day. . . .

On seeing Charles Gould step into the sala he would nod provisionally and go on to the end of the oratorical period. Only then he would say—

"Carlos, my friend, you have ridden from San Tomé at the heat of the day. Always the true English activity. No? What?"

He drank up all the tea at once in one draught. This performance was invariably followed by a slight shudder and a low, involuntary "br-r-r-r," which was not covered by the hasty exclamation, "Excellent!"

Then giving up the empty cup into his young friend's hand, extended with a smile, he continued to expatiate upon the patriotic nature of the San Tomé mine. (pp. 50–51)

Still another indication is Conrad's tendency to address the reader directly with arguments persuading him of the novel's veracity, as when the reader is asked to accept the unusual motives of Pedrito Montero: "Pedrito . . . had been devouring the lighter sort of historical works in the French language. . . . Pedrito had been struck by the splendour of a brilliant court, and had conceived the idea of an existence for himself where, like the Duc de Morny, he would associate the command of every pleasure with the conduct of political affairs and enjoy power supremely in every way. Nobody could have guessed that. And yet this was one of the immediate causes of the Monterist Revolution. This will appear less incredible by the reflection that the fundamental causes were the same as ever, rooted in the political immaturity of the people" (p. 387). In short, Conrad has written a scenario in *Nostromo* without writing a finished narrative, and the creative conflict resulting from this circumstance is visible on almost every page. External evidence suggests that this conflict was with Conrad persistently. According to Gordan, "the serials of *The Rescue* and *Nostromo* differ more from the first editions than do any other of the stories," [12] a pairing which places *Nostromo* in company with the most agonized of all Conrad's creations; and Karl has shown that Conrad tried in his revisions to diminish *Nostromo*'s rhetorical quality, reducing its emphasis on description and expanding the dramatic interplay of characters. [13] Conrad's promise in 1911 to "prune [*Nostromo*] of all redundant phrases" before sending it to a translator [14] almost certainly reflects not only this anxious experience, but the experi-

[12] Gordan, *Joseph Conrad*, p. 217.
[13] Karl, *Reader's Guide*, p. 185.
[14] Aubry, *Life and Letters*, II, p. 137.

ence gained in writing *The Secret Agent* and *Under Western Eyes* as well.

A study of the present kind, which is concerned chiefly to trace Conrad's artistic growth, must pause to ask why Conrad had so much trouble with *Nostromo*, to say, if possible, why the novel falls so far short of the possibilities implicit in its sweeping imaginative range and wealth of characterization. And the answer, I think, is not hard to find: most of *Nostromo*'s defects are the result of carrying over thematic strains and techniques from the Marlow stories, and trying to adjust them to the essentially new purposes of the political tales. If the true moral and artistic center of *Nostromo* lies in a pervasive critical irony like that of *The Secret Agent* (though necessarily lighter and more carefully qualified), then much of the artistic experience Conrad had gained in working his way toward *Lord Jim* is simply irrelevant, and wherever it enters strongly into *Nostromo* is likely to interfere with the novel's development. In its thinness of significant social detail (despite the profusion of scenic and meteorological fact) and in its redundancy and slow narrative movement, *Nostromo* duplicates some of the characteristics of Marlow's oral tales, without the same rhetorical justification. Sometimes there is a valid purpose in the novel's reiteration of physical, especially scenic, detail; so that what may strike the reader at first as mere redundancy is actually Conrad's way of establishing a symbolic background for the events of his story. A phrase like "the snowy dome of Higuerota," which appears, with variations, some twenty or thirty times in the novel, is clearly related to the metaphysical sources of Conrad's political skepticism. " 'Look at the mountains!' " exclaims Decoud, " 'Nature itself seems to cry to us "Separate!"' " (p. 184); and the chief railroad engineer, pointing suddenly to "white Higuerota" in the midst of an idealistic discussion of the Mine, protests, " 'We can't move mountains!' " (p. 41). But even here, Conrad has simply carried over a device from the Marlow tales, as some of his other descriptive language makes clear: after the first failure of the mine, "the very road had vanished under a flood of tropical vegetation as effectually as if swallowed by the sea," a phrase duplicating the central metaphysical metaphors of both *Lord Jim* and "Heart of Darkness"; and only "vestiges of charred timber, some heaps of smashed bricks, and a few shapeless pieces of rusty iron could have been found under the matted mass of thorny creepers" (p. 54), images recalling Conrad's familiar form-and-chaos motif. And for Conrad's political novels, this sort of disruptive background force is less important than the epistemological principle of "chance" or the animal substratum of humanity which interfere so radically with political idealism in *The Secret Agent*. The human presumption and lack of self-knowledge drawn under Conrad's satiric eye in the later novel are largely absent from the attempts to impose a railroad and a political union on the mountain ranges of Costaguana—or are at least qualified by the romantic respect which inevitably attaches to such projects, and to the Lord Jims and Goulds and Ahabs (and even MacWhirrs) who undertake them in fiction. The isolated moral agent confronting forces too powerful and too grand to be resisted by his understanding and will is one kind of hero; the moral agent in society, seeking to impose his will upon other men in the service of some remote idealism, is a different kind of character, and his relation to metaphysical forces less significant.

The same point may be made about the setting of *Nostromo*, which, despite the advantages enumerated earlier, tends in some ways to resist Conrad's purposes. As Hewitt and others have seen, Conrad's isolated settings are especially useful in clarifying the psycho-moral problems he is often concerned with—partly by eliminating the possibility of chance visitors, random conflict, and so on, which would disturb the projective symbolism, and partly by their tendency to magnify the protagonists' stature: "Because they so dominate their surroundings and because there is no interference from outside, their inner problems are mirrored in external events and relationships. The facts of the external world become symbolic of the moral problems with which

they are at grips . . . moral problems which it might otherwise
be difficult to show as other than tenuous, abstract or impossible
of definition." [15] In *Nostromo,* however, this sort of isolation is
less appropriate. Isolated settings are generally primitive settings,
the locus of elemental, prepolitical dilemmas or "plights." But an
isolated setting, with its exotic qualities, may simply interfere
with the concrete development of social detail required by other
fictional themes, like those of Conrad's political tales. Sulaco
must be distinguished sharply from the Eastern, semimythical
settings of the earlier stories; it is essentially a Western locale,
isolated only so that it may be brought suddenly under the ideal
of commercial "progress" as the ships of the O.S.N. steam into its
harbor. Any exotic qualities persisting in *Nostromo* must necessarily disrupt the reader-identification needed to make the social
irony work—a problem which does not arise when the setting is
more nearly a projection of psychological forces. The geography-
with-personality which opens the book, the poetic inversions of
its descriptive style (e.g., "never a strong wind had been known
to blow" upon the Golfo Placido—p. 5), and its aggressive
Latinism, all strain against the counterimpulse to connect Sulaco
somehow with modern European states and thus enlarge the
novel's symbolic scope. Similarly, the isolated setting automatically exaggerates the stature of the major characters, and in so
doing makes Conrad's critical irony more difficult. What Conrad
really needs for the fullest expression of his political attitudes is a
symbolically radical setting which is at the same time closely
integrated with conventional Western society—a setting he finds
in the seamy revolutionary underside of London, in *The Secret
Agent.*

A further reverberation from the Marlow tales—and one,
again, which interferes with the basic critical intention of *Nostromo*—is Conrad's attempt to treat his chief protagonists with
the same complicated respect he had accorded Jim and Kurtz,

[15] Douglas Hewitt, *Conrad: A Reassessment* (Cambridge: Bowes and
Bowes, 1952), p. 13.

While Nostromo is a man "for whom the value of life seems to consist in personal prestige" (p. 248), his vanity, like Jim's, is paradoxically also "that finest form of egoism which can take on the aspect of every virtue" (p. 300). Gould too is like Jim, as Decoud describes him: " 'He cannot act or exist without idealizing every simple feeling, desire, or achievement. He could not believe his own motives if he did not make them first a part of some fairy tale. The earth is not quite good enough for him, I fear' " (pp. 214–215). Again, both Nostromo and the Goulds share the linguistic reserve of Conrad's heroic characters; Gould, especially, is a man of "voiceless reserve" (p. 165) who communicates with his wife chiefly through significant glances, and whose silences have "as many shades of significance as uttered words in the way of assent, of doubt, of negation—even of simple comment" (p. 203). Finally, Decoud—to take perhaps the most important example—exhibits the subtlest form of this thematic perseveration in *Nostromo*. Decoud's experience finally is much like that of Conrad's earlier protagonists. Isolated in the Golfo Placido, he comes to self-awareness too late: "The vague consciousness of a misdirected life given up to impulses whose memory left a bitter taste in his mouth was the first moral sentiment of his manhood" (p. 498). And the proper retribution for his "intellectual audacity" is to be "swallowed up," like Stein's swimmer, in "the immense indifference of things" (p. 501). Thus Decoud's central problem, like Nostromo's hidden passion for Giselle Viola, is thematically anterior to the novel's central concerns. At the same time, since his audacity is "intellectual," Decoud is a step toward the philosophic Heyst of *Victory*: having cut beneath the social illusions that form the chief substance of *Nostromo*, Decoud begins to doubt the significance of his own existence, and thus anticipates the existential motif of the later fiction.

It is precisely where he moves back toward these prepolitical themes, in fact, that Conrad is most successful in *Nostromo*. The book's most extended interior monologues and scenes (especially if we count Decoud's long letter to his sister) are those recording the essentially private dilemmas of Decoud and Nostromo. But so far as this is true, it works against the novel's unity. Nostromo's transgression, moreover, is significantly unlike Jim's or Kurtz's, so that the romantic treatment accorded him is inconsistent with his real moral status. His continuing crime involves none of the paradoxes of will crystallized in Jim's jump from the *Patna*, and his guilt is wholly conscious: after a nocturnal trip to his hidden cache to pick up a couple of ingots, "he would look fixedly at his fingers, as if surprised they had left no stain" (p. 524). When Conrad ends his novel with a reference to "the genius of the magnificent Capataz de Cargadores" dominating "the dark gulf containing his conquests of treasure and love" (p. 566), he accords Nostromo too affirmative a treatment. What has happened is that Conrad has conceived his setting and story partly in the same terms as *Lord Jim* and "Heart of Darkness," while its center is really elsewhere. Gould's politico-economic ideal is not Stein's "dream" or the "light" Conrad's savages seek; and the heart-of-darkness imagery of *Nostromo* suggests that Conrad had not yet quite analyzed the difference: the people of Costaguana's interior are described as "suffering and mute, waiting for the future in a pathetic immobility of patience" (p. 88); the workers of the San Tomé mine survive in a "paradise of snakes" (p. 105); the telegraph wire strung into the great campo is "like a slender, vibrating feeler of that progress waiting outside for a moment of peace to enter and twine itself about the weary heart of the land" (p. 166); and so on.

Finally, however, *Nostromo* is probably hindered most by its retention of certain rhetorical tactics closely associated with Marlow. In a simple mechanical sense, as Baines and others have observed, Captain Mitchell's lengthy narration and Decoud's letter look like truncated forms of the Marlovian voice; and both seem oddly disruptive in the texture of the novel. But more important is Conrad's persistence in symbolic narrative where it is no longer appropriate. As Hewitt observes, "The railway trucks . . . [and] the telegraph wire, are both concrete facts, playing their part in the plot, and symbols of the enslavement of the country. Throughout the book, the moral, the psychological and the spiritual issues are embodied naturally in outward objects." [16] But this is precisely part of the trouble with *Nostromo*. The ironies of political idealism, which by definition have to do with the moral effects of arrogated power, can reveal themselves fully only in the dramatic interaction of characters, in conflicts of motive and need which work themselves out in dialogue and other external situations. This kind of development requires in turn a high proportion of realistic detail. In the Marlow stories, the moral symbol is itself the dramatic fact, since the true narrative movement is in the consciousness of the sympathetic observer and storyteller. Marlow's continually shifting perspective and his externalization of inner discoveries are the proper rhetoric of a pragmatic-symbolist's quest for moral truth, permitting him to juxtapose and hold in balance elements of his experience which seem to him to represent important values and states of mind. But this symbolic reorganization of experience is appropriate only for those spiritual dilemmas which are in fact cognized through some such symbolic process, something akin to the moral philosopher's use of crucial examples. Where value-conflicts are not of this kind—where they are cognized initially through a more nearly inductive process—they can best be dramatized in a concretely developed social setting, particularly if they presuppose economic and political motives. Geographically, the setting of *Nostromo* is highly developed. But the human beings in this setting are rarely brought into conflict; they are more likely to be observed in succession by the narrator, like Marlow's interlocutors in *Lord Jim*.

The subject of *Nostromo* seems to preclude some of Marlow's other tactics, as well. Used too radically, for example, the time-shift will interfere with the development of cause-and-effect

[16] *Ibid.*, p. 54.

patterns which the reader needs to assent to Conrad's ironies; one of the most brilliant aspects of *The Secret Agent* is the success with which Conrad uses the time-shift to create dramatic effects while at the same time preserving the important cause-and-effect relationships of his plot. But the time-shift in *Nostromo* serves a different purpose, something related more closely to the impressionistic effect defined so famously by Ford Madox Ford. The novel's random organization of detail has sometimes been defended on the ground that a visitor fresh to Sulaco would experience the same confusion, and come to his knowledge of place and character in the same fragmentary way. But this is irrelevant unless the learning process is itself an important object of the narrative, as it is in the Marlow tales—and as it is not, in *Nostromo*. *The Secret Agent* establishes its scope by moving from character to character and from social level to social level, but does so without the corruption of a merely associative or impressionistic impulse; and there is no question of disorganization or of lack of clarity in the later novel. As several critics have observed, the time-shifts in *Nostromo* are so frequent and so radical as to negate the sense of time, and so reinforce the book's irony by suggesting an absurd and pointless recurrence of tyrannical exploitation; but the distractions created by this tactic outweigh its positive effects, which may in any case be established more effectively through parallels of imagery and other forms of analogy.

Finally, the abstract passages in *Nostromo* sometimes make it seem more like a political treatise than a novel. Abstract diction in the Marlow tales serves the double purpose of characterizing Marlow and of furnishing the meditative counters with which he controls his experience—in the extreme case, his way of approaching the nearly ineffable. But when the story's chief interest is in the narrator's object, rather than in the narrator himself and his way of telling, an abstract style tends to obscure important detail and oversimplify dramatic issues. *The Secret Agent*, which is often just as abstract as *Nostromo*, does not inspire the same uneasiness; since the novel's intellectual point of view is so firmly established to begin with by the dominant irony of event, detail, and diction, the didactic and expository passages merely reinforce what has already been established esthetically.

Not long after finishing *Nostromo,* Conrad created another Nostromo-like character in "Gaspar Ruiz." The story's first sentence suggests the similarity: "A revolutionary war raises many strange characters out of the obscurity which is the common lot of humble lives in an undisturbed state of society" (*A Set of Six,* p. 3). Like Nostromo, Gaspar dominates other men by the force of his simple personality and his physical strength; and like the novel, his story ends on a note of tribute. But at the same time, Conrad was beginning even here to develop more realistic and analytic versions of political motivation. Like Stevie, Gaspar is a creature of passive intelligence and guileless obedience: "A musket had been thrust into his hands. He had taken it. He had marched" (p. 4). Contemplating his imminent execution, Gaspar is "stirred by a feeling of sluggish anger, which he could not very well express" (p. 5)—the same wordless rage Stevie feels on the famous cab ride. Serving water to the other prisoners, he displays Stevie's "extraordinary air of charity, gentleness, and compassion" (p. 17). And like Stevie, Gaspar has a destructive potential which is "an enormous stone lying on the ground, ready to be hurled this way or that by the hand that picks it up" (p. 27). These and other intimations of *The Secret Agent* are faint in "Gaspar Ruiz," and they are buried in a long and turgid tale; but they mark the beginning of Conrad's movement away from *Nostromo* toward the hard ironic analysis and disciplined structures of the later political fiction.

Nostromo's technical imagination is undeniable. But its pyrotechnics take place largely in a vacuum, and do not illuminate Conrad's subject with anything like the clarity and efficiency a realistic method would provide. For all its strengths, *Nostromo* is little more than a complex parable; and placed beside *The Secret Agent,* it seems coy and calculated. The analogy to the first period of Conrad's career is nearly exact: beginning with the ambitious experiments of *Nostromo,* Conrad was able to work through to the brilliant clear irony of *The Secret Agent,* just as he had gradually found the solution to his earlier artistic problems by working his way through the early fiction toward Marlow. But even if this is true, it takes less away from *Nostromo* than at first appears, since by the time of *Lord Jim* Conrad was an accomplished novelist, and not likely to write anything trivial. In being forced back upon fundamental considerations about the art of fiction in order to articulate his difficulties with *Nostromo,* the reader inadvertently pays tribute to the persistent integrity of Conrad's work.

5

Victory—

The Existential Affirmation

Victory . . . is a book in which I have tried to grasp at more "life-stuff" than perhaps in any other of my works, and the one too of which the appreciation of the public has given me the most pleasure.
—From a letter of Joseph Conrad

In 1959, R. W. Stallman summed up the charges against Conrad's later fiction: "narrators who are unequipped to tell their stories effectively, implausible love-scenes, a new cleansed moral universe marked by sentimental optimism, [and] a reconciliation with the normal and the affirmative which damaged his fiction, his technique and his prose."[1] Readers of the early Conrad have always been struck with his perception of human darkness, his pervasive skepticism and irony, and the "static background" or "void" against which his protagonists work out their destinies. But it has become fashionable to hold that Conrad's later works show an avoidance of this perception of metaphysical and moral evil, as if finally he had lacked the

[1] R. W. Stallman, "Conrad Criticism Today," *Sewanee Review*, LXVII (Winter 1959), 138.

strength and will to face these darknesses, and had evaded them by turning his face to the light.

If it were true that Conrad's later fiction (and his integrity) had declined in this way, a study of his work might stop, for all practical purposes, with *Under Western Eyes*. But in the context of his total artistic growth, the best of Conrad's later works may be seen as complex and satisfying works of art, and as fictional statements of an acceptance which is anything but naïve or evasive. The affirmation of Conrad's later work has been hard won; in the fiction itself, the intellectual processes lying behind that affirmation (and just as importantly, the ironies qualifying it) are recapitulated in tight symbolic form, so that the works establish an emotional and philosophic tension sufficient to do away with any notion of mere slackness or sentimental optimism. In one sense, the affirmation of the later works undergoes even a more severe test than the paradoxical optimism of *Lord Jim* and the other early works: if Jim's moral stature is threatened by the solipsistic quality of his idealism and by his unsuspected weakness, Conrad's later protagonists suffer from conditions far more cosmic in scope and even less remediable by the pragmatic prescriptions of a Stein—metaphysical and epistemological conditions which define the status of the individual and introduce an element of paradox and impossibility into the very notion of moral choice. The metaphysical ideas of *Chance* and *Victory* had been implicit in the earlier fiction, and occasionally even explicit in the meditations of Marlow or some other narrator. But they had not dominated the early work as they dominate *Chance* and *Victory*. These novels set out to examine the very preconditions of moral action; so that while they return superficially to the subjects of the earlier fiction, they focus more closely on the philosophical component of Conrad's characteristically archetypal moral situations, and bring it as close to the foreground of the tale as the narrative form will permit. One may say, for example, that "chance," as Conrad extends the meaning of the term, is the chief barrier to the moral agent's control of the "destructive element," and that the novel *Chance* thus has, as one purpose, a symbolic testing of Conrad's own earlier ethical commitments. The later novels are finally "affirmative" in tone, but not cheaply so.

As might be expected, these later works are often more abstract in style and less sharply individualized in subject matter than the earlier ones, since (at least in *Chance* and *Victory*) Conrad is even more consciously involved in the study of archetypal moral situations. They are intellectually more complex than the earlier works, and more remote in tone. Partly because his own intellectual growth was reaching full fruition, and partly because the philosophical threats to his moral optimism demanded a strong analytic counterbalance, Conrad at times adopts a tone of cold intellectual conviction which tends to freeze the stream of ideas. The tentative, exploratory tone and the ironic self-limitation that had characterized the earlier Marlow are largely absent from the later fiction—an apparent loss of complexity, but a change actually consistent with the direction of Conrad's growth.

The problem of dramatizing his final intellectual and moral beliefs is, however, one which Conrad did not always successfully solve; in general, his later work is successful only where he succeeds in transmuting these convictions into allegorical or near-allegorical form. Where they are given more nearly expository form—as in *Chance*—his work is likely to fail as narrative art. "The Secret Sharer" (which really belongs to this later phase of Conrad's work) and *Victory* are the best of the later works precisely because they succeed most fully in carrying out this symbolic transmutation. "The Secret Sharer" differs from the earlier work not only in its maturer acceptance of the darker sides of the self, but also in its greater degree of intellectual artifice, as revealed in the close control of allegorical and structural devices. Its narrator appropriately fails to achieve the "roundness" of Marlow, since the reader's pleasure is expected to lie instead in the technical ingenuity and symbolic delicacy with which some few profound dimensions of character are explored. The same point holds true roughly of *Victory*, and any criticism which undertakes to examine that novel's characters from the standpoint of psychological realism will quickly run up against an apparent simplicity and naïveté. The pleasure of reading a novel like *Victory* derives less from the recognition of acute psychological or social observation than from the recognition of subtleties in the dramatization of a set of ideas, and to insist on the first at the expense of the second would be to resist the creation of allegory at all. As the next two chapters will suggest, many of the virtues (and the defects) of Conrad's fiction in his third phase result from his effort finally to establish a detailed, semiallegorical symbology of his own; and even the last works, with their apparent relaxation of symbolic tension, take some of their character from this allegorizing impulse, as it perseveres beyond *Victory*.[2]

Victory is the high point of Conrad's third period; yet it has received perhaps the least sympathetic and least adequate readings of any of Conrad's major works. Several writers have offered broad preliminary descriptions of its structure and symbolic methods; and some useful work has recently been done with Shakespearean analogues, to supplement the obvious parallels with Villiers de L'Isle Adam's *Axël*. Beyond this, however, criti-

[2] I am purposely going to use such terms as "allegory" and "symbolic tale" quite loosely here. Even in a single work, Conrad's fiction is likely to approach and recede from one or another of these modes as the needs of plot and structure dictate (*Victory*, for example, as will be seen, moves from an outer periphery of more-or-less realistic narrative to an inner core of conscious allegory, and back again); and the mixture of terms actually gives a truer general idea of what is going on in his later fiction than any one term could. The important point is that his later work, at least up to *Victory*, moves away from the basically realistic techniques of the early fiction and mere dialectical configurations of imagery toward more artificial modes, as the thematic scope of his work becomes more general and philosophical.

cal response has been curiously incomplete, tending either to place the novel in an inappropriate genre like the "popular romance," or to overstress some symbolically subordinate aspect. It is probably the sudden unexpected delicacy of Conrad's symbolic method in *Victory* (although as will be shown, this fine touch is actually the end product of a series of lesser works) that has thrown so many expert readers off balance—his apparently sudden transition from the heavy analytic development of *Chance* to the light allegorical development of the later novel. In any case, the result has been to leave *Victory* with no clear niche in the Conrad canon.

Conrad's letters and conversation stress the importance he placed on *Victory;* and for his only public reading from his works, he chose Lena's death scene. The Author's Note is his longest and most analytic; he not only provides an extended explication, but confesses his own "mixed feelings" in the face of the novel's first critical notices, and calls attention to some elements that superficial reviewers might have missed: the quality of Lena's "victory," the symbolic status of Jones, Pedro, and Ricardo, and so on. And his very first sentence stresses *Victory*'s intensely personal quality: "The first thing I am conscious of is the actual nearness to me personally" (p. ix). Unless we are simply to dismiss Conrad's strongest intuitions about his own art, we must somehow account for his feeling about *Victory;* and this, I think, requires an acknowledgment that the novel is considerably more complex than it has usually been taken to be. *Victory* is not thematically obscure—especially for the reader who has read Conrad's earlier works—but the metaphysical and mythical dimensions gradually developed in the narrative give it an intellectual depth and symbolic subtlety which raise it far beyond the usual formulas offered in interpretation.

Before turning directly to the novel, something must be said about the value-claims being made here for *Victory* and some of Conrad's other later work. An essential premise of this study has been that Conrad necessarily wrote different *kinds* of fiction as he moved from major period to major period; that his growth cannot be seen simply in terms of subject matter, since technique and subject matter are two aspects of a unified whole; and that in consequence considerable technical discussion would be necessary if the lines of Conrad's career were to be marked off successfully. Viewing it solely in terms of subject matter, Conrad's fiction seems uneven, with inexplicable shifts of interest; if the critic happens to prefer the earlier subjects, he will praise and blame accordingly. Viewing the fiction in terms of a single technical criterion will have a similar result: a preference for realism will yield the fundamentals of an achievement-and-decline theory, a preference for symbolic narrative will elevate the later work, and so on. When such methods are brought to bear on a novelist whose works are basically similar, as for example Jane Austen, the kind of critical differences engendered by Conrad's work generally do not arise; the critic will discuss the fiction if he finds it congenial, and if not, will let it rest. But with a writer like Conrad the case is different. His work is all of a piece, but only at the basic level of ethical commitment defined earlier; beyond that, it is diverse both in theme and technique. In its growth toward the firm (if enigmatic) affirmation of *Lord Jim,* and then again toward its equally firm converse in the relentless irony of *The Secret Agent,* Conrad had worked toward essential meanings in two different fields of experience, and simultaneously had worked out the techniques that had enabled him to project these meanings in fictional form—or more exactly, the technical and intellectual efforts had been one. The same thing happens in his third major period; and since *Victory* is the period's effective terminus, the first problem is to mark off its technical and thematic differences from the earlier work, before venturing value judgments or importing irrelevant tools of analysis. The view taken here is that *Victory* sets out to develop, in symbolic form, the metaphysical and epistemological beliefs that had always been implicit in Conrad's fiction, and that the proper route for technical analysis to take is accordingly toward the novel's symbolic and allegorical subtleties. Seen in this light, *Victory* emerges as a significant achievement in a difficult technical mode.

But here a rhetorical problem arises. Most modern readers are unsympathetic with this kind of defense: they simply do want their fictional realism, at any cost. The erosion of metaphysical and ethical certainty since the Renaissance has meant also an erosion of allegory; the modern fictionist is more likely to turn to realism and its associated forms, and to obtrude himself as little as possible into his narrative. Insofar as allegory results from the marriage of ethical or metaphysical certitudes with narrative art, it is out of the question so long as these certitudes are lacking. But with Conrad the case is different. The dominant motifs and ideas of *Victory* are themselves, in large part, the premises which have undermined modern intellectual certitude, or the existential moral inferences which have been built upon them—or, finally, the contrary and analogous beliefs, myths, and symbolic systems which might help to give Conrad's own narrative ironic depth. As one critic has observed, "Conrad is not the only modern writer to find that the tragic or ironic rehandling of a myth which had an optimistic meaning in its original form fits the modern sensibility of disillusionment and regret." [3] Conrad's allegory in *Victory* is probably the only kind of allegory that *could* be written for a sophisticated modern audience: sufficiently congruent with its skeptical assumptions to be regarded as intellectually respectable. The degree of understanding and technical facility with which Conrad develops these central concerns is of course a further matter, but the usual prejudice against allegory ought not to gain footing here.

From this first difficulty, however, follows a second. The normal use of critical analysis is to crystallize the reader's perception into some significant pattern; if he is told, for example, that the central concerns of Conrad's early fiction are the psycho-moral

[3] David Lodge, "Conrad's *Victory* and *The Tempest*: An Amplification," *Modern Language Review*, LIX (April 1964), 198.

dilemmas defined by critics like Guerard, he can view that work with an instrument which will give it focus and unity, and can extend his own insights into passages not discussed by any critic. And where such a critical proposition deals largely with content, rather than technique, the rhetorical negotiation between critic and reader is usually successful. But description of technique is another matter, particularly where technique departs from the familiar analogues of photography and exposition. Usually it is possible to interest the reader in image-patterns, since these are like sensory configurations; sometimes it is possible to interest him in structure, since this bears a close relation to the geometrical properties of his own physical environment and his own expository discourse. But to move on to metonymy, allegorical representation, mythical parallels, literary allusion, and the like —devices which depend on logical, rather than physical analogues—is more difficult; few readers attend closely to them, and the popular critical literature, particularly, is unlikely to give them due weight. Thus an analysis of technique may not succeed at all in crystallizing the reader's responses; and if not, he may be thrown back once again upon the elementary realistic or expository criteria more appropriate to another kind of work. Something like this has happened, I think, even with sophisticated critics of *Victory*—partly because Conrad's other novels tend to establish critical assumptions which simply will not work here, and partly because *Victory* itself does start out realistically, and only gradually draws the reader into a core of allegory.

The superficial story and characterization of *Victory* (as befits an allegorical narrative) are not difficult to summarize. The skeptically detached protagonist Heyst, yielding to his compassion for the unfortunate orchestra girl Lena (as he had yielded earlier to his sympathy for Morrison), involves himself in the commitment to action which his temperament and philosophy had renounced. When as a result the world intrudes upon his retreat at Samburan, in the persons of Jones, Ricardo, and Pedro, he finds himself unequipped to cope with the forces they represent; and the novel's final dramatic and spiritual ironies are generated by this defect of moral responsibility. Conrad draws attention in his Author's Note to some of the obvious inadequacies of Heyst's character: the "fine detachment" and "habit of profound reflection" that interfere finally with his power to assert himself against "the universally irremediable," as represented by Jones and company, and so on (pp. x–xi). But to stay very long within the conventional categories of "plot" and "character" will make *Victory* seem shallow and absurd. A better lead can be found in Conrad's famous letter to Barrett H. Clark, who had just written him a personal analysis of *Victory*: "A work of art is very seldom limited to one exclusive meaning and not necessarily tending to a definite conclusion. And this for the reason that the nearer it approaches art, the more it acquires a symbolic character." [4] *Victory*'s character as a secular allegory is announced in the epigraph from *Comus*: "Of calling shapes, and beckoning shadows dire,/ And airy tongues that syllable men's names/ On sands and shores and desert wildernesses"; and the careful reader will discover that Conrad's simple "plot" and "characterization" rest upon a fairly complex structure of multivalent moral and archetypal symbols.

The best way to approach a work as tightly organized as *Victory* is to borrow one of Conrad's own characteristic methods: examine first what is most obvious, then work beyond these superficial appearances toward a core of deeper meaning. And certainly the most obviously symbolic element of *Victory* is the triumvirate of evil which invades Sourabaya and then Samburan, and brings Heyst to his self-destructive moral test. The apparition of Jones, Ricardo, and Pedro—"a spectre, a cat, an ape" (p. 148)—introduces lines of imagery which are to be developed and magnified as the novel progresses, and which more than any other dominate its descriptive passages. Mr. Jones, the leader, who stands at one end of this evil spectrum, is

---

[4] Aubry, *Life and Letters*, II, pp. 204–205.

corpselike, almost skeletal, with a "dark, sunken stare," "clean-shaven, extremely thin face," "long and loose-jointed" frame (pp. 98–99), and "feminine eyelashes," all of which gives him "a used-up, weary, depraved distinction" (p. 102). The catlike Ricardo has "a thin, dishevelled moustache sticking out quaintly under the tip of a rigid nose" (p. 100), "phosphorescent" eyes (p. 123), and a jaguar's grin. His sensuality is savage ("Take 'em by the throat or chuck 'em under the chin, it's all one to me—almost"—p. 166), his aggression coyly cannibalistic (he looks at Schomberg "with the expression of a cat which sees a fish in the pantry out of reach"—p. 117); and even his loquacity is feline ("Schomberg experienced mingled relief and apprehension, as if suddenly an enormous savage cat had begun to wind itself about his legs in inexplicable friendliness"—p. 126). At the bottom of this spectrum is the "shaggy, hair-smothered" Pedro: "The lower part of his physiognomy was over-developed; his narrow and low forehead, unintelligently furrowed by horizontal wrinkles, surmounted wildly hirsute cheeks and a flat nose with wide, baboon-like nostrils" (p. 99). The suggestions of these images are plain enough, but lest the dense Schomberg miss the trio's allegorical bearing, Mr. Jones calls attention to it: " 'You don't think, by any chance, that you have to do with ordinary people, do you?' " (p. 112). By the end of the novel, these villains have been developed sufficiently so that even the detached Heyst is able to articulate some of their significance: " 'Here they are, the envoys of the outer world. Here they are before you—evil intelligence, instinctive savagery, arm in arm. The brute force is at the back . . . fantasms from the sea—apparitions, chimaeras! And they persist. . . . They have no right to be—but they are' " (p. 329). When Mr. Jones and company arrive at Samburan, *Victory* becomes like one of "those myths . . . of amazing strangers, who arrive at an island, gods or demons, bringing good or evil to the innocence of the inhabitants" (p. 228); and the novel is released from all superficial claims of realism.

Implicit in the character of Mr. Jones, however, is a further allegorical element. If Mr. Jones is "used-up, weary," "feminine," and, as it were, "attenuated" (p. 117), then, seen from Conrad's vigorously masculine point of view, he is the devil himself: pure anticreativity and antienergy. Jones's Satanism is confessed in his own characteristic idiom, but the novel's other characters perceive it too, each in his own way. The maliciously aware Ricardo speaks of Jones not as an "upright" gentleman, but as a "downright" one (p. 126); and the unaware Schomberg inadvertently recognizes the same thing: " 'I've been already living in hell for weeks, so you don't make much difference' " (p. 115). By the novel's end, Heyst is prepared to formulate this aspect, too, of Mr. Jones: " 'Having been ejected, he said, from his proper social sphere because he had refused to conform to certain usual conventions, he was a rebel now, and was coming and going up and down the earth. . . . I told him that I had heard that sort of story about somebody else before' " (pp. 317–318). Mr. Jones assumes finally the burden of the total existential situation: " 'I am he who is' " (p. 317); " 'I am the world itself, come to pay you a visit' " (p. 379); and Lena recognizes finally that Ricardo is "an unavoidable presence, which had attended all her life . . . the embodied evil of the world" (p. 298).[5]

Some readers have found this particular symbolic dimension of *Victory* a little tedious, particularly the proliferating cat-imagery used of Ricardo. Yet, as will be suggested, the gradual intensification of Ricardo's character does conform to the general structural principle of the book as the reader moves closer and closer to the moral inwardness of Heyst's situation: beginning with a reasonably realistic presentation of the externals of Heyst's life, the novel gradually becomes an allegory as it moves toward Samburan and the final conflict with Mr. Jones. Moreover, the ultimate development of this allegory, and its final

[5] Seymour L. Gross, "The Devil in Samburan: Jones and Richardo in *Victory*," *Nineteenth-Century Fiction*, XVI (June 1961), 81–85, is excellent on details of this Satanism in *Victory*, though it probably offers too Manichean a reading of the novel, based on this single focus.

resolution, are presented partly in sexual terms, so that the gradual growth of Ricardo's voluptuousness—a feline association confirmed by a wide range of folklore and archetypal symbolism —assumes crucial importance. As the narrative progresses, Ricardo leers more, undulates more, purrs and rubs himself more, and finally springs at Lena in a direct sexual attack. Simultaneously, Ricardo's "peculiar idiom" (p. 277), which consists of a heavy use of zoological metaphor, becomes more pronounced, including, among other creatures, moles, wasps, dogs, apes, and salamanders; and even Heyst is finally drawn into this metaphorical system: "a prancing beast" (p. 277).

Lena, too, of course—the descendant of a whole line of cosmic seductresses in Conrad's fiction—gradually becomes agent of a broader force: "She was not automatically obeying a momentary suggestion; she was under influences more deliberate, more vague, and of greater potency. She had been prompted, not by her will, but by a force that was outside of her and more worthy"; and her purpose becomes no less than that of "capturing death—savage, sudden, irresponsible death" (p. 394). When Lena first appears, she is under persecution and necessarily passive (" 'You do something!' " she tells Heyst) and has reached a state of desperation sufficiently intense to make her threaten suicide (pp. 78, 80). But even here she has begun to assume metaphysical dimensions (Heyst finds something "indefinably audacious and infinitely miserable" in her face, and hears "a voice fit to utter the most exquisite things"—p. 74). As many readers have observed, Lena's name (like Heyst's own "Axel") is allegorically significant: she is called both Alma (soul) and Magdalen. Lena's whorish side—certainly not much developed in the novel—is suggested by her reiterated confession that " 'I am not what they call a good girl' " (p. 198) and by the vulgarity of her speech in the opening scene with Heyst; and is confirmed in Ricardo's recognition of her as a sexual object. It is to be Heyst's unconscious privilege to give Lena's energies a spiritual direction, so that she may evade the mere whoredom offered by

Ricardo. Jones and company break in on this dream at a promis-
ingly creative moment, in the midst of Lena's "sudden and close
embrace" with Heyst (p. 223); and from this moment forward
she is on the passionate defensive; but by this time her symbolic
functions have become clear.

There is also, however, much of Jones's infernal character in
Heyst. Like Heyst, Jones is a "gentleman at large" (p. 100); and
both have drifted and survived in "unexplored countries, in the
wilds" (p. 211). Both laugh at the "ridiculous position" in which
their final conflict places them (p. 339). Finally Jones charges
Heyst with the identity: " 'We pursue the same ends . . . only
perhaps I pursue them with more openness than you—with
more simplicity' " (p. 320). All this is merely a special case of
something that is generally true of *Victory*'s symbolic method:
that Heyst is identified somehow with all the other characters,
because they are all symbolic vectors in a crucial moral case of
which he is protagonist (there is a close analogue here to the
early Marlow's symbolic relationship to his narrative scene).
Everything that happens on Samburan happens under the
brooding mentality of Heyst, just as everything that happens in
the parlor of his house happens under the stern eye of his
father's portrait. But it is important to see that the identity
between Heyst and Jones is not exact; rather, they are inverted
images of one another. Heyst reflects, Jones merely broods;
Heyst is drawn into action through loneliness or sympathy, Jones
merely through fits of boredom; Heyst feels a kind of abstracted
love for Lena, but Jones feels only a pathological revulsion
toward all women; Jones is physically effete but morally resolute
(in his own inverted terms), while Heyst is physically strong
and resolute, but morally effete. Jones is, in fact, the anticreative
second term of Heyst's ambivalence toward Lena, and the narrator explicitly accounts for Jones's misogyny in these terms:
"There is no strong sentiment without some terror, as there is no
real religion without a little fetishism" (p. 161). Jones's homosexuality is a way of symbolizing the inwardness and potentially

involuted direction of Heyst's creative energies, and Heyst's dilemma at the end of the novel is presented finally in terms of
competing sexual solicitations: peering in at what seems to be
Lena's seduction of Ricardo, and feeling a deep jealousy and
disillusion, he becomes aware of Jones's gentle blandishments—a
hand laid on his arm, an elbow touching his, and a "thin, bony
grasp"; and feels a "hot breath" in his ear proclaiming its disgust
at the heterosexual "spectacle" (pp. 390–393). It is to Heyst's
credit (in this symbolic universe) that he fends off the advance:
" 'Ouch!' " cries Jones unexpectedly in the midst of his seductive
monologue (p. 391). Lena, meanwhile, is intent on capturing
Ricardo's phallic knife: at his first allusion to it, she stoops
toward Ricardo "eagerly" and remains "expectant, the lips girl-
ishly parted, red in the pale face, and quivering in the quickened
drawing of her breath" (p. 398); and ultimately she takes the
knife unto herself: "She let it slip into the fold of her dress, and
laid her forearms with clasped fingers over her knees, which she
pressed desperately together. The dreaded thing was out of sight
at last. She felt a dampness break out all over her" (p. 400).
Supplementing this symbolic self-sacrifice is the bullet from Mr.
Jones's revolver, which is, like the knife, a "sting of death" (p.
405)—one of the many "wasp" images associating Jones with
Ricardo's dagger, just as Ricardo's excitement at the prospect of
using his knife on other men is a more aggressive equivalent of
Jones's weary homosexuality, and helps to suggest the essential
identity among the triumvirate of evil.

As the last few paragraphs suggest, any effort to discuss the
more obvious symbolic aspects of Conrad's characters leads very
quickly to other symbolic overtones and conceptual relationships.
Quite aside from the larger question whether allegory is even a
feasible option for the modern fictionist, this raises a second,
more technical question which has been at the center of some of
the disagreement over *Victory*—namely, to what extent allegorical characters need to be "human" or "real." Some writers, notably achievement-and-decline critics, have taken it as a conclusive

criticism of *Victory* that its characters are psychologically uncon-
vincing; others have seen that "Conrad is not interested, or not
only interested, in creating a humanly realistic love-drama; he is
concerned to create a drama of conflicting ideologies or value-sys-
tems," and that "the characters must therefore be 'larger than
life,' free to adopt postures that would be extravagantly histrionic
within the conventions of naturalistic prose fiction"; [6] that they
are, in brief, "generalized into a connection with prototypes." [7]
Still others, while willing to admit the validity of allegory when
the characters are also psychologically convincing, deny that this
is the case with *Victory*.

A few points about the art of fiction needed to be explored, I
think, if we are to arrive at any coherent resolution of these
differences. To begin with, the very play of image and symbol, if
it is complex enough, is itself a literary pleasure; so far as narrative approaches the delicacy and compression of a lyric, it need
not invite the commonsense assent of realistic fiction: the pleasures are different, but equally legitimate. Moreover, the successful allegorical symbol itself invites a kind of assent based on
previous learning and experience, in the manner of successful
abstraction in expository writing. But the issue is confused, in
Victory, by Conrad's unusual structural methods. At the beginning of the novel, the reader is confronted by what looks like
conventional realistic narrative—experience seen from the nor-
mative public point of view. But gradually the symbolic overtones accumulate, as the book moves toward its inner core of
allegory; and the reader must shift his stance, undergoing a
progress from one kind of pleasure at the beginning to another
kind at the end—a gradual penetration through externals to the
essential truths of Heyst's metaphysico-moral situation, much on

[6] Lodge, "Conrad's *Victory* and *The Tempest*," 199.
[7] Donald A. Dike, "The Tempest of Axel Heyst," *Nineteenth-Century
Fiction*, XVII (September 1962), 107. As this article demonstrates, there
is in any case considerable psychological and moral complexity of a
"realistic" kind in the relations among the characters of *Victory*.

the order of Marlow's meditative journeys. As the allegory becomes firmer, the need of fictional realism lessens; and Conrad has the additional advantage of having begun in a reasonably straightforward way, so that the reader carries his assent with him into the heightened experience of Samburan. Not surprisingly, it is the characters who belong chiefly to the allegory, like Jones and company, who have suffered the most abuse from unsympathetic critics, and have proved most difficult for the naturalistic drama of modern stage and cinema: Conrad's collaborator in the first dramatization of *Victory* was simply bewildered as to Jones's motivation; and Conrad himself, in desperation, proposed a "florid final scene, ending with Jones, alone on the island, setting fire to the bungalow, and presumably about to perish in it, screaming 'I am a force!' over and over." [8] To be really successful, a dramatization of *Victory* would have to begin looking something like Maugham's *Rain* and end looking like *The Tempest*; and so far, no playwright of sufficient agility has undertaken that task.

Judgment of this aspect of *Victory* has been further confounded, it seems to me, by a more sophisticated form of the realist's claim: the theory that "every great work of art operates on multiple levels of meaning and suasion," [9] and that these multiple levels make separate and simultaneous demands. If this theory is correct, *Victory* is defective insofar as it fails to meet the credibility tests of a popular romance, since that is after all its first and most obvious "level." But the whole question of levels of meaning needs further study, bearing as it does not only on Conrad, but on any complex novelist or playwright. As a rhetorical convenience, the idea is undeniably attractive; it limits the area of immediate discussion to this or that aspect of a work, and so serves as a principle of organization in controlling the varied

[8] Robert S. Ryf, "Conrad's Stage *Victory*," *Modern Drama*, VII (September 1964), 158.

[9] *'Heart of Darkness' and 'The Secret Sharer,'* with Introduction by Albert J. Guerard (New York: New American Library, 1950), p. 9.

responses a sensitive reader has to any piece of literature. Yet these "levels" cannot finally be judged separately, since it is the relationships between them which create much of the meaning in successful works. The critic's obligation is not (to borrow a figure from another discussion of this subject) to take his mental elevator to whatever level he wishes, but rather to get off on all levels at once; and the arduous critical efforts to specify the artistic center of such eclectic works as *Moby-Dick* show this assumption of esthetic unity in action. The use of an expression like "levels of meaning" is made more plausible by the fact that the "levels" are usually given different degrees of abstractness: this is true, for example, of the list Guerard gives for *The Nigger of the 'Narcissus'* (see Chapter 2). Thus on the surface, the various levels cannot stand in contradiction to one another; and taken together, they seem to suggest an admirable fullness of content in the work, and a commendable breadth of interpretation in the critic. But in considering the work's unity and coherence, the critic may discover that some of these levels interfere with one another: it would be impossible, for example, to carry the "travelogue" level of "Heart of Darkness" very far up the river without interfering with the chaos imagery that is such an essential part of Marlow's experience. Similarly, *Victory* cannot sustain its opening level of psychological realism without interfering seriously with the development of its symbolic motifs. Whichever level of a work dominates and limits the others may properly be called its thematic level; and in *Victory*, this is the allegorical level which culminates in Samburan.

Clarifying the structural relationship between "levels" in *Victory* can also help obviate a familiar criticism: that Davidson's final visit to Samburan, and his subsequent interview with "the Excellency," is a lapse of integrity, making possible a final summary and stage-cleaning without any solid narrative justification. Some critics have objected to Davidson's presence in *Victory* at all. But the book's structural principles amply justify both his appearance at the beginning and his reappearance at the end.

Davidson returns to Samburan not as a *deus ex machina* (after all, he does nothing that the external narrator might not have done), but to restore the level of normality and realism with which the novel had begun, by reversing the gradual process of allegorization that had drawn the reader toward Samburan. Once again, for example, Davidson returns to the notion that Heyst's father " 'seems to have been a crank, and to have upset his head when he was young' "; and he restores the public level of mild irony and mere empirical understanding: " 'Yes, Excellency,' said Davidson in his placid voice; 'there are more dead in this affair—more white people, I mean—than have been killed in many of the battles of the last Achin war' " (pp. 408–409). To move from a more-or-less normal point of view and setting into a more remote and mysterious one, and then back to the starting point, is a structural principle perfectly familiar in Conrad—in "Heart of Darkness," *Lord Jim,* and *Chance,* just to name a varied sampling—and it should be no more objectionable in *Victory* than elsewhere. Moreover, the particular form which that structural principle takes in *Victory* permits Conrad to do away with the meditative narrator, who runs the risk of speeding ahead of the narrative movement and establishing tones and attitudes before they are justified by the story itself, as in *Chance.* And to shift the point of view from a meditative protagonist, like Marlow, to a more active and involved one, like Heyst, provides some assurance that the narrator will not be tempted to excuse himself from the human condition, and like Hardy's gods, indulge in a "most improper fit of laughter" at pathetic or tragic moments: Heyst's detachment, in fact, is a product of his awareness that he, perhaps more than lesser figures, is subject to that condition. On the whole, it is probable that both the structure and point of view of *Victory,* Davidson included, are the best that Conrad might have devised for his special artistic purposes.

The remote island, the symbolic villains, and other features of *Victory* naturally suggest *The Tempest.* Donald Dike and others have discussed this aspect of the novel in detail: the scholar's dream of radical innocence and escape from experience that Heyst must finally abandon, his private universe of Calibans and Ariels, and the like; and of course the essential difference: Prospero's real victory of social commitment and forgiveness, as against Heyst's tragicomic confrontation of the absurd.[10] Like Prospero's island, Samburan is the stage of a masque or myth with profound implications. Heyst looms up "largely" before Jones and Ricardo, "fascinating and defenceless in the middle of the sea, filling the whole field of their vision" (p. 269). "'This is like no other job we ever turned our minds to,'" Ricardo warns; and Jones agrees: "'It's a different thing. It's a sort of test'" (p. 335). At the final moment of crisis, it is "as if the heart of hearts had ceased to beat and the end of all things had come" (p. 373). Here, then, is the final extreme of Conrad's device of geographic distancing for the purpose of symbolic exaggeration. And it is important to see that in his techniques for establishing this symbolic exaggeration in *Victory,* Conrad recapitulates much of his own intellectual and artistic history. There are first of all the usual techniques of description and characterization to set Heyst and Lena apart from the rest of the world—passages implying qualities of delicacy, humanity, sensitivity, intelligence, and so forth, which underscore their moral stature from the beginning. There is a certain stature implied in Heyst's very taste for solitude, in his attracting such diction to himself as "Enchanted," "pilgrimage," "hermit," and the like; and Lena is clearly a special case among the orchestra girls, as suggested both by her living accommodations and by the special treatment accorded her by Mrs. Zangiacomo. Lena seems to Heyst to be stranded "in a moral desert as arid as the sands of Sahara" (p. 80); and in the opening stages of their love, especially, they are surrounded with Edenic associations and with images of deluge, cataclysm, and

---

[10] Dike, "The Tempest of Axel Heyst," is the best treatment of the subject; Karl and Baines had earlier suggested some parallels; and Lodge, "Conrad's *Victory* and *The Tempest*," adds some useful observations of detail.

metaphysical loneliness. But what is more interesting is that Heyst has arrived at his moral hermitage through a process of social and economic disillusionment much like that implied by the irony of the political novels; his final disenchantment, after all, is with the failure of the Tropical Belt Coal Company, in which he had placed an optimistic faith reminiscent of Charles Gould. (Even *Chance*, as will appear, suggests the same movement on the part of the meditative protagonist Marlow, as he works through the economic follies of de Barral and the inadequacies of the public and bourgeois minds, toward the deeper moral perplexities of Flora and Anthony.) The "decaying bones of that once sanguine enterprise" are made to reflect the houses of London: "tombs of an unvisited, unhonoured cemetery of hopes" (pp. 173–174), phrases which project the reader once again into the malignant urban setting of *The Secret Agent*. But to this clear foundation of social disillusionment now is superadded the epistemological complexity of *Chance*: Heyst is "done" with the observation of "facts" which had enchanted him for so long, just as Marlow is impatient with the mere observation of sensory surfaces. The novel's opening pages play disrespectfully with the scientific metaphors of chemistry and economics; and even the good Davidson, like Powell, is gently chided for his lack of intuitive or analytic penetration: he is likely to discover "the fact without discovering the reason" (p. 177). Finally, Heyst, in the presence of Morrison's simple faith in providence, can only incline his head "as from respect for a conviction he could not share" (p. 17), a favorite posture of the later Marlow.

This epistemological point merges with the general point that has already been made about the novel's structure: that *Victory* progresses away from the outer facts of Heyst's situation toward its moral core, away from mere realism toward the symbolic projection of more general truths. At the beginning of the novel, the reader is momentarily shown Heyst smoking meditatively on his island, for the purpose of identifying immediately the locus of the book's final interest. But then the narrator drops back to the periphery of Heyst's social history, as viewed first by the eye of public opinion and then by the somewhat more humane and tolerant Davidson. The first chapters of each of the novel's first three parts are parallel in their content and purpose—in each case, an examination of Heyst's character and motives; but in each case, on a deeper psychological and intellectual level. And each part concludes with a chapter which pulls the previous psycho-moral threads together. This process of gradual penetration is something like Marlow's meditative movement toward the heart of the Congo; but its organized and symmetrical character helps to establish an allegorical firmness missing in the earlier work, and to create some of the circular structures noted long ago by R. W. Stallman.[11] The terms used in describing Davidson— "a good, simple fellow" (p. 29), "delicate, humane and regular" (p. 52), "prudent" (p. 35), "shrewd" (p. 38), "sensitive" (p. 42), and the like—all tend to give him a limited choral status. Like Captain MacWhirr, Davidson is one step better than most people; and his refusal to condemn Heyst, along with his clear and commonsense premonition of disaster ("You don't take a woman into a desert jungle without being made sorry for it sooner or later"—p. 51), establish a kind of moral norm for those who lack the spiritually heroic complexity of a Heyst. In the chapters dominated by Davidson and the outside narrator of the story, the reader gains his first insights, if superficial ones, into Heyst's moral defects and the difficulties to come in the wake of his flight with Lena. There is, for example, the telling distinction between mere "politeness" and genuine "cordiality" in Heyst's dealings with Morrison—a distinction prefiguring the later and more important distinction between the sympathy which Heyst can feel for Lena and the love he cannot feel: his excessive courtesy and humanity are in themselves, paradoxically, a kind

[11] Robert W. Stallman, "The Structure and Symbolism of Conrad's *Victory,*" *Western Review,* XIII (Spring 1949), 146–157; reprinted in Ray B. West, Jr., and Stallman, eds., *The Art of Modern Fiction* (New York: Rinehart, 1949), pp. 607–620.

of destructive detachment from the world. Then Heyst is introduced to the reader in his hermitage on Samburan (significantly, through a dialogue with Davidson), and the novel's point of view shifts toward Heyst himself; at first in Schomberg's hotel, in the social relations which Heyst finds so superficial, and then finally back on Samburan, with Lena. And as this movement progresses, all the motives and symbolic motifs of the novel expand and deepen.

One may illustrate this point briefly by examining the gradual revelation of Heyst's skepticism, and at the same time, the expansion of the father-and-son motif that attends this development. At the opening of the novel, Heyst's character is revealed chiefly through gross public labels like "Enchanted Heyst" (p. 7) and "Hard Facts" Heyst (p. 8); or in the ironic descriptions of him as an "inert body" (p. 3) and a "queer chap" (p. 4). But gradually a clearer formulation of his motives begins to emerge. There is first of all the simple statement Heyst regards as fit for Davidson's ears: " 'All action is bound to be harmful. It is devilish. That is why this world is evil upon the whole. But I have done with it! I shall never lift a finger again. At one time I thought that intelligent observation of facts was the best way of cheating the time which is allotted to us whether we want it or not; but now I have done with observation, too' " (p. 54). Then follows —symmetrically enough, in the first chapter of Part II—a more complex and more exact formulation: "His scornful temperament, beguiled into action, suffered from failure in a subtle way unknown to men accustomed to grapple with the realities of common human enterprise. It was like the gnawing pain of useless apostasy, a sort of shame before his own betrayed nature" (p. 65). Finally there are the deeper psychological and intellectual causes suggested by the word "apostasy": the "pitiless cold blasts of the father's analysis" which had blown away Heyst's "blessed, warm mental fog" (p. 92); and (symmetrically again) the philosophic dialogue at the beginning of Part III during which Heyst's father advises him on rational grounds to

" 'cultivate that form of contempt which is called pity' " and to
" 'look on—make no sound' " (pp. 174–175). Accompanying
this development is a set of filial metaphors which gradually take
on Adamic overtones, in ironic opposition to the teachings of the
father. The first term in this series is Davidson's commonsense
formula: " 'He told me that directly his father died he lit out into
the wide world on his own, and had been on the move until he
fetched up against this famous coal business. Fits the son of his
father somehow, don't you think?' " (p. 33). Then Heyst himself adds a little to the metaphor: "He meant to drift altogether
and literally, body and soul, like a detached leaf. . . . 'This shall
be my defence against life,' he had said to himself with a sort of
inward consciousness that for the son of his father there was no
other worthy alternative" (p. 92). And finally, Heyst's patri-
mony of guilt and responsibility begins to interfere with his
inheritance of skeptical detachment: "There was in the son a lot
of that first ancestor who, as soon as he could uplift his muddy
frame from the celestial mould, started inspecting and naming
the animals of that paradise which he was soon to lose. . . .
'And I, the son of my father, have been caught too, like the
silliest fish of them all,' Heyst said to himself" (pp. 173–174).
This irony persists through the rest of the novel, and coalesces
with the Edenic and Satanic imagery to create a consistent
overtone of Christian allegory.

Perhaps the most important substructure of *Victory*, however,
is the gradual deepening of the concept of "love," which finally
occupies such a high place in the novel's dramatic conclusion.
Here again, the reader proceeds from an outward and somewhat
conventional view to a metaphysical complexity in which Lena
represents a creative force and Heyst, until too late, the uncom-
mitted and only potentially creative moral agent. This motif
begins with the initial loneliness and awakened sexual interest of
Heyst in Schomberg's hotel: his awareness of Lena's "well-
formed arms," "thick brown tresses," "slender white bust," and
the like (p. 70); and proceeds through his admiration of Lena's

smile and voice (features gradually to assume a metaphysical depth); to the intimacy of a kiss in Schomberg's garden (recalling *Chance*'s Anthony and Flora); and finally to the more complex courting behavior and sexual play on Samburan, before the arrival of Jones and company—once again, a progress from the physical to the symbolic. But even at this point Lena is aware that Heyst's feeling for her is something short of "love": " 'You should try to love me!' . . . 'Sometimes it seems to me that you can never love me for myself, only for myself. . . . Do try!' " (p. 221). Here the feelings and awareness of Heyst and Lena begin to diverge even more sharply than before. In Lena's mind, "love" acquires a connotation of self-sacrifice, an "inconceivable intensity of existence" (p. 364), and a "blinding, hot glow of passionate purpose" (p. 367) in which she determines to serve the principle of life by disarming the death that threatens Heyst. Simultaneously, Heyst undergoes an expansion of self-awareness, stimulated by Lena and ultimately directed toward the creative possibility she represents—a process which goes through too many stages to illustrate adequately, but terminates finally in Heyst's famous final outcry to Davidson: " 'Ah, Davidson, woe to the man whose heart has not learned while young to hope, to love—and to put its trust in life!' " (p. 410). Heyst discovers gradually that Lena gives him "a greater sense of his own reality than he had ever known in all his life" (p. 200); his "cherished negations" (p. 222) fall away one by one; he feels a vague sense of "obligation" (but "no line of action"—p. 258); and in his sharp description of Jones, Ricardo, and Pedro in terms of the animal metaphors previously developed in the novel, he exhibits the gradual convergence of his own point of view with Lena's and with the reader's. But at the same time, he also recognizes his own final powerlessness: " 'There is a strain in me which lays me under an insensate obligation to avoid even the appearance of murder' " (p. 329); and thus the moral forces are poised for the novel's final events. Ultimately, Heyst's inbred reserve forces a suicidal expression of pure life on Lena's part to resist the destructiveness represented by Ricardo; and as a final crushing melodramatic irony, Heyst finds it impossible to utter a word of love even in the moment of Lena's death: "Heyst bent low over her, cursing his fastidious soul, which even at that moment kept the true cry of love from his lips in its infernal mistrust of all life" (p. 406). Lena dies in illusory triumph: "He was ready to lift her up in his firm arms and take her into the sanctuary of his innermost heart—for ever! The flush of rapture flooding her whole being broke out in a smile of innocent, girlish happiness; and with that divine radiance on her lips she breathed her last, triumphant, seeking for his glance in the shades of death" (p. 407). Just as in *Chance,* love and death are here conjoined in a final catharsis. And the novel's villains, defeated on some high metaphysical level, suffer their own appropriate ends: Wang emerges to destroy the bestial Pedro; and Jones, in a final involuted and decadent denial of life, commits suicide (p. 411). In this dramatic resolution, in Lena's persistent illusion and Heyst's despairing acknowledgement of it, *Victory* ends on a note of affirmation; but it is an existentially aware affirmation, projected against the backdrop of Davidson's final emphatic "Nothing!" (p. 412).

Attention to these major symbolic motifs can help explain details which otherwise may seem forced and awkward—Heyst's strange scheme of signaling the hidden Lena by a complicated system of lighting and extinguishing candles, for example; or the statuary imagery used of Lena in her death scene; both of which have been questioned by skeptical critics. Conrad's statuary imagery helps both to confirm Lena's status as a "love goddess" and to establish the irony of Heyst's final impotence. And Heyst's candle system may be read in terms of a symbolic language already established in the book, with each candle representing a life: if Lena sees three candles blown out and one relighted, that is Heyst's signal that he has destroyed the three villains and that Lena is to re-emerge from the darkness to join him (p. 372). Lights and candles have previously been associated with "life" in the novel: the meditative and potentially explosive volcano; Heyst's lamp, lit uncertainly in defiance of the villains; Heyst's cigar-tip glowing on the verandah; the suddenly flickering gleams of anger in Jones's eyes and of lust in Ricardo's; and so on. And Heyst's calculated mathematical affirmation of the possibilities of continuing life, in his system of candle-counting, are to be contrasted with the "intolerable brilliance" of the "eight candle-flames" (p. 392) Lena lights for her reception of Ricardo. *Victory* has its defects, but the novel's symbolic play is still too little analyzed to permit easy judgment.

The preceding remarks have identified, I think, the chief symbolic structures of *Victory,* but they have by no means exhausted its subtleties. There is, for example, Wang, the fathomless coolie, whose instinct for survival and deeply inbred Oriental negation stand in ironic counterpoint to Heyst's suicidal and artificial detachment. Like Heyst, Wang prefers Samburan to the outer world; and like Heyst, he is an orphan and a "restless vagabond" (p. 307) whose only tie is to a recently acquired woman. But unlike Heyst, Wang instinctively recognizes certain necessities of preservation against the destructive element, building a fence around his garden and ultimately, in effect, around his end of the island, by blocking the path to it with a wall of spears.[12] There is also Conrad's curiously powerful extension of

[12] The importance of Wang's being Chinese can hardly be overestimated, in view of the social position of Chinese in the rest of Conrad's fiction. Occasionally one finds a "high" Chinese, like Davidson's employer. But on the whole Conrad's Orientals are as low on the scale of civilization as possible. In *Almayer's Folly,* it is Jim-Eng the opium-smoker who is the lowest figure on the human scale, and introduces Almayer to his final degradation, in which he symbolically becomes a Chinese himself (p. 205). In *An Outcast of the Islands,* coolies are represented as the most primitive form of humanity (e.g., on p. 364), or likened to ferocious animals (pp. 161–162). It is a group of coolies who riot subrationally in Captain MacWhirr's hold in "Typhoon." And in "A Smile of Fortune," coolies are placed on a level with Negroes (p. 61)—an equation which sends them far back on the evolutionary and moral scales, in Conrad's symbolic universe. There are other examples.

his own allegory into Christian terms of punishment, redemption, mercy, and hope—a development which begins all the way back with Morrison's naïve faith in Providence and gains ironic headway through the Adamic and Edenic associations connected with Heyst and Lena. Heyst's superior skepticism (" 'Ah, you remember what you have been told—as a child—on Sundays' " —p. 359), is met by Lena with a perfectly innocent nostalgia for her Christian friends; and Ricardo is daunted later by the silent prayerful movement of Lena's lips. In an extraordinary fusion of this allegorical strain with the extensive animal-imagery (this is the kind of ingenious stroke that yields a constant delight for the attentive reader of *Victory*), Conrad suddenly shifts Ricardo's personal idiom, retaining its characteristic syntax, but replacing the final term, which would ordinarily be the name of some animal, with the appropriate Biblical expression: " 'What does he think a fellow is—a graven image?' " (p. 370).

There are two further aspects of Conrad's symbolism, however, which deserve special attention, since they help to demonstrate the many senses in which *Victory* is the culmination of Conrad's creative growth. The first of these is the notion of an evolutionary continuum among the three villains of the novel— Pedro, with his primeval anthropological associations; Jones, at the other end, with his superrefined decadence; and Ricardo in between, retaining his jungle associations in his resemblance to a jaguar, yet inspired to emulate his "governor," and mediating neatly between Pedro and Jones: clubbing and choking the one, and serving the other with a treacherous cat's-loyalty. This notion of an evolutionary continuum appears repeatedly in the dialogue—for example, in Ricardo's observation that Jones " 'wasn't so young as he looked—not by a long chalk' " (p. 128), or his order to Pedro to " 'keep back where you belong, you murdering brute, you slaughtering savage, you!' " (p. 231), and is confirmed in the villains' behavior. But it also leads to some subtler effects. On their own evolutionary scale, Jones and company strive toward a formal perfection just as Conrad's early primitives had done (" 'Ferocity ain't good form,' " Ricardo tells Schomberg—p. 136) and in a sharply significant phrase, Pedro is identified with Kurtz in the last depths of his degradation: " 'He has no restraint, no restraint at all' " (p. 233). The three villains recognize a social and temporal hierarchy of weapons: Mr. Jones, the most progressive of the lot, employs the delicate revolver; Ricardo uses " 'shooting irons' " or "the still less aristocratic knife" (p. 239); and Pedro clutches a stone-age blade. Heyst at one point perceives the immense ironic regression that has come to Samburan: " 'A creature with an antediluvian lower jaw, hairy like a mastodon, and formed like a prehistoric ape, has laid this table' " (p. 358). And Ricardo's animal-idiom, which begins harmlessly enough with dogs and cats and bears and apes, gradually regresses also, as the book proceeds, toward earlier evolutionary forms, terminating finally in salamanders and vipers, imagery which not only underscores Ricardo's essential continuity with Pedro, but also reaffirms some of the Christian elements of the allegory. Even more interesting is the ease with which the villains—especially Ricardo, who stands in the middle —can move back and forth, progressing or regressing along their own evolutionary axis. Ricardo's expressions of lust, for example, are at one moment "obscene" and at the next moment "tender" as he wavers between the sheer savagery of Pedro and the femininity of Mr. Jones (p. 396). In his moments of keenest ferocity, he is likely to slip back a little toward Pedro: threatening Schomberg, he shows him the knife "strapped to a very hairy limb" (p. 136); but under the stimulation of Lena and the educational advantages provided by Mr. Jones, he gradually begins to encroach on his leader's authority: by becoming theoretical and "warmly argumentative" (p. 263), by dissimulating to Jones about the presence of Lena, by "moralising" (p. 268), and even by usurping Mr. Jones's hairlessness (" 'And he shaved —shaved under my very nose,' " says Jones furiously—p. 387).

Conversely, under the stress of his violent anger, Mr. Jones adopts Ricardo's feline idiom: " 'I might have smelt a rat!' " (p. 389). Conrad's villains in *Victory* are more complex than they have been made out to be, and the reader is likely to be surprised at any moment by some device of this kind. Simultaneously, there is a civilized human continuum mirroring that of the villains. Heyst himself is the most advanced evolutionary product: " 'You,' " he tells Lena, may " 'represent something as old as the world,' " but " 'I date later—much later. I can't call myself a child, but I am so recent that I may call myself a man of the last hour—or is it the hour before last?' " (p. 359). Heyst's hair is elegantly diminished; his head is "largely bald," but he has "long, horizontal moustaches of crinkly bronze hair," an inverted image of Ricardo's cat-whiskers (p. 73). On the lower end of the scale are the chestnut-bearded Schomberg and the purple-bearded Zangiacomo. Schomberg is the mirror equivalent of Pedro, a "lazy beast" (p. 59), who prowls around Lena "mute, hungry" (p. 79), and is repeatedly called an "ass," an animal bearing roughly the same status in domestic life that Pedro bears in his jungle society. Schomberg is not quite inarticulate, like Pedro; but his gossip is the lowest form of human speech. His taste for Zangiacomo's music is contrasted with Heyst's taste for "the music of the spheres" (p. 66). And in his choking, rolling battle with Zangiacomo (" 'Chinamen up the trees' "—p. 48), Schomberg grotesquely mirrors the jungle battle of Pedro and Ricardo. Schomberg is then, naturally enough, the point of civilized contact for the evil triumvirate; given purchase on the human scene by Schomberg's fear, the villains rise by a kind of Satanic reflex to attack the highest human form in Heyst.

There is thus a pervasive doubling effect in *Victory*, not only in the relation between Heyst and Jones, but between the entire civilized continuum of humanity and the dark, regressive spectrum of figures which is the underside of the same humanity. Critics have recently pointed out a variety of other suggestions of doubling and mirroring—the ironic parallels between the book's four "rescue" scenes, the affinities between Jones and the elder Heyst, and so on.[13] And the most pronounced moral effect of this mirroring (an effect which is also grotesquely comic) is to produce some of the full inversions of value which Conrad had earlier satirized in other contexts. Some of them cluster about the notion of Jones's evolutionary and social superiority: " 'I am an Englishman,' " Ricardo tells Schomberg, " 'and I know a gentleman at sight. I should know one drunk, in the gutter, in jail, under the gallows' " (p. 125). Ricardo assures Jones that " 'with your looks, sir, it will be easy enough' " to appear ill—"a naïve tribute to the aspect of his physique" which Mr. Jones appreciates with "a silent smile" (pp. 272–273). When Mr. Jones suggests jocularly that Heyst's restiveness may proceed from a " 'bad conscience,' " the distracted Ricardo fails to "see the joke" (p. 264). And so on, inversion following inversion. The entire jungle scene, in which Jones and Ricardo acquire their faithful servant Pedro by the expedient of killing his brother, is an extended demonstration of upside-down ethics—a comic masterpiece in which diction, syntax, and dialogue all serve Conrad's purposes. But perhaps the most curious twist of all, in this specially conceived universe, is Mr. Jones's inversion of Conrad's principle of "chance" into a means of aggression and survival, making him a metaphysical as well as a sexual invert: " 'Gamble? That's nature. What's life itself? You never know what may turn up. The worst of it is that you never can tell exactly what sort of cards you are holding yourself. What's trumps—that is the question. See?' " (pp. 146–147). Heyst toys with the counters of a skeptical philosophy which recognizes "chance" as a cosmic determinant and therefore a reason for inaction: Jones, on the other side of the mirror, satanically takes "fortune by the scruff of the neck" (p. 149). The phrasing of

[13] See, e.g., Sharon Kaehele and Howard German, "Conrad's *Victory*: A Reassessment," *Modern Fiction Studies,* X (Spring 1964), 55–72; Gerard A. Pilecke, "Conrad's *Victory,*" *Explicator,* XXIII (January 1965), Item 36.

Jones's question gives some credence to the notion that Conrad was thinking a little of Hamlet when he created Heyst. And there are other characteristic philosophic concepts of Conrad which are projected into the allegory of Victory: Chance's pervasive distinction between appearance and reality, for example, which is implicit not only in the structure of Victory, as it progresses from illusory externals toward a core of truth, but also in the experience of all the major characters.

This clarifying of philosophical motifs is perhaps the most important observation that might be made about Victory. Donald Dike, who has probably written the best article on the novel, has pointed out that the partial and incomplete views of Heyst expressed by other characters, "however derelict their spokesmen . . . draw on philosophic ideas which are part of the history of the western mind"; [14] and these implicit frames of reference give Victory a greater allegorical density than is usually thought. But they also illustrate something that had been happening on a broader scale in all Conrad's fiction—namely, the shifting of his thematic interests away from the essentially inner psycho-moral perplexities of his early work toward the external conditions which define the status of the moral agent: toward metaphysico-moral perplexities, one might say. Very recently, critics have begun to comment on the affinities between Conrad and such writers as Sartre and Camus; [15] and despite some obvious differences, these comparisons are useful. Themes of isolation, alienation and guilt, a willed commitment to human solidarity in the face of a metaphysical void, and the like, exist in all these writers, in some broad form. But it is important to see that Conrad's affinities with existentialism developed only gradually.

[14] Dike, "The Tempest of Axel Heyst," 102.

[15] Two studies of special interest in this connection, especially as they take care to discriminate between Conrad and the existentialists on some important points, are Gillon, The Eternal Solitary, Ch. 7; and Watt, "Joseph Conrad: Alienation and Commitment." I have not seen Joan Parsons Wang's unpublished dissertation, "Joseph Conrad, Proto-Existentialist: A Comparative Study of Conrad, Camus and Sartre" (Indiana, 1965).

His earlier commitments had tended to invoke such terms as "dream" and "illusion" and paradoxically to commend both a romantic distortion of reality and a pragmatic coping with the "destructive element," so that the dream might be sustained. Some other order of commitment was implicit in Marlow's skeptical metaphysics; but it lay largely dormant, on the ideational level, until after the period of Conrad's political fiction. The isolated protagonist of Conrad's early fiction is likely to be alienated from human history, or the community at large, and to suffer more from his own inner darkness or self-aggrandizement than from any outer metaphysical condition. Conrad's ethical conservatism and mistrust of society, plus a skeptical naturalism, had yielded the paradoxical affirmations of *Lord Jim* as a kind of reflexive counterbalance. But as the intellectual presuppositions of his own commitments and beliefs became ever clearer to Conrad—a process visible in his letters and essays, as well as his fiction—the locus of his analytic and symbolic interests moved outward and broadened. Heyst is *dis*illusioned, yet finally affirms; M. George of *The Arrow of Gold* (that *bête noire* of recent Conrad studies) relinquishes romantic illusion for a maturer kind of affirmation; and so on. This general intellectual movement of Conrad's is visible even in his political fiction, to the extent that some few critics have tried to read the political novels in terms of the existential absurd [16]—a mistake, I think, since the absurdities in the existence of Conrad's political protagonists really have less metaphysical causes, but nonetheless a sensitive observation of intellectual undercurrents that were gathering strength in Conrad's fiction. And to turn back to the earlier works of Conrad's third period—among them the enigmatic *Chance*—will enable us to perceive not only the growth of these philosophic attitudes, but the growth also of the symbolic and rhetorical techniques Conrad needed to give them expression.

[10] See, e.g., Lois A. Michel, "The Absurd Predicament In Conrad's Political Novels," *College English*, XXIII (November 1961), 131–136; and Tony Tanner, "Nightmare and Complacency: Razumov and the Western Eye," *Critical Quarterly*, IV (Autumn 1962), 197–214.

6

Knights and Damsels—
The Growth of a Symbology

Marlow's omniscience . . . is a prolonged hovering flight of the
subjective over the outstretched ground of the case exposed. We
make out this ground but through the shadow cast by the flight. . . .
The dénouement gives us the system fighting in triumph, though
with its back desperately to the wall, and laying the powers piled up
at its feet.

—Henry James, on *Chance*

In tracing the origins of *Victory*, there is no better place to
begin than with *Chance*, its popular but puzzling precursor. Of
all Conrad's novels, *Chance* is most likely to give the modern
reader a severe shock when he first tries to read it, and to raise
questions whose answers will help illuminate Conrad's later
techniques. Despite its welcome commercial success, *Chance* is
finally an unpleasant and unsatisfactory novel. In trying to say
why this should be, the reader discovers that he is formulating
some of Conrad's basic artistic aims; and in light of these aims,
both *Chance* and the shorter fiction of Conrad's third period take
on new significance, as a series of preliminary essays toward the
existential clarity and allegorical firmness of *Victory*.

[198]

The most striking feature of *Chance* is the return of Marlow as narrator, and the most striking feature of this new Marlow is his self-conscious intellectualism. The reflective, self-qualifying moralist of *Lord Jim* has become a more dogmatic philosopher and a crueler ironist; and the reader who remembers the earlier Marlow is likely to feel that these changes are distinctly for the worse. *Chance*'s Marlow displays all the paraphernalia of the high intellectual: the classical allusion, the abstract logical terminology, the meticulous concern with exact shades of meaning, the elegant syntax, and the aggressive insistence on the universal relevance of his own reading and powers of inference. Marlow points to his own logical devices: of his country acquaintances' existence in town, for example, he knows "no more than may be inferred from analogy" (p. 41). He pauses to refine his own diction: "Her last sleep, I won't say of innocence—that word would not render my exact meaning, because it has a special meaning of its own—but I will say: of that ignorance, or better still, of that unconsciousness" (p. 99). He regards his own intellectual interests as obligatory upon everyone: "Don't you know that people laugh at absurdities that are very far from being comic? Didn't you read the latest books about laughter written by philosophers, psychologists?" (p. 283). He denies responsibility for the obscurities in his own narrative: "Dark and, so to speak, inscrutable spaces being met with in life, there must be such places in any statement dealing with life" (p. 101). And at one point (perhaps unconsciously), he even identifies himself with Socrates: " '. . . a true friend of youth. He lectured them in a peculiarly exasperating manner. It was a way he had' " (p. 13). *Chance* is itself an exasperating lecture for the reader whose metaphysics and morals are inadequately fused, and Marlow's aggressive intellectualism does nothing to ease the pain of being lectured.

Nor is Marlow's condescension confined to intellectual matters. He "gently" corrects his friend Powell's view of his own experiences (p. 23), and adopts a "conciliatory tone" when contradicting him in nautical matters (p. 35). His "retrospective smile" is "kind as though he bore no grudge against people he used to know" (p. 37). He is well aware of his "vindictiveness" (p. 151) and of the "chaffing" quality of his humor (p. 149), but makes no effort to leave off indulging them. He confesses that it is impossible for him to say anything stupid even if he tries (p. 147); and believes that he, unlike the heroine Flora de Barral, has the "power of evoking sympathy, that personal gift of direct appeal to the feelings" (p. 142). He contains a "drop of superior essence" (p. 146). And lest his auditor think that Marlow is pushing these claims too far, Marlow assures him that "this is not vanity; it is analysis" (p. 145). Marlow's condescension and contempt are at their fiercest in dealing with the Fynes, his country-holiday acquaintances and ultimately Flora's imperceptive in-laws. Fyne is "good little Fyne" (p. 90), "solemn little Fyne" (p. 41), "my simple Fyne" (p. 38), and the like. At one point Marlow is good enough to acknowledge the Fynes' "undeniable humanity" (p. 135), and on one occasion he even admits that Fyne "came very near showing something like insight" (p. 89). But on the whole he indulges in a gratuitous malice, and his case is not helped any by his own hypocrisy: he cultivates the Fynes in the country but avoids them in town (p. 41), praises Fyne's sagacity to his face but laughs at his stupidity behind his back (p. 135), and so on. Judging from external appearances, Marlow's integrity and tolerance seem to have deteriorated over the years since *Lord Jim*.

And the reader's confidence is undermined even more by Marlow's visible failures of insight and rhetoric. There are, to begin with, a number of propositions so obvious as to be unworthy of Marlow (e.g., "Nothing is more disturbing than the upsetting of a preconceived idea"—p. 289; "things are not always what they seem"—p. 201). There are some too naïvely simple analyses of public events and public institutions, such as his explanation of Flora's father's financial career: "He was a clerk in a bank, like thousands of others. . . . Then one day as though a supernatural voice had whispered into his ear or some invisible fly had stung him, he put on his hat, went out into the street and began advertising. That's absolutely all there was to it" (p. 78). There is a good deal of defective psychologizing (e.g., "You will tell me perhaps that children's impressions are not durable. That's true enough"—p. 138). And there is even some mere nonsense: "You know more women than I do. . . . Well, just try to remember how many instances of compunction you have seen. . . . Compunction! . . . I tell you it is so rare that you may call it non-existent. They are too passionate. Too pedantic. Too courageous with themselves—perhaps" (pp. 158–159). In this last example Marlow's intellectual gymnastic has merged with his rhetorical reaching for effect; and the reader who studies the word "pedantic" is likely to decide that it is there merely for the alliteration. *Chance* is marred by bad jokes and arbitrary figures of speech. There is, for example, Marlow's self-consciously humorous remark that if women had cautiousness, "they would make of it a thing of passion, so that its own mother—I mean the mother of cautiousness—wouldn't recognize it" (p. 63), or his cheap punning on the hiker Fyne's "high pedestrian faculties" (p. 48). There is his embarrassing attempt to cancel out the effect of a cliché-ridden description with a final intellectual allusion: "It was a fine day; a delicious day, with the horror of the Infinite veiled by the splendid tent of blue; a day innocently bright like a child with a washed face, fresh like an innocent young girl, suave in welcoming one's respects like—like a Roman prelate" (p. 64). There are figures of speech wholly dissociated from their context, some of them even creating tonal contradictions to ideas and attitudes already established, as when Fyne scolds his barking dog and Marlow remarks that his "deeply modulated remonstrances abashed the vivacious animal no more than the deep, patient murmur of the sea abashes a nigger minstrel on a popular beach" (p. 141). There is a good deal of unnecessarily pompous diction ("'The daughter of a poet and the daughter of a convict are not comparable in the consequences of their conduct if their necessity may wear at times a similar aspect"—p. 161; "She did not know how to defend herself from their importunities, insolence and exigencies"—p. 164). And, apparently under the influence of James, there is a good deal of unnecessary syntax shuffling ("At the proper season you would meet in the fields Fyne"—p. 37; "The difficulty here is to keep steadily in view the then conditions of her existence" —p. 223). In all these ways, *Chance's* Marlow displays a self-conscious intellectual subtlety which fails precisely because it is so calculated and self-aware. None of the foregoing, of course, has the purpose merely of attacking a fictional character for his personal failures. But Marlow is once again established as a choral figure, and his defects of sympathy and judgment and expression do irremediable damage to Conrad's novel.

The devices which establish Marlow's choral status in *Chance* are of great interest, however, since they contrast sharply in several ways with the similar devices in *Lord Jim* and "Heart of Darkness," and so in themselves help illustrate the direction of Conrad's growth during the intervening period. The frame narrator's descriptions of Marlow are generally more abstract and more elegantly figurative. He is "lanky, loose, quietly composed in varied shades of brown, robbed of every vestige of gloss," with a "narrow, veiled glance" and "neutral bearing" (p. 32); and like the earlier Marlow, he is a compulsive traveler and at heart a sea-dweller: "From year to year he dwelt on land as a bird rests on the branch of a tree, so tense with the power of brusque flight into its true element that it is incomprehensible why it should sit still minute after minute" (pp. 33–34). His nautical status is once again of utmost importance: "Profane men living in ships, like the holy men gathered together in monasteries, develop traits of profound resemblance . . . because the service of the sea and the service of a temple are both detached from the vanities and errors of a world which follows no severe rule. . . . Simplicity is a good counsellor and isolation not a bad educator. A turn of mind composed of innocence and scepticism is com-

mon to them all, with the addition of an unexpected insight into
motives, as of disinterested lookers-on at a game" (pp. 32–33).
This passage is remarkable. Not only does it insist once again, in
the context of an obviously complex novel, on the familiar
themes of "isolation" and "simplicity"; but it also gives an abstract expansion to the Buddha-imagery that had earlier been
associated with Marlow. The generally more expository method
and more dogmatic tone of *Chance* also permit the frame narrator to declare the virtues of Marlow's understanding with more
directness than the earlier frame narrators had been allowed:
having " 'gone about the seas prying into things considerably' "
(p. 35), Marlow " 'appears to know something of every soul that
ever went afloat in a sailor's body' " (p. 36), and so on. To
complement this broad empirical knowledge, Marlow has "the
habit of pursuing general ideas in a peculiar manner, between
jest and earnest" (p. 23). And in case the reader fails to respond
appropriately to this "justification" of Marlow (to use Ford's
term once again), the frame narrator demonstrates: "Marlow
looked at me with his dark penetrating glance. I was struck by
the absolute verisimilitude of [his] suggestion" (p. 102); "I
couldn't refuse Marlow the tribute of a prolonged whistle" (p.
103); and so on. By the time the frame narrator is ready to draw
the moral—" 'We, my dear Marlow, have the inestimable advantage of understanding what is happening to others' " (p. 117)—
the reader is prepared to admit that such at least is Conrad's
intention, despite the narrator's grudging irony.

Some of these changes in Marlow, and in the devices used to
justify him, can be attributed to Conrad's own personal development since *Lord Jim*. The tone of his letters during these years
gradually becomes more dogmatic, and their content more
learned and analytic, paralleling Marlow's intellectual authori-
tarianism and contempt for the "public mind" (p. 87): "People
don't want intelligence. It worries them." Marlow's "chaffing
humour" is undoubtedly Conrad's: "I am proud of my powers of
stately invective combined with that art of putting the finger to

the nose." And Marlow's laughter in the face of tragedy is echoed in Conrad's response to his own family's ill fortunes: "By Jove! I've got to hold myself with both hands not to burst into a laugh which would scare wife, baby and the other invalid." [1] But there is a crucial difference here. The real-life Conrad threatens a stoical laugh at his own pain, while Marlow laughs at the pain and limitations of others. If Marlow had been able to identify with the Fynes and Flora and Anthony as the earlier Marlow had identified with Jim, his laughter might have taken on some of the heroic quality of Conrad's. Unhappily, however, the partnership in suffering which would justify Marlow's tragicomic tone is outside the novel, in Conrad's personal life; and Marlow emerges in the novel as the cynic who repeatedly implies, but never identifies, some secret hurt. Marlow is an incomplete projection of Conrad, his intellectual and skeptical side dissociated firmly from the rest in order to control the peculiar materials of *Chance. Chance* is an ambitious and radically new attempt to sum up old themes, clarify them sharply, and push beyond them to the metaphysical substructure which gives them their existential overtones. In striving toward this philosophic universality, Conrad necessarily moves toward greater abstraction and a higher degree of symbolic artifice; Marlow becomes less a person than an intellectual voice; and elements of his personality which would, in a more realistic context, guarantee his emotional complexity and human sympathy, simply drop away from the novel.

The most obvious precondition of moral action in Conrad's earlier work is the power of chance; and understood properly, in all the breadth and complexity Conrad gives the idea, "chance" may be said to be the theme of the novel. Conrad points this focus at the beginning of his Author's Note: "It is a mighty force

---

[1] Aubry, *Life and Letters,* II, pp. 24, 59, 52. An earlier letter illustrates the same point, and gives the psychologist an intriguing suggestion about Conrad's inhibitions: speaking of marionettes, Conrad observes that "their impassibility in love, in crime, in mirth, in sorrow,—is heroic, superhuman, fascinating" (I, p. 213).

that of mere chance; absolutely irresistible yet manifesting itself often in delicate forms such for instance as the charm, true or illusory, of a human being" (p. vii). Marlow reiterates the same idea: Flora de Barral's "unconsciousness was to be broken into with profane violence. . . . And if you ask me how, wherefore, for what reason? I will answer you: Why, by chance! By the merest chance, as things do happen, lucky and unlucky, terrible or tender, important or unimportant; and even things which are neither, things so completely neutral in character that you would wonder why they do happen at all if you didn't know that they, too, carry in their insignificance the seeds of further incalculable chances" (pp. 99–100). The Stein-like construction of Marlow's question and answer gives some idea of the distance he has come since *Lord Jim*. And it is worth remembering how pervasive, if implicit, the idea of "chance" had been in the earlier fiction. Willems, whose chance vision of Aissa in the forest ultimately destroys him; Jim, whose chance illness brings him aboard the *Patna* and whose chance encounters with a sunken derelict and with Gentleman Brown are his undoing; and a whole range of other major and minor characters learn the power of chance in the earlier fiction. In *The Secret Agent*, the principle of chance has been expanded into an even more emphatic counterpoint to the characters' calculation of their own destinies. Winnie meets Verloc by chance, and is abetted by chance in her apparently most efficient murder of him, since it is only an accident that her knife strikes so neatly between Verloc's ribs ("Hazard has such accuracies," Conrad remarks wryly—p. 263). Stevie trips over a root by accident (note the clear symbolic similarity to Jim's sunken derelict). Heat gets his clue by accident. And so on, indefinitely. Conrad's conscious awareness of this metaphysical condition (it is also, as will presently be shown, an epistemological condition) grows until it achieves full thematic status in *Chance*.

There are, first of all, the many etymological and philosophical variants of "chance" caught in Marlow's diction and meditative asides; as well as a structure of events based largely on coincidence and accident, and determined very little, if at all, by the conscious intentions of the major characters. Just as a sampling, the word "chance" is used variously to denote a piece of luck (p. 27), an opportunity (p. 28), an abstract force (p. 28), an accident (p. 40), and a cosmic plan imperceptible to mortals (p. 128). As for narrative events, Anthony and Flora meet by chance at the Fynes', and again by chance on one of Flora's walks; Marlow chances along just in time to forestall Flora's possible suicide; Powell just happens to look through the skylight (which in turn has accidentally been broken earlier in the day) in time to see de Barral poison Captain Anthony's drink; and so on. The variable denotation of "chance" yields multiple ironies, as when de Barral, drinking his own poison finally in an admission of defeat, raises the glass to Powell and exclaims, " 'Here's luck' " (p. 433); and the principle of chance extends even into the narrative method: for example, it is Marlow's accidental intimacy with Flora over the matter of her attempted suicide that gives him access to the most personal parts of her story.

Still another definition Marlow provides of "chance," however, points to a more important kind of development. If the "workmanship" of "chance, fate, providence, call it what you will," is "precise" (p. 411), then the appearance of accident is an illusion maintained only from the human point of view, and the problem of chance reduces itself to one of knowledge. Many of *Chance*'s peculiarities of structure and content can be traced to this epistemological subtheme, as for example the epiphenomenalist's description of Captain Anthony under the stress of passion: "He would jump up to rush on deck and tramp, tramp up and down that poop till he felt ready to drop, without being able to wear down the agitation of his soul, generous indeed, but weighted by its envelope of blood and muscle and bone; handicapped by the brain creating precise images and everlastingly speculating, speculating" (p. 379). In his constant effort to distinguish appearance from reality, Marlow utters a good deal of epistemological theory, including some theories about language. There is his intuitionist notion of the inferior status of empirical knowledge: "Information is something one goes out to seek and puts away when found as you might do a piece of lead: ponderous, useful, unvibrating, dull. Whereas knowledge comes to one . . . a chance acquisition, preserving in its repose a fine resonant quality" (p. 88). Or again, he speaks of "the inability to interpret aright the signs which experience (a thing mysterious in itself) makes to our understanding and emotions" (p. 282). He hints at a theory of descriptive language something like that of the early logical positivists (p. 101), and adumbrates a theory of the social power of words which might be the starting point for a later semanticist (p. 74). And he offers repeated assurances to the frame narrator about his sources of knowledge: "I am telling you at once the details which I heard from Mrs. Fyne later in the day, as well as what little Fyne imparted to me" (p. 107); "You understand I am piecing here bits of disconnected statements" (p. 222); and the like. Occasionally this subtheme too yields a multilayered irony; looking back on her illusion-filled, luckless life at the end of the novel, Flora Anthony indulges in a cliché whose implications have by this time become incredibly complex: "Truth will out, Mr. Marlow" (p. 444). This subtheme helps explain some of Marlow's unpleasantness: it is his function to raise the factual, imperceptive reports of characters like Fyne and Powell to another level of truth, so that his condescension toward them is thematically important. Just as the other major figures of *Chance* are symbolic, partially allegorical constructs, so Marlow is an intellectual construct. A single example will show this refining, analytic function: when Powell recounts his paralysis of feeling in the presence of the poisoner de Barral, Marlow observes that " 'all he could do was to look at the surface. The inwardness of what was passing before his eyes was hidden from him, who had looked on, more impenetrably than from me who at a distance of years was listening to his words. What presently happened at this crisis in Flora de Barral's fate was beyond his power of comment' " (p. 426). If Marlow is to help reveal the "inwardness" of events, he must—at least in the terms which *Chance* imposes on itself—adopt a self-consciously superior attitude.

Marlow's analytic improvement of other characters' understanding extends even to their unconscious motives—emotional forces which go unrecognized by the characters themselves, and thus fall within Conrad's comprehensive definition of "chance." Here Marlow is brilliant, despite the fact that the motives he perceives are rarely allowed to reveal themselves through the concrete detail of dialogue and action. The insights he offers into minor characters are perhaps ordinary: Mrs. Fyne's "unconscious Machiavellism" (p. 194) in sending her husband to protest the elopement of Flora and Anthony; or the "malice" in the way Powell, the shipping master, seizes the opportunity to "serve" his namesake young Powell (p. 23). But when Marlow approaches his major characters, with the intent of analyzing those "troubles which are subtle often to the extent of not being understood by the very hearts they devastate or uplift" (p. 272), his psychologizing necessarily becomes more complicated. His characters are aware of inexplicable feelings: Powell feels "sorry" for Captain Anthony "without being able to discover the origins of that sympathy of which he had become so suddenly aware" (p. 394); Anthony, persuaded that Flora feels a "completely justifiable" fear and detestation of him, nevertheless finds that he resents it (p. 397); and so on. The main characters' motives are permeated with ambivalence and paradox: Anthony's exultation in his love seems "to take him by the throat like an enemy" (p. 339); his behavior toward Flora is "stupidly sublime" (p. 395); he wishes both to "console" and to "cherish" her sorrow (p. 348). Similarly, Flora, living away from the ship and visited only intermittently by her husband, discovers that "the absence of Anthony was a relief and his visits were pleasurable" (p. 388). There would perhaps be nothing remarkable in these conflicts if they were not so sharply caught in paradoxical phrases and were not so pervasive; as it is, they form a separate strain of meaning. The common notion that *Chance* shows a sentimental simplification of motive needs reconsideration in the light of passages like these; the novel seems to suggest instead a still-growing awareness of psychological complexity.

These observations tend to confirm a view sometimes offered of *Chance*: that its title is ironic, that what Conrad really sees in his characters is a rigidly determined behavior, and that much of Marlow's amusement is Bergsonian, the by-product of this perception.[2] These observations help account, I think, for some of Marlow's cerebral irony. His dissociation is so pronounced that he can be "amused by the misfortunes of a fellow-creature" (p. 49) and allude "playfully" to "the distress of the poor Fynes" (p. 45). He finds the trial of de Barral a "sinister farce," and the laughter at its disclosures "irresistible" despite his clear awareness of the "mute anguish" of de Barral's bankrupted depositors (p. 81). He sees a tortured confession as an "untimely joke" (p. 212). And like the narrator of *Under Western Eyes,* he sees a close alliance between cruelty and absurdity (p. 169). At the same time, this tragicomic laughter is not the final attitude of *Chance.* To discover the novel's profounder meanings, it is necessary to follow Marlow as he assesses the impact of this psychological necessity on the archetypal moral situation of Flora and Anthony: to see where the laughter stops, as it were, and freedom for these characters, however limited, begins.

Marlow is, then, a philosophic and analytic voice concerned not so much with the external events of Flora de Barral's life as with their inner meaning; and since the meaning he sees often contradicts the conventional or commonsense view, an important nonchronological element of structure may be identified: a continuous symbolic opposition or tension in which Marlow's skepti-

[2] See, e.g., Bruce Harkness, "The Epigraph of Conrad's *Chance*," *Nineteenth-Century Fiction,* IX (December 1954), 209–222; and Wolfgang B. Fleischmann, "Conrad's *Chance* and Bergson's *Laughter*," *Renascence,* XIV (Winter 1961), 66–71.

cal, analytic reserve is placed over against a moral melodrama populated with superficially simple characters whose conscious motives are often "romantic" or sentimental, but whose true motivation and significance are more profound. It is this ironic interplay between an archetypal "love" story and the cynical philosophic temperament which gives *Chance* much of its charm and defines most of Marlow's function in the novel. What ought to be clear and cleanly creative between Flora and Anthony comes to the reader reduced and corroded by Marlow's intellect; conversely, at the novel's end the reader finds that Marlow's skepticism permits a higher and more carefully qualified level of affirmation in terms of precisely the same sort of archetypal situation the novel had begun with. The story of Flora and Anthony is something for Marlow's irony to work against; and as in "Heart of Darkness" and *Lord Jim*, he becomes the novel's meditative protagonist.

Something has already been said of the reasons for Marlow's correction of other characters' observations in *Chance*. When he penetrates beyond Powell's mere topographical understanding of the story's climactic events, Marlow is simply exercising his proper analytic function. And this in turn implies that Conrad had by this time gone a little beyond the esthetic outlined in the Preface to the *Nigger*. Powell's report is, after all, stubbornly visual; and it is significant that Marlow emphatically removes the locus of truth from mere sensory detail: meditating on the meaning of de Barral's behavior, using his "mind" instead of his eyes, Marlow reports that "the disclosure which so often rewards a moment of detachment from mere visual impressions gave me a thrill very much approaching a shudder" (p. 87). In another context he deplores the influence of sense experience on judgment: "Our mental conclusions depend so much on momentary physical sensations—don't they?" (p. 56). Remarks of this kind tend to confirm what has already been suggested—that by the time of *Chance*, Conrad had moved away from his earlier methods toward a more highly symbolic, near-allegorical mode, in which imagery is more nearly the projection of an idea than a sensory report.

As in the case of "chance," many of the ideas projected by Marlow are simply more cleanly functional versions of ideas that had appeared, explicitly or implicitly, in Conrad's earlier work. In one sense this crystallization represents a growth, and in another it does not. So far as ideas remain abstract, dry, and mechanical—as they too often do in *Chance*—they are useless to a novelist. If, however, they can be placed over against an archetypal human situation which has its own independent movement, so that a species of rhetorical tension is generated which engages the reader's interest in much the same way as an emotional conflict in realistic fiction, then the work will begin to achieve some positive esthetic excitement. *Chance* sometimes succeeds in achieving this rhetorical tension, and sometimes not. But the *kind* of fiction Conrad tried for here—not realistic, and above all not a "love story"—might be successful enough. There is, however, as we have seen, a more promising mode for Conrad: the projection of ideas into a detailed symbolic narrative, so that the reflective component of *Chance*'s rhetorical structure can disappear entirely, along with Marlow. Insofar as *Chance* is a philosophical summing-up for Conrad, and insofar as it eliminates certain impossible technical gambits by trial and error, it represents an essential preparation for *Victory;* and seen in this light—despite its own radical defects—it is a sign of growth in Conrad's art.

The structure of *Chance*, then, is generated by a kind of truth-seeking rhetoric, in which Marlow's skeptical intellect, equipped with a body of broad generalizations, is set in tension with an archetypal romantic affair.[3] Marlow's first problem is to knock apart the shell of conventional opinion surrounding such

[3] For discussions of rhetorical structures in *Chance*, see Curtis C. Smith, "Conrad's *Chance*: A Dialectical Novel," *Thoth*, VI (Spring 1965), 16–24; and Jerome Zuckermann, "Contrapuntal Structure in Conrad's *Chance*," *Modern Fiction Studies*, X (Spring 1964), 49–54.

universal institutions as love, marriage and filial obedience, an effort which obligates him to undertake a certain amount of cynical reductionism. Captain Anthony's love for Flora is reduced to a combination of pity and tenderness (p. 261), to a perverse possessiveness (p. 224), and, in what must surely be the last analysis, to a growling, fierce, savage passion (p. 226)—prefiguring at least some of the elements of Heyst's love for Lena in *Victory*. Carleon Anthony is the "poet-tyrant," and de Barral the "financier-convict" (p. 148). Anthony himself, with ironic reiteration, is "the son of the poet—you know." Marlow offers some explicit analytic simplification, as in his account of de Barral's financial success quoted earlier. (Aware that his explanation has seemed too simple, Marlow defends himself, and in doing so points to the antirealistic thrust of *Chance*: "I exaggerate! . . . My dear fellow, I have merely stripped the rags of business verbiage and financial jargon off my statements. . . . I am giving you the naked truth"—p. 80.) And sometimes he simply expresses a very general skepticism toward the human condition, either through abstract philosophizing ("The incapacity to achieve anything distinctly good or evil is inherent in our earthly condition. Mediocrity is our mark"—p. 23) or through passages of description which have the same effect ("It was one of those dewy, clear, starry nights, oppressing our spirit, crushing our pride, by the brilliant evidence of the awful loneliness, of the hopeless obscure insignificance of our globe lost in the splendid revelation of a glittering, soulless universe"—p. 50).

Against this dark cosmic background, in an analytic universe which tends to reduce all human behavior to its psycho-moral essentials, Flora and Anthony are pushed toward a symbolic extreme of human fortune. "The girl's life had presented itself to me," says Marlow, "as a tragi-comical adventure, the saddest thing on earth . . . and the most common" (p. 310). Flora is at once radical and ordinary in her range of reference: few "real" people have millionaire-convicts for fathers, or marry sea captains (themselves moral radicals in Conrad's universe); but Flora's fate is nonetheless universal: " 'Of all the forms offered to us by life it is the one demanding a couple to realize it fully, which is the most imperative. Pairing off is the fate of mankind. And if two beings thrown together, mutually attracted, resist the necessity, fail in understanding and voluntarily stop short of the—the embrace, in the noblest meaning of the word, then they are committing a sin against life' " (pp. 426–427). Passages like these silence any reading of *Chance* in terms of mere sexual love; Anthony and Flora are presented as the symbolic root case in a rendition of the existential situation of "mankind." Marlow's metaphors repeatedly enforce the point: Anthony restrains himself "from shaking an indignant fist at the universe" (p. 344); his ship is "unrestful in the sense . . . [in] which this planet of ours is unrestful" (p. 376); and so on; and Conrad employs a variety of devices to render Flora and Anthony archetypally male-and-female. One of these is the Knight-Damsel motif, which, while it does not dominate the novel to the extent suggested by the subtitles of the sections, does receive some gently ironic development. More interesting are the Edenic overtones in Marlow's descriptions of Flora and Anthony, whom he sees as "outside all conventions," and "as untrammelled in a sense as the first man and the first woman" (p. 210). Their first intimate meeting is in a "little garden" where they can "just make out each other" (p. 230); later, aboard Anthony's ship, expelled from their garden and tortuously self-aware, it is "as if they both had taken a bite of the same bitter fruit" (p. 342). Anthony's "dithyrambic" expressions of love (p. 234) are related to this strain of imagery; and much of Marlow's own exaggerated diction is explicable in terms of this basic symbolic intention.

In three or four important passages, Marlow explains Flora's archetypal status: "Flora de Barral . . . was thoroughly feminine. She would be passive (and that does not mean inanimate) in the circumstances, where the mere fact of being a woman was enough to give her an occult and supreme significance. And she would be enduring, which is the essence of woman's visible, tangible power" (p. 310). Flora's essential passivity accounts for her inability to correct the situation aboard the *Ferndale* with the single aggressive speech some readers have called for: a real-life woman might make such a speech, but as a "thoroughly feminine" figure Flora cannot. At the same time, to be passive is not to be inanimate, as Marlow points out; and Flora is given a dimension of imagery that goes all the way back to Aissa and the proliferating, formless tropical life of the Malayan tales: her eyes suggest an "unexpressed menace in the depths of the dilated pupils within the rings of sombre blue. It was—how shall I say it?—a night effect when you seem to see vague shapes and don't know what reality you may come upon at any time" (p. 215). The notion of Flora as a creative principle is further reinforced by the reiterated comparison of the depth and color of her eyes to the depth and color of the sea, imagery which associates her with Conrad's favorite archetypal life source. And the dominant irony of her fate derives from this symbolic overtone: her creative energy has absolutely no "footing in this world" (p. 196); she is "fated to be always surrounded by treachery and lies stifling every better impulse, every instinctive aspiration of her soul to trust and to love" (pp. 174–175). Marlow sees Flora as the extreme case of frustration: "Was there anything more to disclose—some other misery, some other deception of which that girl had been a victim? It seemed hardly probable. It was not even easy to imagine" (p. 207). Because of *Chance*'s excessive reliance on abstract development, the reader may not be convinced; but it is clear that Conrad wishes to represent the sum of Flora's misfortunes—social, filial, romantic, sexual—as a paradigm of all human misfortune. And it is because a kind of nihilism has been pressed on her from without that Flora is constantly on the brink of suicide: " 'If he bolts away,' she thought, 'then I shall know that I am of no account indeed! That no one loves me, that words and actions and protestations and everything in the world is false—and I shall jump into the dock. *That* at least won't lie' " (p. 370).

Conversely, Anthony is the archetypal activist—significantly, in the context of *Chance*, the son of an erotic poet (it is probably a promotion for Heyst, in a similar situation, that he is the son of a skeptical philosopher). Anthony's stature is underscored by his unique moral position: "The captain of a ship at sea is a remote, inaccessible creature, something like the prince of a fairy-tale, alone of his kind, depending on nobody, not to be called to account except by powers practically invisible and so distant, that they might well be looked upon as supernatural" (p. 288). At the same time, the crew feels that Anthony is "our property" (p. 412), as if his fate somehow reflected theirs. And just as Flora's "endurance" carries its own implicit weakness ("one may die of too much endurance"—p. 310), so does Anthony's chivalric idealism. Othello-like ("there was something African, something Moorish in Captain Anthony"—p. 424), he is the victim of his own jealous misconstruction and rejection of love. He displays a "satanic conceit" (p. 351) which identifies a part of him with de Barral's possessiveness (de Barral's place of confinement as a convict is referred to as the "Nether Regions" —p. 347, an "infernal" prison—p. 352, and so on; and much is made of his later referring to Captain Anthony as his "jailer"). Marlow sums up the extremes of Anthony's personality (and incidentally reminds the reader of Heyst) when he describes him as a man "trying to act at the same time like a beast of prey, a pure spirit and the 'most generous of men' " (p. 415). And the reader is made to feel Anthony's self-imposed paralysis: Flora "existed, unapproachable, behind the blank wall of his renunciation. His force, fit for action, experienced the impatience, the indignation, almost the despair of his vitality arrested, bound, stilled, progressively worn down, frittered away by Time" (p. 396). Placed in opposition to Flora's essential passivity, Anthony's "renunciation" generates the same sort of elemental moral irony that the reader sees later in *Victory*.

This complex of artistic purposes explains some of the most puzzling technical features of *Chance*, as for example the cu-

rious narrative sequence and painful slowness of its "story." If
the most important movement is Marlow's, as he guides the
frame narrator through a periphery of illusions, prejudices, inadequate conventional views, and the like, toward the central psycho-moral truths about Anthony and Flora, then the complicated
patching together of information and continual analysis are essential aspects of structure. Marlow's narrative is itself an exercise illustrating some of the novel's major ideas; in the end, it
takes Powell's "ugly spying" aboard the *Ferndale* (p. 413) to
ferret out the final moral truths—or to give Marlow the materials
for his final analytic penetration. Marlow works through an
outer shell of social illusion and domestic situation toward a
morally archetypal core—a process somewhere between the more
randomly associative movements of *Nostromo* and the more
highly schematized movement of *Victory*. At the same time, this
movement is for Flora a progress toward more fundamental
psycho-moral levels—from her utterly dependent childhood role,
through such roles as those of house guest, companion, tutor, and
unwanted cousin, toward her final conflicting identities as protective daughter and wife: gradually taking more responsibility
onto herself, and gradually becoming aware of deeper levels of
perfidy in her very existence as a feminine being. De Barral's
appearance is thus delayed until the second part (he might, after
all, have emerged from prison at any convenient moment): as
Flora's deepest emotional tie (except for Anthony), he does not
figure strongly until late in the book; and his betrayal of Flora is
the most grotesque and shocking of all. When Flora begins to
detect "some rather ugly shades" in the "invariable gentleness"
which had been her father's claim on her, and finds herself
"wondering" that his declarations of affection do not "warm her
heart more" (p. 357), she is thrown back with utter finality on
her own feminine passivity, which is to say, on her own creative
potential. Her heartfelt cry to Anthony—" 'But I don't want to
be let off' " (p. 430)—is a final renunciation of her resistance,

and thus the high point of her "passive" femininity. Anthony seizes his "opportunity" (note even at this crucial point of masculine decision the persistence of the diction of chance), and this chapter of Flora de Barral's life may be said to end on an affirmative note. But it is an affirmation deeply qualified by Marlow's skepticism and by Flora's paradigmatic history; and it is to be qualified even further by the final mockery of Anthony's absurd accidental death.

As the foregoing discussion of *Victory* has suggested, a final ironic fusion of destruction and affirmation is thoroughly appropriate to Conrad's existential stance. This is clearer, of course, in *Victory*. *Chance* appears at first to end more optimistically, in line with the traditional catharsis of melodrama. A new series of actions is begun, once again in "the fragrant darkness of the garden"; [4] at the very last Marlow suggests to Powell that there is after all a " 'science of life,' " consisting in " 'seizing every chance that presents itself' "; his final view of Flora and Powell is once

---

[4] It is Marlow who confronts Flora in this particular garden. But he is there, in a sense, on Powell's behalf, and he has become sufficiently identified with Anthony by this time to serve as a surrogate for any lover Flora might choose. Marlow does not identify with Flora and Anthony as intensely as he does with Kurtz and Jim, because he is essentially a dissociated intellect in *Chance*. But he does confess to a small portion of femininity (p. 146), and notes parallels between his own experience and Flora's. With Anthony the identification is more obvious. One detail is especially interesting, however, and pertains directly to the garden theme. In his passion for Flora, Anthony finds himself in the "enchanted gardens of Armida" (p. 396). As Tasso's sorceress in *Jerusalem Delivered*, who seduces the knight Rinaldo and is finally converted by him, Flora makes a good Armida, especially in view of de Barral's satanic associations (Armida is the niece of Satan). But it is Marlow who has undertaken Rinaldo's task of persuading Armida not to commit suicide; and thus he shares in the allusion and can legitimately appear in the garden with Flora. For a further discussion, see Gerald H. Levin, "An Allusion to Tasso in Conrad's *Chance*," *Nineteenth-Century Fiction*, XIII (September 1958), 145–151.

again Edenic; and he ends his narrative with the declaration, "Hang it all, for all my belief in Chance I am not exactly a pagan" (pp. 445–447). But it must be remembered how much of Flora's and Powell's opportunity has been lost—to put it simply, how old they are at this point—and also what obstacles the novel's first romantic effort, proceeding from the Fynes' garden, had encountered. This is hardly a "happy ending," and it invites the reader to define the novel's final moral attitudes, if he can.

There is, of course, the epigraph: " 'Those that hold that all things are governed by fortune had not erred, had they not persisted there'—SIR THOMAS BROWNE"; and this in itself supports Marlow's denial of mere paganism and nihilism. Conrad's Author's Note reiterates "the solidarity of all mankind in simple ideas and in sincere emotions" (p. ix); and Marlow repeatedly confirms the validity of elemental presocial values. But there are new qualities in this later affirmation, elements of stoicism and existential acceptance and a new esthetic dimension (in the broadest sense of the word) that need to be identified, if Conrad's growth is to be seen fully. The idea of "endurance," for example, is new, though it might have been anticipated: the novel was begun during Jessie Conrad's invalidism, and continued through a series of medical and economic crises. Conrad's letters of the period are despairing; at one point, with unintended irony, he even associates the novel with his family's misfortunes: "Really I haven't got my share of the commonest sort of luck. I suppose *Chance* will have to pay for all this."[5] The stoical strain of *Chance* thus has a poignancy and force not wholly derived from the novel. And there is another element which is absent from the earlier fiction (unless it is seen somehow in the Malayan and Congo natives' striving toward light and form): what Marlow defines succinctly as "the joys of form, colour, sensations—the only riches of our world of senses" (p.

[5] Aubry, *Life and Letters,* II, p. 48.

62). In a significant passage near the end of *Chance*, Flora de Barral expands this idea:

"I have had a fine adventure."

"It was fine, then," I said, interested.

"The finest in the world! Only think! I loved and I was loved, untroubled, at peace, without remorse, without fear. All the world, all life, were transformed for me. And how much I have seen! . . . The most familiar things appeared lighted up with a new light, clothed with a loveliness I had never suspected. The sea itself! . . . You are a sailor. You have lived your life on it. But do you know how beautiful it is, how strong, how charming." (pp. 444–445)

Far from being destructive, "peace" is held out here as an essential precondition of significant experience. This motif extends into the later fiction: in the Edenic associations of *Victory*; in Lena's naïve appreciation of the charms of Samburan; in Peyrol's direct, monosyllabic appetite for the contours of his childhood home; and the like; but these peaceful pleasures, like Flora's, have been won only through the catharsis of suffering.

Chance was Conrad's first important commercial success. Its appeal to female readers perhaps accounts for some of this popularity; and Marlow raises some other matters of obvious interest to the novel reader of 1912: agnosticism, moral relativism, the mechanisms of sudden financial greatness and financial ruin, and so on. The novel's secular-ironic tone is reminiscent of such writers as Shaw, Hardy, Robinson, Dreiser, and the naughtier Marlow-to-come, H. L. Mencken. In its superficial attitudes and subjects, *Chance* moved with the currents of its time. But in these respects it is also, of course, a period piece. For all its popularity, and for all its interest to the student of Conrad's growth, *Chance* is not a good novel. There is a close analogy here to *Nostromo*. Like *Nostromo*, *Chance* is a brilliant technical experiment (we would know this simply from Henry James's interest in it), but an unfinished work of art. And the reemergence of Marlow involves Conrad in difficulties that can be resolved only by turning to a more thoroughly symbolic method. So long as Marlow is permitted to develop the novel's ideas abstractly—and the more concrete he becomes, the less reason there is for his existence—he will create as many problems as he solves. It is only in a spirit of extreme critical objectivity that the reader can make the proper allowances for Marlow's condescension and cynicism. Faced with a fairly realistic and colloquial beginning, the reader does not learn the book's purposes soon enough, and some of Marlow's early descriptions strike him as too incredibly generalized: the hysterically deprived depositors laughing in unison at de Barral's trial, for example, or Flora's face being white and bloodless "for a couple of years" after her bad experience with the Governess (p. 122). Moreover, to place so many of Marlow's theme-defining ruminations in series near the beginning of the novel makes it drag intolerably, as if the story had fallen behind Marlow's epistemological screen and gotten lost. Ultimately, of course, the reader sees the purpose; but meanwhile his confidence has been put to a severe test. And to develop each segment of Flora de Barral's history in order—to give the Fynes, for example, a full development, and then the Governess, and so on—precludes the reader's identifying Flora as the central source of interest until late in Part I. For a hundred pages or so, the negative pole of Conrad's symbolic opposition in *Chance*—Marlow's corrosive intellect, against which the romantic motives of "the Knight" and "the Damsel" are to be tested—is developed in isolation, through a kind of empirical method, at the expense of the Fynes, de Barral, the Governess, the public, and even the Fynes' dog; until the reader begins to forget the promised human story, and to see only random destruction. Individual items in the series, like the cruelty of Flora's cousins, are likely to seem gratuitous, since Marlow has no time to pause for details; and some of his insights, while perfectly plausible (like Mrs. Fyne's unconscious Machiavellism), are simply sprung on the reader. Many of these difficulties disappear on rereading, but only for the reason that the difficulties of *Nostromo* disappear: the generosity of the reader, who has become aware of a respectable creative purpose and is willing to join in achieving it.

One need only compare *Chance* to another novel with a similar intention, a similar heroine, and even a similar final affirmation, complete to a symbolic recoupling of the major characters—*Tess of the D'Urbervilles*—to see how far short of his subject Conrad falls. There are of course important differences between the two novels. But Hardy's ability to refrain from extended exposition, his delicate irony of detail, and his ability to generate emotional power despite his own detachment, all suggest shortcomings of *Chance*. *Chance* does generate some emotional power, but largely near the end of Part II, where the development has become less abstract and meditative, and Marlow has begun to exploit the dialogue and dramatic conflict so sorely lacking in the earlier pages. Perhaps the secret is Conrad's divided intention about Marlow: he is to tell the story, and thus must inevitably transmute it into his highly personal idiom; but at the same time, he is, for much of the novel, the essentially negative intellect which is only a part of the novel's moral machinery. His domination of the narrative inadvertently destroys the emotional appeal of such people as the Fynes and Flora's relatives, and even of such important figures as Captain Anthony. The other characters naturally turn out to be no match for Marlow, since he is holding all the strings. And the reader inevitably feels a sense of artistic injustice. What Conrad really needs is a protagonist in whom the value conflicts and philosophic conflicts of *Chance* can appear as a dramatic unity, as well as some method of giving both concrete form and universal scope to the forces that threaten that protagonist—and this points ahead to *Victory* and Axel Heyst.

As early as 1907, when Conrad started *Chance,* he had begun to break away from the political interests of the previous half-decade, and once again to extend the thematic scope of his fiction. Some of this later work returns to the psycho-moral base of his early fiction, as the starting point for a new kind of development. "The Secret Sharer," which stands at the beginning of Conrad's third period, has a subject with affinities to "Heart of Darkness," but transmuted into highly symbolic form, thus signaling the direction of Conrad's future growth. It is also a highly controversial story, and deserves the closest attention of anyone interested in Conrad's artistic development.

Albert Guerard, whose discussions of "Heart of Darkness" and "The Secret Sharer" are basic reading for the student of Conrad, holds that "in broad terms 'The Secret Sharer' concerns the classic night journey and willed descent into the unconscious. But even broader terms may be as true: that Conrad apparently detected in himself a division (possibly damaging, possibly saving) into a respectable traditional rational seaman-self and a more interior outlaw-self that repudiated law and tradition." [6] Most readers would agree that Leggatt somehow represents the darker side of the Captain-narrator's self. But he has also been seen as a projection of the Captain's maritime ideal, and conversely as a total failure. And the story's conclusion is likewise controversial. According to Guerard, the moral is that "we cannot be good seamen, alone with our ships, until we have faced out, recognized, and subdued those selves which interfere with seamanship (i.e., action)." [7] This represents perhaps the most common reading; and since it sees the story as recommending that the darker sides of the self be "subdued," it is in accord with the larger view of Conrad's later fiction as sentimental and evasive. Read more closely, however, "The Secret Sharer" seems to show its narrator arriving finally at an acceptance, rather than a repression, of his own dark complexity; so that what Conrad has achieved here, if the story is to be taken as a document in his own psycho-moral history, is a legitimate self-integration. If Con-

[6] Guerard, *Conrad the Novelist*, p. 26.   [7] *Ibid.*, p. 31.

rad's later work is to be seen clearly, these issues must somehow be resolved.

Guerard is right, I think, in saying that Leggatt represents a lawless, subrational side of the self which may lie dormant until some moment of moral stress (the narrator at first believes that Leggatt is dead), and then must somehow be encountered. But it is important to give this idea sharper focus by considering the specific details through which Leggatt is revealed to the reader. And the first point to emphasize in this regard is Leggatt's utter lack of rationality (despite the Captain's descriptions of him as "intelligent" and "sane"—details to which we must return in a moment). In his own element, the fishlike Leggatt loses even the appearance of rationality: "With a gasp I saw revealed to my stare a pair of feet, the long legs, a broad livid back immersed right up to the neck in a greenish cadaverous glow. . . . He was complete but for the head. A headless corpse!" (p. 97). If Leggatt symbolically lacks a head, as this description and his name both imply, then there is little surprise in his finding the narrator's hat useless when at the end of the story he returns to his native element. This notion of subrationality is confirmed by imagery familiar to readers of "Falk" and Lord Jim and Victory: not only is Leggatt "fish-like" (p. 98); he is also like a terrier or its jungle counterpart ("'I had him by the throat,'" Leggatt tells the narrator, "'and went on shaking him like a rat'"—p. 102) and a "wild beast" (p. 109). As suggested above in discussing "Falk," this device is most effective where the bridge between the reader's conscious mentality and his regressive self is as direct as possible. Here "The Secret Sharer" succeeds better than any other of Conrad's stories. The notion of a regressive animalism, for example, is implied both in Leggatt's unflagging appetite and in his instinctive alertness: "I had to shake him for a solid minute, but when at last he opened his eyes it was in the full possession of his senses" (p. 114). His processes of decision are distinctly subrational: "'I just took it into my own hands and

went away from him, boiling' " (p. 124); and the narrator formulates a significant distinction in his description of Leggatt's
"thinking out" of his escape from the *Sephora:* "a stubborn if not
a steadfast operation" (p. 106). Leggatt himself recognizes the
impulsive quality of his motives: " 'I strolled out on the quarter-
deck. I don't know that I meant to do anything. . . . Then a
sudden temptation came over me. I kicked off my slippers and
was in the water before I had made up my mind fairly' " (p.
108). And when Leggatt finally makes his departure, he returns
to the two archetypal life sources in Conrad's fiction: the sea,
and the heart of darkness (Koh-ring, a "towering fragment of the
everlasting night" among islands "unknown to trade, to travel,
almost to geography"—pp. 139, 133).

Two or three details in this development, however, deserve
special attention. For one thing, Leggatt's language, at least as
the narrator describes it, relates him to such deep primitives as
the finally inarticulate Kurtz, the mute Pedro, and the grotesquely articulate Yanko Goorall: "He told me the story roughly
in brusque, disconnected sentences" (p. 102). On his first appearance, Leggatt too, of course, is "mute." This subrational and
even subconceptual status explains Leggatt's resistance to the
anxiety that grips the narrator; since insanity is by definition a
disruption of rationality, Leggatt cannot be susceptible to it:
there was "something unyielding in his character," the narrator
reports, "there was no agitation in his whisper" (p. 131). Leggatt
is "sane" and "intelligent"—or appears so, to the distracted narrator—only because the opposites of these terms have no meaning
when applied to him. Correlatively, the narrator finds that Leggatt's experiences will not yield to rational analysis: "There was
something that made comment impossible in his narrative, or
perhaps in himself; a sort of feeling, a quality, which I can't find
a name for" (p. 109). What Leggatt represents (or perhaps less
allegorically, what he has experienced so sharply that it has
stamped itself indelibly into his character) resists conceptual
identification just as Kurtz's final "horror" does. And yet what-

ever it is seeks the same light and freedom that all Conrad's primitives strive for: "'I didn't mind being looked at,'" Leggatt says, thinking of his nakedness in the water, "'I—I liked it. . . . I don't know—I wanted to be seen, to talk with somebody'" (pp. 110–111). If "Heart of Darkness" and "The Secret Sharer" dramatize a willed descent into the unconscious, they also both dramatize the surging will of the unconscious to escape the bonds of repression imposed upon it.[8]

Once it is seen that the impulse toward identification and communication is shared by the narrator and Leggatt, "The Secret Sharer" becomes a story of integration, rather than conflict and repression. To "subdue" Leggatt would be a mistake (delegated here to the legalistic Captain Archbold of the *Sephora*); the narrator must instead fuse Leggatt's subrational personality with his own rational and civilized one, to emerge as a conceptually imperfect but pragmatically effective and healthy moral agent. It is not that the Captain cannot be commander of his ship until Leggatt has left it, but rather that until he has made his full and active practical commitment to Leggatt— risked everything to guarantee Leggatt's freedom and survival, instead of his repression—he cannot feel the self-assurance and practical force necessary to command either himself or his ship, just as Captain Anthony, in a similar situation, cannot acquire command until he has accepted the force and unruliness of his own passion for Flora. "The Secret Sharer" in a sense dramatizes Stein's paradox; the Captain fuses his dual nature, and in so doing makes the destructive part of himself serve his ideal ends.

[8] Robert A. Day, "The Rebirth of Leggatt," *Literature and Psychology*, XIII (Summer 1963), 74–80, is a provocative treatment, finding striking similarities between Leggatt's story and the rebirth archetype of "The Ancient Mariner." Leggatt does emerge from the Captain into a new life; but through his identification with Leggatt, the Captain, too, may be said to be reborn; and what is important is not their separation, but their final union. The conscious symbolic system of the story modifies the archetype in a way that Day's article misses, but it does point the way toward a valid Jungian explanation of some of the story's emotional power.

The process of identification and integration is revealed in the narrator's language, which proceeds in such a way as to draw Leggatt and himself into continuously more intimate relations, until finally at the end they are indistinguishable—a fact which helps resolve the puzzle of the story's last sentence. When Leggatt first boards the narrator's ship, their similarity is expressed in a variety of half-whimsical similes: Leggatt "followed me like my double on the poop" (p. 100); "the shadowy, dark head, like mine, seemed to nod imperceptibly" (p. 101); and so on. But soon the narrator has progressed to metaphor: Leggatt becomes "my double" (p. 102), my "own grey ghost" (p. 103), "my other self" (p. 111), and finally "the secret sharer of my life" (p. 114). And as the narrator progresses from playful and loose figures of speech to ever-more-intense metaphors, his self-descriptions reveal his sense of identity with Leggatt: from at first a mere "excitement" and "confused sensation" (p. 111) and a confession that "I felt dual" (p. 112), to a distraction which is almost insanity (p. 114), to a "queer sense of whispering to myself" (p. 115), to an inability to detach himself from a mental vision of Leggatt. At this point the notion of separate identities is dropped entirely and the series is begun again. The narrator accepts his identity with Leggatt, but again only in the form of a simile: "I felt as if I, personally, were being given to understand that I, too, was not the sort that would have done for the chief mate of a ship like the *Sephora*" (p. 119). The narrator's "feeling of identity with the other" (p. 120) is then developed through a second series of gradually intensifying metaphors: "I felt . . . torn in two" (p. 123); "part of me was absent" (p. 125); and the like; and gradually the narrator's syntax and pronoun reference begin to reflect a full fusion, as when the steward enters the Captain's cabin and miraculously fails to discover its secret: " 'Saved,' I thought. 'But, no! Lost! Gone! He was gone!' " (p. 129); or when the Captain finds Leggatt planning his route of escape: "On opening the door I had a back view of my very own self looking at a chart. He had come out of the recess and was standing near the table" (p. 137). Finally, the two characters begin to share the position of grammatical subject in major clauses (e.g., "The double captain slipped past the stairs"—p. 138); and the story's final sentence—"The secret sharer of my cabin and of my thoughts, as though he were my second self, had lowered himself into the water to take his punishment: a free man, a proud swimmer striking out for a new destiny" (p. 143)—seems paradoxical only because it applies both to Leggatt and to the Captain. Leggatt's "punishment" is to return to the unconscious sources from whence he came; but since during the course of the story he has become identified with the narrator, he has also achieved his freedom and a "new destiny" in the fierce self-command of the Captain. (It is fascinating to observe also that in his final sentence—one of the many marvels in Conrad's story—Conrad has increased the paradoxical tension, and also permitted the narrator to return to his original level of consciousness, by once again employing the mere similes of the story's first few pages.)

Paralleling this linguistic development is a more obvious dramatic and emotional identification. When he first sees Leggatt in the water, the Captain finds that he wants him to emerge into the light and air: "He made no motion to get out of the water. . . . It was inconceivable that he should not attempt to come on board, and strangely troubling to suspect that perhaps he did not want to. And my first words were prompted by just that troubled incertitude" (p. 98). Leggatt is hidden first in the Captain's cabin, then in bed and bathroom (inviting all amateur Freudians to go to work); and finally, in a significant bit of maritime intimacy, he shares the Captain's bunk (p. 127). The Captain's sympathy with Leggatt progresses from his first protective impulses, to his generous description of Leggatt's murderous behavior as a mere "fit of temper" (p. 101), to his conflict over whether to lie directly to the Captain of the Sephora (he does, of course, lie indirectly), and finally to an explicit recognition that he wishes Leggatt's freedom: "My hesitation in letting that man swim away from my ship's side had been a mere sham sentiment, a sort of cowardice" (p. 132). Their final symbolic union is, significantly, wordless: "Our hands met gropingly, lingered united in a steady, motionless clasp for a second. . . . No word was breathed by either of us when they separated" (p. 138). And in the end, of course, his identification with Leggatt saves the Captain's command. Having rammed his floppy hat onto Leggatt's head to protect him from the sun ("I saw myself wandering barefooted, bareheaded, the sun beating on my dark poll"—p. 138), the Captain sees it floating on the water after Leggatt has returned to the depths, and is able to save his ship by using it as a navigation point. If the Captain is saved by his impulsive gesture of capping Leggatt with the rationality symbolized in the hat, it is Leggatt's acceptance, and not his repression, that matters. This reading is confirmed finally by one striking detail which simply rules out the notion that Leggatt is "subdued" at the end of the story: the first emphatic gesture of self-determination the Captain makes in the story's final moment of crisis, drifting under the shadow of Koh-ring, is to sublimate the murderous behavior of Leggatt and use it as an instrument of just-barely-legal discipline. Leggatt had held his victim by the throat and shaken him like a rat; the Captain disciplines his fear-ridden chief in the same way:

I caught his arm as he was raising it to batter his poor devoted head, and shook it violently.

"She's ashore already," he wailed, trying to tear himself away.

"Is she? . . . Keep good full there!"

"Good full, sir," cried the helmsman in a frightened, thin, child-like voice.

I hadn't let go the mate's arm and went on shaking it. "Ready about, do you hear? You go forward"—shake—"and stop there"—shake—"and hold your noise"—shake—"and see these head-sheets properly overhauled"—shake, shake—shake. (p. 141) [9]

[9] E. Arthur Robinson has also observed this detail, in an excellent note in *Explicator*, XVIII (February 1960), Item 28.

In this fusion of conscience and daring lies the secret of self-determination: the sails are properly raised before the breeze, the
ship is filled with "cheery cries," the mate assumes his proper
function of giving "various orders," and the Captain feels himself in "the perfect communion of a seaman with his first command" (p. 143). The "ideal conception of one's own personality
every man sets up for himself secretly" (p. 94), which the
narrator had meditated upon at the beginning of the story, is
neither the nautical priggishness of Captain Archbold nor the
uncontrolled impulse of a Leggatt, but something emerging from
their conflict and superseding both.

Two further aspects of "The Secret Sharer" deserve brief
attention, since they parallel important motifs in other works of
Conrad. There is, first of all, the use of a placid sea to symbolize
a state of rational self-confidence soon to be disrupted by a
submarine threat: ". . . a blue sea that itself looked solid, so still
and stable did it lie below my feet . . . the straight line of the
flat shore joined to the stable sea, edge to edge, with a perfect
and unmarked closeness, in one levelled floor half brown, half
blue under the enormous dome of the sky" (p. 91). The same
sort of description appears in the account of the *Patna*'s voyage
in *Lord Jim*, and is to reappear later in two semiallegorical short
stories, "Freya of the Seven Isles" and "The Tale." At the same
time, the Captain notices "a mysterious system of half-sub-
merged bamboo fences, incomprehensible in its division of the
domain of tropical fishes, and crazy of aspect" (p. 92), a line of
counterimagery which, in its primitive associations and lack of
conceptual form, looks ahead to the emergence of Leggatt
(whose remedy for his difficulties aboard the *Sephora* during the
storm, by the way, had been devised under the pressure of "a sea
gone mad!"—p. 124). Secondly, there is the curious epistemological hierarchy formed by the officers of the narrator's ship, beginning with the Captain's own final self-aware pragmatism at the
top and descending through the mere rationalism of the chief
mate (it is pure theory that convinces him at the end that the

ship is lost) to the scornful empiricism of the second mate. The chief mate, for example, undertakes to explain a mysterious fact by a priori processes: "As he used to say, he 'liked to account to himself' for practically everything that came in his way, down to a miserable scorpion he had found in his cabin a week before. The why and the wherefore of that scorpion—how it got on board and came to select his room rather than the pantry (which was a dark place and more what a scorpion would be partial to), and how on earth it managed to drown itself in the inkwell of his writing-desk—had exercised him infinitely" (p. 94). The second mate, on the other hand, is full of facts: in response to the chief mate's speculation that the *Sephora* was a "ship from home lately arrived" he replies, " 'That's so. . . . She draws over twenty feet. She's the Liverpool ship *Sephora* with a cargo of coal. Hundred and twenty-three days from Cardiff' " (p. 94). But both of these characters are subordinated to the Captain by story's end; and in this relationship the reader sees prefigured exactly the epistemological convictions articulated by *Chance*'s Marlow and built into the structure of *Victory*.

"A Smile of Fortune," which appears along with "The Secret Sharer" and "Freya of the Seven Isles" in *'Twixt Land and Sea*, is a half-hearted creative effort; but it is worth pausing to see even here Conrad's experimentation with rhetorical and symbolic devices that are to be brought into finished form in *Chance* and *Victory*. The story's narrator shares Marlow's later satirical tone and high diction: "In the instability of his emotions man resembles deplorably a monkey"; "Theirs was a callous, abominable, almost revolting, pertinacity" (p. 16); and so on. And he stands at the same distance from human misery: "I listened with horribly critical detachment to that service I had had to read myself, once or twice, over childlike men who had died at sea. . . . What was the use of asking Death where her sting was, before that small, dark hole in the ground?" (p. 16). But more interesting are some mild experiments with mythical imagery—

in this case not the Edenic overtones of *Chance* and *Victory*, but the Satanic undertones. The opening description of the ship's anchorage is Melvilleian: "Clouds swirled down the porphyry crags under which we lay. The rising wind made a great bullying noise amongst the naked spars, with interludes of sad moaning. . . . Ah, but it was an exasperating, weary, endless night, to be lying at anchor close under that black coast! The agitated water made snarling sounds all round the ship" (pp. 4–5). These demonic suggestions are extended through such words as "infernal" (p. 42), "satanic" (p. 82), and "furnace" (p. 67), all of which stand in opposition to the island's proud legend ("Pearl of the Ocean"), and help define the true nature of the "sacred business" (p. 50) that has brought the narrator to it. The title, "A Smile of Fortune," exploits this irony: a subterranean crop, potatoes, is finally forced into the hold of the narrator's ship and quite by accident brings him a tidy profit (" 'A wonderful piece of luck!' " cries the mate). *Victory*'s heavy animal metaphors are also anticipated, particularly in the cat and swine imagery used of Alfred Jacobus. Alice Jacobus, the issue of Alfred's compulsive sexual passion and the inspirer of similar feelings in the narrator, is also feline, and is reminiscent of Aissa, with her primitive innocence and supple sexuality and her "long eyes, a narrowed gleam of liquid white and intense motionless black, with their gaze so empty of thought" (p. 63). But none of these strains of meaning is developed enough to invite further analysis.

"Freya of the Seven Isles" is more exciting for the reader interested in Conrad's technical growth. Written during an interlude in his reworking of *Chance*, "Freya" is a companion piece to the longer work: a romantic allegory with strong pessimistic overtones and a pessimistic conclusion (so pessimistic, in fact, that one reader complained to Conrad that the story "gratuitously and intolerably" harrowed his feelings—p. x). Once again the narrator bears striking similarities to *Chance*'s Marlow, seeing a "crude and savage jesting" (p. 231) in "the common

cudgel-play of Fate" (p. 167), and even descending, like Marlow, to some disreputable puns: Nelson traveled the Eastern
Archipelago "in an eminently pacific way" (p. 147); ever since
Jasper Allen had bought his beautiful little ship, "his heart [had
been] in the brig" (p. 156); and so on. He stands at the same
tragicomic distance from his tale: the unfortunate Nelson is a
"comedy father" (p. 173). And he shows the same intellectual
pride and condescension—even remarking of Nelson at one
point, as Marlow might remark of Fyne, that "he was angry,
angry enough to achieve irony; yes . . . irony! Just a gleam of it"
(p. 200). In its allegory, however, "Freya" is even better developed than *Chance*. Freya Nelson (or Nielsen) stands at the apex
of a romantic triangle involving Jasper Allen, the resolute, sprite-
like lover; and Heemskirk, the sensual and devilish destroyer.
But to this conventional melodrama Conrad brings symbolic
modifications distinctly his own, and the result is a curious
mixture of Wagnerian romance and ironic analysis—with the
temperament and philosophic vision of the narrator set over
against an archetypal situation, as in *Chance*. Freya herself is a
principle of creativity, the model of female vigor and optimism,
and thus something of a divinity (" 'You Scandinavian Goddess
of Love!' " cries Heemskirk in his frustration—p. 195). Like
Lena near the end of *Victory*, Freya is seen in terms of statuary
imagery, her "beautiful white arms" held high and motionless as
she is admired by Allen and the skulking Heemskirk. As she
stands flinging kisses to Jasper, "the slowly ascending sun" brings
"the glory of colour to the world, turning the islets green, the sea
blue, the brig below her white"; and at each kiss she murmurs
"with a rising inflexion: 'Take this—and this—and this' " (p.
204). This cosmic sexuality is not destined, however, for the
romantic Jasper, with whom Freya has planned an " 'ever after'
happiness" (p. 178); for in the offing is the "malevolent" (p.
159) Heemskirk, who represents a Satanic principle (old Nelson
must offer up bottles of his best claret "on the altar of concili-
ation"—p. 176) and in other ways anticipates the villains of

Victory. Like Schomberg, he works himself up into a "heavily breathing state of passion" (p. 181). Like Ricardo, he is a hissing sexual "tiger" whose "absolute stillness [is] impressive" (p. 187). Like the ape-man Pedro, he has a "straddling, broad figure" (p. 205). And like Jones, he prides himself on being a "gentleman" and a "man of family" (p. 195). Germinal experiments like this almost certainly enabled Conrad to arrive at his sharp symbolic analysis in *Victory*, just as analogous experiments in the political short stories had helped sharpen his political psychology in *The Secret Agent*. And certainly Flora de Barral—whose name, history, and symbolic function all bear close similarities to Freya's —must have profited from Conrad's having done this story. There are difficulties with the resolution of "Freya" (if such a bizarre story can be said to have a "resolution"). Freya's passivity and erotic postponement are viewed finally with self-reproach, instead of being integrated into her essential character, as in Flora's case; and her status as a fertility goddess interferes somewhat with Jasper's masculinity, giving the reader full license to speculate about Conrad's sexual powers (" 'If I had been a man I would have carried her off,' " the defeated Jasper confesses at story's end, " 'but she made a child, a happy child, of me' "—p. 236). "Freya" is a weirdly interesting exercise for the tolerant reader, however, and not at all devoid of its own special pleasures.

Two stories from *A Set of Six*, "The Duel" and "Il Conde," also deserve attention here. Together, they represent Conrad's first extended exercise in the ironic analysis of romantic clichés and stereotypes (excepting perhaps the autobiographical "Youth"), and thus help prepare both for the sharp Marlovian irony of *Chance* and for some of the comic elements of *Victory*, particularly in the treatment of Axel Heyst. Caution is required, of course, in identifying lines of growth, since any novelist's techniques are likely to have a highly personal stamp which will create parallels among his works. But not until "The Duel" and

"Il Conde" did Conrad begin to exploit the combination of pathos and intellectually distant irony that gives *Chance* its peculiar flavor, and, in gentler and more carefully transmuted form, establishes the emotional tone of *Victory*. And both these stories prefigure some of *Victory*'s symbolic characterization.

"The Duel" tells of an "affair" between the French officers D'Hubert and Feraud, a matter of honor which originates absurdly in the sanguine temper of Feraud and pursues the two through sixteen years of bloody Napoleonic history; and the tale is developed with all the relish Conrad could bring to the examination of high moral folly. Nevertheless, whether because of his own romantic respect for the Napoleonic past, or because of his affection for any sort of steadfastness in a spiritual cause, Conrad retains a clear sense of the humanity of both Feraud and D'Hubert. This sympathetic overtone of Conrad's irony is perhaps most noticeable near the beginning of the story, when the supports of cliché are first being removed from under the reader's romantic expectations. Faced with Feraud's first "mad declaration" of intent ("I mean to cut off your ears to teach you to disturb me with the general's orders when I am talking to a lady!"), D'Hubert suddenly becomes aware of "the little birds singing sanely in the garden" (pp. 175–176); and the witnesses of their first encounter confirm this suggestion of wild irrationality: the old lady "projected out of a window upstairs," waving her arms and scolding "in a cracked voice"; and the gardener, with his "toothless mouth" and "idiotic astonishment" (p. 179). Presently Feraud, who has suffered the first fall, has a chance to reconsider: "Lieut. Feraud had raised himself on his good arm. He was looking sleepily at his other arm, at the mess of blood on his uniform, at a small red pool on the ground, at his sabre lying a foot away on the path. Then he laid himself down gently again to think it all out, as far as a thundering headache would permit of mental operations" (p. 183). Feraud does not desist, however; and the duelists pursue their mad (and ultimately legendary) affair through a series of meetings with swords, sabres, and pistols, on foot and even on horseback. The end comes finally in a farcical confrontation in a secluded wood, in which the strategist D'Hubert emerges victorious through a combination of accident, instinct, and mutual misapprehension. Despite its redundancy, "The Duel" for the most part will bear the close scrutiny of scene and dialogue that Conrad's fiction usually does not invite; and his high ironic diction in dealing with the duelists is a continual pleasure.

"The Duel" also anticipates some of *Victory*'s most important symbolic motifs. The opposition between Feraud and D'Hubert, for example, bears a similarity to the later oppositions between Jasper Allen and Heemskirk and between Heyst and the Jones gang. Feraud is dark, hirsute, and Southern, the embodiment of sheer impulse and fierce absurd aggression. Like Alice Jacobus and Heemskirk and Ricardo, he is compared to a giant cat; and like Mr. Jones, he is inclined grotesquely to invert normal values: "The horrible view of a world at peace . . . frightened him" (p. 230). On the other side, D'Hubert is faintly Heyst-like: "Rejected by his old friends, and mistrusting profoundly the advances of Royalist society, the young and handsome general (he was barely forty) adopted a manner of cold, punctilious courtesy, which at the merest shadow of an intended slight passed easily into harsh haughtiness" (pp. 221–222). Like Heyst, D'Hubert has a high fair brow and blue eyes that turn cold and brittle in response to an indelicacy or an insult. And like Heyst, he is forced to contend with an aggressive force from which he would rather just dissociate himself. It is doubtful that Conrad consciously modeled Heyst on any previous character, but experiments like these probably helped him achieve *Victory*'s clarity of characterization.

For present purposes, the chief interest of "Il Conde" is in its central character, the old Count of the title, who is a clearer forerunner of Heyst even than D'Hubert. The Count is less isolated and of a lesser stature than the Baron of *Victory*, but in his personal characteristics and his central moral recognition he is much like Heyst. His white hair, "brushed upwards off a lofty forehead," gives him "the air of an idealist, of an imaginative man." His moustache is "carefully trimmed and arranged" (p. 270). Like Heyst, he is "a man of the world" (p. 269) and a lover of good books, but essentially a transient who had never had "any grave affairs to attend to in his life" (p. 272). And like Heyst, he suffers an external challenge from the world and an internal challenge from his own nature that both enlighten and destroy him. The Young *Cavaliere* who robs the Count of his money and his delicate illusions looks ahead sharply to *Victory's* villains. Like Mr. Jones, the *Cavaliere* sits "moodily" in an attitude of "peevish discontent" (p. 278); and at one point is seen in Jones's posture of a draped skeleton: "his legs stretched out, his arms folded and his head drooping on his breast" (p. 279). His weapon, "a long narrow blade"; his gnashing white teeth and "leering" eyes (p. 278); and his air of general "ferocity" (p. 280) suggest Ricardo. And in the face of the *Cavaliere's* hissing demands, the old Count finds distinctly Heystian reasons for nonresistance, or at best passive resistance. In the end, he is fully aware that his loss has been a spiritual one: "He was shocked at being the selected victim, not of robbery so much as of contempt. His tranquillity had been wantonly desecrated. His lifelong, kindly nicety of outlook had been defaced" (p. 284). And the ultimate result is for him, as for Heyst, a kind of self-immolation in the name of honor. In each instance, the Count's lineaments are softer and his responses more effete than Heyst's; his antagonist is less complex, and his experience of disillusionment and self-recognition less severe. But these are matters of degree. With the antagonists of "Il Conde," the metaphysical interests of *Chance,* and the conscious allegorical methods of "Freya of the Seven Isles" and other stories of this period, Conrad had begun to assemble the ingredients of *Victory*.

One more volume of short stories intervenes between *Under Western Eyes* and *Victory*, however; and these stories too need to be taken into account to see the genesis of the later novels. Although *Within the Tides* was not published until 1915, everything in it except "The Planter of Malata" had been written before *Chance*; and "The Planter of Malata" was done during a break in *Victory*. None of these stories excites much sustained interest, but in each of them Conrad moves in some explicit way toward the techniques of *Chance* and *Victory*. The epigraph to *Within the Tides*, Hamlet's command to the Players to "Go, make you ready," reflects Conrad's growing concern with the conscious artifices of his fiction; and it is useful to identify, if possible, the specific elements which help prepare the way for his later work.

"The Inn of the Two Witches" and "The Partner," two pieces of small virtue, can be dealt with summarily. Both touch upon the characteristic symbolic opposition in Conrad's fiction of this period, the romantic or isolated innocent in conflict with subterranean forces; and the occasional hell-and-devil imagery in each story relates it, however tenuously, to the central axes of Conrad's moral interests. Captain Harry of "The Partner" is undone by the "devil" in the persons of Stafford and Cloete; the witches of "The Inn" are, naturally enough, "affiliated to the devil" (p. 142), and house a female "child of Satan" (p. 149) who (like Alice Jacobus and Ricardo) displays the "sensual ferocity of a baffled cat" (p. 153). More importantly, both stories suggest some conscious experimentation with the later Marlovian point of view. The old stevedore who is the internal narrator of "The Partner" is, like the grounded bird Marlow, ideally equipped to tell his story of transactions between sea and shore; his professional viewpoint enables him to perceive both the amorality and greed of commercial motives and the simple goodness of the mariner. And the experiment Conrad makes with the old stevedore's syntax—in an effort, apparently, to find a way of suggesting the skeptical detachment which is later to characterize Marlow so strongly—is fascinating precisely because it is such a failure: "Without moving a muscle of his face he emitted a powerful 'Rot,' from somewhere out of the depths of his chest, and went on in his hoarse, fragmentary mumble. 'Stare at the silly rocks—nod their silly heads. . . . What do they think a man is—blown out paper bag or what?—go off pop like that when he's hit—— Damn silly yarn—— Hint indeed! . . . A lie?' " (pp. 90–91). Luckily, Conrad was able to try this device and find it wanting before coming to *Chance*. "The Inn of the Two Witches," on the other hand, achieves its skeptical distance (though perhaps "skeptical" is the wrong word for this odd little horror story) by more conventional Marlovian means: intellectualized irony, urbane diction, abstract psychological analysis, and the like. The story's protagonist is sent into terrain that gives him "the oppressive sense of an uninhabited world" (p. 146), and he suffers a nightmare experience with his murderous hostesses; but these devices are more like Poe's methods of bringing a rational narrative surface into tension with subrational forces than like anything else in Conrad. What is more interesting about the story is its concern, even in this unlikely context, with the narrator's sources of knowledge: he explains precisely the means by which he acquired the protagonist's written account of his adventure, justifies some of his information on the basis of "internal evidence" (p. 133), remarks that other facts "can be only inferred from the preserved scraps" (p. 134), and so on. There seems to be nothing about the subject of "The Inn of the Two Witches" which would invite Conrad's treating it in just this way—certainly he could not have hoped to persuade the reader of the story's veracity, as perhaps he did when he employed similar devices in *Under Western Eyes*—and the answer probably is simply that in "The Inn of the Two Witches" one of Conrad's deeply pressing interests emerged in spite of an incompatible subject and intention.

"Because of the Dollars" is a better story, and Conrad obviously had it in mind when he began *Victory*. Davidson appears in both, with the same Chinese employer and the same permission to deviate from his normal course to visit an isolated white man: "All right, Captain. You do what you like" (p. 174; cp. *Victory*, p. 30). Bamtz, the degraded drifter whom Davidson's humanity compels him to help, has certain superficial similarities to Heyst: "He had been known to loaf up and down the wilderness as far north as the Gulf of Tonkin" (p. 178), and had "vanished from Saigon" (p. 180) with a woman in distress after meeting her "in some low café" (p. 178). The woman, in turn, bears resemblances to Lena both as "a painted woman" (p. 184) and in her final self-sacrificing service to Davidson. Here Davidson himself prefigures Heyst; it is he who has the treasure and is attacked for it by a radically unrealistic triumvirate of evil: Fector, Niclaus, and the Frenchman. And it is interesting to see Conrad experiment in this story with a device for giving these villains symbolic universality that had appeared usefully in his earlier work, most notably in *Nostromo* and *The Secret Agent*. Fector, the English blackmailer, visits Niclaus and the Frenchman in a low hotel kept by "the usual sort of Portuguese and a very disreputable Chinaman"; and Niclaus is in turn a "nondescript beggar" with "a tartar moustache and a yellow complexion, like a Mongolian," who flies the Dutch flag from his Malay prau and speaks only English (p. 186). The greater symbolic scope of *Victory*, when compared with the political novels, is suggested in Conrad's dissatisfaction with this merely geographical way of universalizing his villains, and the more highly allegorical techniques he accordingly worked out for them in *Victory*. Bamtz, too, becomes analogous in the course of the story to one of *Victory's* villains: like Schomberg, he is pretentiously bearded, is forced to join the other villains through funk, and is betrayed by a dissimulating "wife" whose real loyalties lie elsewhere. In all these ways, "Because of the Dollars" explores moral and symbolic relationships which are to be developed more fully in *Victory*. And it is worth noting that Davidson is represented here as a "*really* good man" (p. 171), one whose "moral excellence" was "quietly appreciated by those who knew him well" (p. 175). Davidson's character may have changed between the story and the novel; but he is transplanted so nearly intact in other respects that the story probably may be taken as an external endorsement of his limited choric judgment in *Victory*.

"Because of the Dollars" also reminds the reader a little of *Chance*. Its internal narrator, Hollis, "a firm believer in the final value of shades" (p. 171) and a man of the Eastern world with "dark, keen eyes" (p. 172), is Marlow under another name, even to his interest in feminine physiognomy: "What I noticed under the superficial aspect of vapid sweetness," he says of Mrs. Davidson, "was her convex, obstinate forehead, and her small, red, pretty, ungenerous mouth" (p. 176). The murdering Frenchman of the story is finally laid low by "a chance shot" (p. 208); and Hollis explains the origin of the whole villainous plot as a matter of accident: "Accident, mere accident put in its work by providing a pair of fine ears close behind Davidson's chair" (p. 185). The story's relationships to *Victory*, however, are much more pronounced and significant.

The final story in *Within the Tides*—first in the volume, but last in order of composition—is a romantic curiosity called "The Planter of Malata," a work which has occasionally attracted favorable comment, but is marred by uncertainty of purpose and excesses of development. Its protagonist, Geoffrey Renouard, is again something like Heyst: a wanderer who had left school at an early age and had settled on a private island "after five strenuous years of adventure and exploration" (p. 5), and is now inclined to "a shrinking from contests with certain forms of vulgarity—like a man who would face a lion and go out of his way to avoid a toad" (p. 55). Like Heyst, he has chosen his isolation partly as a way of "holding aloof from these [urban] agglomerations of units in which one loses one's importance even to oneself" (p. 35). He is also a descendant of Stein, which gives him some further status in the pantheon of Conradian heroes: his "five-years' programme of scientific adventure, of work, of danger and endurance [had been] carried out with . . . distinction and rewarded modestly with the lease of Malata island" (p.

6), and he is engaged in developing a special kind of silk plant. But under the stress of his passion for Felicia Moorsom, Renouard's character begins to disintegrate; he undertakes behavior that would be unthinkable to Heyst, and finally sacrifices principle to his barely sublimated lust. Heyst would not likely take an "anguished tone" (p. 24) in conversation; nor would he "give the last shred of his rectitude" to secure an extra day of Felicia Moorsom's company (p. 56). And Renouard in love is perhaps the best evidence of all in support of Thomas Moser's theories: "Directly he saw her in the distance at the other end of the terrace he shuddered to the roots of his hair" (p. 30); "He fought down the impulse to seize her by the hand, lead her down into the garden away under the big trees, and throw himself at her feet uttering words of love" (p. 47); "He got down on his knees in silence, bent low to her very feet . . . [and] remained bowed to the ground pressing the hem of her skirt to his lips" (pp. 77–78). Under the circumstances, it would be unwise to lay too much stress on the similarities between Heyst and Renouard.

It is clearly Conrad's intention, however, to extend the story's scope by presenting Geoffrey and Felicia as figures more significant than mere lovers. Felicia Moorsom stands somewhere between Freya, the metaphysical sexpot of the earlier story, and the humbler figures of Flora de Barral and Lena. Felicia appears to Geoffrey as "a tragic Venus arising before him, not from the foam of the sea, but from a distant, still more formless, mysterious, and potent immensity of mankind" (p. 36)—a vision one step removed from Freya's direct creation of the sunrise, but probably still too close to raw mythology for Conrad's purposes. Felicia has a "pagan" head, "magnificently red" hair and "very black" eyes, and walks "as if she were restraining herself . . . with a rhythmic upward undulation of her whole figure" (p. 9). Like both Lena and Freya, she is seen in statuary images, coming to Geoffrey in a dream as a head with "marble hair . . . done in the bold lines of a helmet" (p. 31). Geoffrey's own meditative profile vaguely recalls "a Minerva's head" (p. 38), and on an-

other occasion "the profile of Pallas, still, austere" (p. 75).
Emerging together from the shadows, Geoffrey and Felicia seem
"statuesque in their calmness and in their pallor" (p. 50). When
at the end of the story the tormented Renouard tells Felicia,
" 'Felicia, a woman like you and a man like me do not often come
together on this earth' " (p. 75), the reader is prepared to agree.
But the basic trouble with "The Planter of Malata" is that
Conrad has chosen too explicitly sensual a figure to represent
Renouard's romantic commitment. The story is another of Conrad's attempts to bring into opposition the "crude impulses of old
humanity" (an expression recalling the evolutionary dimensions
of both "Heart of Darkness" and *Victory*) with the "mere pure
froth and bubble on the inscrutable depths" (p. 77). But Conrad
was unable in this instance to free his allegorical devices from
the fetishistic symbolism of his own unconscious conflicts. And
the difficulty is even greater in "The Planter of Malata" because
of his mixed intentions with respect to Felicia—she is seen on
the one hand as a " 'Divinity' " who is " 'the eternal love itself,' "
but on the other hand as a vain and fundamentally purposeless
creature who has " 'moved, breathed, existed, and even
triumphed in the mere smother and froth of life—the brilliant
froth,' " and whose " 'thoughts, sentiments, opinions, feelings,
actions too, are nothing but agitation in empty space—to amuse
life—a sort of superior debauchery, exciting and fatiguing,
meaning nothing, leading nowhere' " (pp. 40–41). Conrad's an-
tisocial attitudes have mixed here with his deeper purpose, and
Felicia emerges as an impossible contradiction. Conrad does
make some effort to reconcile these aspects of Felicia's personality, as in Geoffrey's tortured cry, " 'O Divinity, it isn't your body,
it is your soul that is made of foam' " (p. 77); and one might
conceivably work out some consistent set of meanings for the
tale. But as it stands, "The Planter of Malata" is opaque and
unintentionally comic.

With the exception of "The Secret Sharer," all the short
stories of Conrad's third period are artistically deficient. But at

the same time, Conrad was trying some difficult experiments here; and he was more consciously writing for money than ever before. His own sense of the stories' inadequacy is suggested in the fact that only one of them proliferated into a novel. To measure his true stature during these years we must look first at the novels, and then somehow account for the rest. And whatever the deficiencies of Conrad's later short stories, neither *Chance* nor *Victory* could have been written without Conrad's first having done them.

7

"After Stormie Seas"

When Paul Claudel first introduced the name Conrad to André Gide, Gide asked him what books of Conrad's he should read. "All of them," answered Claudel. The advice is still valuable. . . . The world is too poor, at the present moment, in writers who show us how it takes the whole strength and dedication of a lifetime to achieve literary endurance, to permit us to minimize Conrad's example.

—Morton Dauwen Zabel, in *The Portable Conrad*

Conrad's artistic growth ends with *Victory*. Having drawn together the lines of insight and technical invention that had begun with *Almayer's Folly* some two decades before, Conrad relaxed in the later work into a calmer and more empirical mood, as if aware that his finest achievements lay behind him. Some of the later fiction, like *The Shadow-Line* and *The Arrow of Gold*, is heavily autobiographical, as his earliest work had been; some of it, like *The Rescue* and *Suspense*, resumes creative projects postponed from earlier years. Despite their lessening of imaginative tension, however, these final works generally have more integrity than recent criticism has been willing to grant. Each of them shows Conrad's continuing use of the technical devices he had painfully evolved between *The Secret Agent* and *Victory*;

and each of them exhibits, in some mature and attractive form, the qualified spirit of affirmation that had gradually emerged in his work—a kind of existential pragmatism, lightly ironic, curious, appreciative of esthetic values. Thus, as in Conrad's first and second major periods, certain themes and techniques tend to perseverate beyond the major achievements of the period; and wherever this is true, the fiction has a special flavor for the admirer of Conrad.

The Shadow-Line needs no particular defense. A straightforward account of a young Captain's assumption of his first command, the story bears certain obvious similarities to "The Secret Sharer"; and some critics have even preferred it to the earlier story, on the ground of its greater concreteness and clarity. There are enough differences, however, to weaken any such comparison. Conrad describes The Shadow-Line as "personal experience seen in perspective with the eye of the mind and coloured by . . . affection" (p. vii), a formulation ruling out the allegorical depths of "The Secret Sharer." Conrad's purpose in The Shadow-Line is to recount his earlier experience in such a way that it may be seen as morally archetypal: "To Borys," the epigraph reads, "and all others who like himself have crossed in early youth the shadow-line of their generation." When the young Captain crosses his own shadow-line, he is suddenly projected into a primordial state of self-reliance: "Ransome stepped back two paces and vanished from my sight. At once an uneasiness possessed me, as if some support had been withdrawn. I moved forward too, outside the circle of light, into the darkness that stood in front of me like a wall. In one stride I penetrated it. Such must have been the darkness before creation. . . . I was alone, every man was alone where he stood" (pp. 112–113). But except for some metaphysical malice in the descriptive imagery and some unfocused anxiety on the Captain's part, the evils to be met aboard this ship are concretely identifiable—the tropical fever that attacks the crew, the mate's idée fixe about his dead

Captain, and so on. The story's psychology is clear and conscious, giving the reader an admirably detailed account of the Captain's state of awareness during his ordeal. His descriptions of the environment are interfused with his feelings and moral anxieties in a way worthy of a Marlow: "Mysterious currents drifted us here and there, with a stealthy power made manifest by the changing vistas of the islands. . . . And there were winds too, fitful and deceitful. They raised hopes only to dash them into the bitterest disappointment, promises of advance ending in lost ground, expiring in sighs, dying into dumb stillness in which the currents had it all their own way—all their own inimical way" (pp. 83–84). The story's central power, however, derives from certain elements of controlled simplicity: the clarity and coherence of its narrative line, for example, which stands over against the maturely reflective mind of the narrator; and the almost epigrammatic quality of some of its interpretative equipment: "I was like a mad carpenter making a box. Were he ever so convinced that he was King of Jerusalem, the box he would make would be a sane box" (p. 101). When these elements are added to Conrad's close control of symbolic description, the impression gained is one of disciplined nostalgia and psychological power.

The Shadow-Line also, however, extends some of the intellectual attitudes and symbolic methods Conrad had already worked out in his later fiction. His suggestion that the story is personal experience "seen in perspective with the eye of the mind" indicates this intellectualizing tendency. But even a reader who had not had this warning would be struck by the sharp Marlovian tone of the story's opening:

Only the young have such moments. I don't mean the very young. No. The very young have, properly speaking, no moments. It is the privilege of early youth to live in advance of its days in all the beautiful continuity of hope which knows no pauses and no introspection.

One closes behind one the little gate of mere boyishness—and

enters an enchanted garden [cp. *Chance* and *Victory*]. Its very
shades glow with promise. Every turn of the path has its seduction.
And it isn't because it is an undiscovered country. One knows well
enough that all mankind had streamed that way. It is the charm of
universal experience from which one expects an uncommon or personal sensation—a bit of one's own.

One goes on recognising the landmarks of the predecessors, ex-
cited, amused, taking the hard luck and the good luck together . . .
till one perceives ahead a shadow-line warning one that the region of
early youth, too, must be left behind. (p. 3)

The repeated negatives and universal propositions in this passage
give *The Shadow-Line* a didactic tone which is never quite lost;
and in the narrator's easy references to the "enchanted garden"
and "the hard luck and the good luck" the motifs of the later
fiction are implicitly at work, modifying a direct personal experience. There is some of the diction used in *Chance* and other
works for esthetic distancing: "evil spell" (p. 83), "bewitched"
(p. 84), and the like. There is even one passage which so closely
duplicates a similar passage in *Chance* (quoted above) that it
suggests Conrad was thinking of *Chance* when he wrote it: "My
sensations could not be like those of any other man on board.
In that community I stood, like a king in his country, in a class all
by myself. I mean an hereditary king, not a mere elected head of
a state. I was brought there to rule by an agency as remote from
the people and as inscrutable almost to them as the Grace of
God" (p. 62). Sometimes this consciously archetypal overtone
introduces an unpleasant dissonance, as when the narrator com-
pares Captain Ellis, the Harbour-Master, to "a fierce sort of
fairy," or likens himself to Cinderella (p. 40). But on the whole,
allusions of this sort are well under control, and give the story a
pleasant ironic flavor.

The most important aspect of the story's method, however, is
the persistent element of psychological analysis, undertaken not
from the standpoint of the youthful protagonist, but from the

standpoint of the mature narrator. The descriptions of the steward as a person of "gratuitous impertinence" (p. 10), or of
Captain Giles as a man "possessed of a deeper philosophy" (p.
14), or of Captain Ellis as an "inquisitorial and peremptory"
man who was "redoubtable, not in virtue of his office, but because of his unwarrantable assumptions" (p. 30), must necessarily be assigned to the older man. But the narrator habitually
breaks down this distinction, so that the reader encounters passages of refined dialogue or monologue on the part of the young
protagonist: passages which are actually a combination of the
young man's perceptions with the older man's reflective mentality. When the young Captain first sits in his new chair, a
"composite soul, the soul of command" seems to whisper to him:
" 'You, too!' it seemed to say, 'you, too, shall taste of that peace
and that unrest in a searching intimacy with your own self—obscure as we were and as supreme in the fact of all the winds and
all the seas, in an immensity that receives no impress, preserves
no memories, and keeps no reckoning of lives' " (p. 53). This is
an unlikely hallucination for the young man who shortly before
had found it impossible to perceive what the rather simple Captain Giles was trying to tell him. The protagonist's character at
the beginning is one of self-righteous innocence (an instance of
Conrad's retrospective irony at his own expense), and it is thoroughly inconsistent with the subtle interpretations of his experience provided by the narrator. Conrad is not concerned much to
preserve the distinction—even the young Captain's diary, supposedly transcribed directly, shows a maturity and an intellectual
grasp which were supposedly beyond him at that stage. This
fusion of psychological report and *post hoc* meditation removes
the story from the level of hard realism to which it has sometimes
been assigned. Conrad points out as much: "The effect of perspective in memory is to make things loom large because the
essentials stand out isolated from their surroundings of insignificant daily facts" (p. vii). Conrad returns to autobiography in

The Shadow-Line, but it is autobiography transmuted into moral archetype by the narrative methods of his later work.[1]

To see this point with respect to *The Shadow-Line* prepares the reader to view *The Arrow of Gold* with more sympathy and comprehension, I think, than most recent writers have brought to it. From the technical standpoint alone, *The Arrow of Gold* represents an advance over *The Shadow-Line.* Conrad is undeniably better at sea than in a drawing-room. But *The Arrow of Gold,* which also takes a retrospective view of a part of Conrad's own life, more successfully exploits the devices which can give depth and subtlety to such a narrative. The similarity of purpose between these two works is suggested by Conrad's remark that *The Arrow of Gold* is a "story of young, very young love told with a depth of emotion pointing to experience";[2] and the suggestion is confirmed by his bracketing the story between two "Notes" which project it into the past and bring it under the scrutiny of a mature intelligence. Much of the novel's strangeness is traceable to this point of view, particularly to the narrator's practice of fusing his mature reflection with the direct record of events. Like *The Shadow-Line, The Arrow of Gold* sets out to heighten Conrad's private experience so that it may be seen as archetypal. M. George's adventure "might have happened anywhere" (p. 4); and in the elusive Rita is " 'something of the women of all time' " (p. 28), an "indefinable quality of charm beyond all analysis [which] made you think of remote races, of strange generations, of the faces of women sculptured on immemorial monuments and of those lying unsung in their

[1] Sherry, *Conrad's Eastern World,* pp. 211–249, offers an exhaustive study of the extent to which *The Shadow-Line* is and is not "exact autobiography." A careful effort to account for all the differences between fact and fiction in this case might tell us a great deal about Conrad's later methods.

[2] Aubry, *Life and Letters,* II, p. 224.

tombs" (pp. 66–67). Just as Heyst is a descendant of Geoffrey Renouard and other characters in the earlier fiction, so Rita is a descendant of Freya and Felicia Moorsom, even to her luxuriant rust-colored hair, penetrated by the phallic Arrow of Gold. Rita is identified with a "fleshy and very much foreshortened goddess . . . in the Italian style" (p. 17), with Cleopatra and La Vallière (p. 24), with a Byzantine Empress (p. 28), and with a wide range of other highly sensual females—a process which George sums up, finally, in his recognition that "the Rita that haunted me had no history; she was but the principle of life charged with fatality" (p. 268). The continual use of highly intellectualized symbols, especially of an exotic cast, is a striking feature of *The Arrow of Gold*; and it is again reinforced by some elegant psychologizing. At the beginning of his affair, for example, M. George is "inconceivably young—still beautifully unthinking—infinitely receptive" (p. 8); he represents "a perfect freshness of sensations and a refreshing ignorance" (p. 31). As in *The Shadow-Line*, these phrases force the reader to dissociate protagonist from narrator, especially in view of sophisticated, Jamesian passages like the following: "That woman was revealed to me young, younger than anybody I had ever seen, as young as myself (and my sensation of my youth was then very acute); revealed with something peculiarly intimate in the conviction, as if she were young exactly in the same way in which I felt myself young; and that therefore no misunderstanding between us was possible" (p. 70). The older narrator occasionally acknowledges the difference: "The years have chilled the blood without dimming the memory" (p. 125). The fantastically involuted dialogue George enters into with Rita, his complicated psychological insights, his introspective self-awareness at moments of crisis, and so on, all must be understood as the narrator's articulation of feelings and intuitions which in the younger man would have been half-conscious at best. There is a question, of course, how much of this fusion of mature intellect with the innocent experience of the younger man is intentional, and how much acciden-

tal. But it is worth noticing that in the narrator's transcription of
M. George's diary, he makes no pretense of an exact copy, as the
narrator of *The Shadow-Line* had, instead permitting the temporal reference point and verb tenses to shift as convenience
dictates, so that the diary is clearly a joint creation of the older
and the younger man.

There is still another sense in which *The Arrow of Gold*
extends the technical methods evolved in the earlier fiction. It
has sometimes been charged that the novel lacks form. But *The
Arrow of Gold* is in fact structured along lines analogous to those
of *Victory,* and thus exploits one of Conrad's most effective
devices for dramatizing the process of moral discovery. As Conrad suggests, the novel's central subject is M. George's "initiation
(through an ordeal which required some resolution to face) into
the life of passion" (p. ix). From a starting point of mere
historical circumstance, the reader is led through an outer periphery of more-or-less reliable reports about the legendary Rita
de Lastaola toward the woman herself, and finally, at the novel's
end, to the consummation of George's passion; a process strictly
analogous to the movement from the outer narrator in *Victory* to
Davidson and then to Heyst himself. "For me," the narrator says
in the first paragraph of his story, "[the Cannebière] has been a
street leading into the unknown" (p. 7); and it leads M. George
through a series of strangely disturbing experiences toward an
unsuspected core of passion. (There is even a note of similarity
here between the Cannebière and Marlow's river.) From his
vision of the pink tongue of the figure of Night in the opening
carnival scene, to his shock at the moral realities revealed in the
conversation of Blunt and Mills, to an "obscure premonition" (p.
19) of significant experience to come, George moves steadily
toward his union with Rita: first merely hearing about her from
Blunt and Mills, then joining her guests, then engaging her in
private conversation in a social setting, then in conversation
alone, through stages of greater and greater intimacy, until at the
very end of the novel his perception of her is supraliterary and

necessarily brings the tale to a close: " 'Speak no words of love,
George! . . . I shall seal your lips with the thing itself' " (p.
336). Along the way George encounters slander, blackmail, jealousy, and the like; and even receives a rough sexual education
from the redoubtable Dominic. Occasionally, George's disillusionment takes a delicate and surprising form, as when Mills, in
the midst of a discussion of costly *objets d'art,* tosses "down his
throat some wine out of a Venetian goblet" (p. 22); or when
George, near the end of the novel and the final consummation of
his love for Rita, is forced to encounter the sexual demon of her
agrarian past—one Señor Ortega, who knew Rita when she
herded goats and now invisibly pounds and clamors to be let into
her room. The repressed Ortega burns out all his energy in this
wild behavior and then accidentally injures himself with his own
monstrously phallic weapon, taken straight from the Heart of
Darkness: "an Abyssinian or Nubian production of a bizarre
shape; the clumsiest thing imaginable, partaking of a sickle and a
chopper with a sharp and a pointed end" (p. 325). George's
romantic clichés and vague perceptions are elements of just that
chivalric innocence his experience is designed to destroy; and the
book's esthetic clutter is there partly to stand in tension with the
clearer truths he is to discover by the end. In the novel's final
scenes he begins to reach toward an "assurance" (p. 307) and
"authority" (p. 329) in his dealings with Rita, and is ready to
be freed. The novel releases him through a mechanism remarkably like the mechanism at the end of *Victory* that releases the
reader from the catharsis of Samburan: in *Victory* the reader
passes quickly backward through the stages of his original approach to the island, from Davidson back to the outer narrator; in
The Arrow of Gold, George is returned to normalcy through a
violent meeting with Blunt and then a quieter meeting with
Mills, who had been his original point of contact with Rita and
the Carlist intrigue. (This is one reason why Mills, like Davidson, must be left behind as the novel develops.) *The Arrow of
Gold* has its defects, but a broad lack of structure is not one of

them; and criticism of this novel on the whole has not analyzed Conrad's intentions or techniques sufficiently to isolate those defects.

The Rover—Conrad's last completed novel—is superficially less complex than The Shadow-Line and The Arrow of Gold. Its narrative thread seems simply a romantic adventure tale, reflecting Conrad's calmness of spirit and his interest in French history. But behind this simple surface lies a highly personal allegory—personal not in the sense that it reflects the events of Conrad's own life, but rather that it expresses in simple and final form the existential affirmation that had been at the root of Conrad's fiction from the beginning. The Rover is a resigned and yet stoically optimistic book, and much of its charm proceeds from this calm resignation.

There is little doubt that Conrad's artistic judgment had deteriorated by the time of The Rover. He seems no longer to be able to hear the characteristic rhythms of English and of his own earlier idiomatic style, and it is easy to point to tasteless metaphors and syntactical errors. At the same time, some of the technical features which have seemed weaknesses may actually be organic to Conrad's later attitude: the angular syntax, the absence of a militant motive toward originality (a willingness to use clichés, for example, with only the faintest irony), and the gently undercut romanticism of the later fiction may amount to a subtle affirmation of human community—the same commitment which, seen earlier in a more defensive and energetically moralistic way, had helped define the assumptions of works like Lord Jim and The Secret Agent. In its humility of diction, The Rover even approaches the stoical immediacy of a Hemingway or Camus: "The whole neck of land was so low that it seemed to have no more thickness than a sheet of paper laid on the sea. Citizen Peyrol saw on the level of his eye, as if from a mere raft, sails of various craft, some white and some brown, while before him his native island of Porquerolles rose dull and solid beyond a wide strip of water" (p. 15). The whole question of Conrad's later style is a difficult one, and must be approached first of all in the context of his later artistic aims.[3]

Perhaps the first thing to notice, in relating *The Rover* to the other work of Conrad's third period, is a similarity between Heyst and old Peyrol. Peyrol is "tired of rolling about the seas" and longs for "a period of repose on shore" (p. 3). Like Heyst, he is scornfully antipolitical, able to observe the irony in "Immortal Principles causing the death of many people" (p. 25) and to dissociate himself bluntly from the "'damned nonsense'" of revolutionary jargon (p. 22). (Scevola, a bloodthirsty relic of the revolution, is on the other hand a distinct echo of the anarchist Professor: "There was a time when civic virtue flourished," he tells Peyrol, "but now it has got to hide its head. And I will tell you why: there has not been enough killing"—p. 27.) Again like Heyst, Peyrol is projected from detachment into action by an irresistible claim on behalf of "life" and "love," as represented in Lieutenant Réal and Arlette. Arlette is the final type of Conrad's long line of love goddesses and metaphysical seductresses, and

[3] As Guerard and others have noted, this problem is complicated by the necessity of dictation imposed on Conrad in his later years. Moser discounts this, pointing to Henry James as proof that dictating novels need have no ill effect. But for James, a gregarious man and polished conversationalist whose first language was English, oral composition no doubt came more easily. And in his letters Conrad does complain both about the haphazard process of proofreading and about his secretary's introduction of errors into his manuscripts. Moreover, some of the unconventional syntax and grammar in Conrad's later work seems to be the result of conscious experiment. Some of it appears influenced by James; some of it, like the missing "and" in the first sentence of *The Rover,* appears in positions of such high emphasis it is unlikely Conrad would simply overlook it. It has even been suggested that some of *The Rover*'s syntactical difficulties represent a purposely unidiomatic translation from the French. In any case, it is probably too extreme to find "sheer mechanical faultiness," "slovenliness," "simple clumsiness," and "downright gibberish," as Thomas Moser does in *Joseph Conrad: Achievement and Decline* (Cambridge: Harvard University Press, 1957), pp. 193 ff.

Réal the final type of his proud romantic heroes. The wanderer Peyrol, returning to the place of his earliest memories to re-establish his roots, becomes a symbolic father for Arlette, drawing her out of the terrified silence that had held her captive since the bloody destruction of her parents; and Catherine, the virginal aunt who had cared for Arlette, joins Peyrol in this symbolic parenthood. This motif is only gently developed, but it shows a surprising subtlety: the very notion of setting the morally heroic but infertile Peyrol and Catherine over against the young lovers, as a way of heightening Peyrol's obligation to sacrifice himself by taking over Réal's suicidal mission, is itself a piece of symbolic delicacy. Arlette and Réal are gradually given special allegoric status, she in her growing awareness of an "instinctive seduction" (p. 175) and "strength" (p. 176), he in his "sense of remoteness from ordinary mankind" (p. 209); and they emerge finally from a rainstorm which is like "the beginning of a destroying and universal deluge" (p. 248)—Arlette to follow Réal "to the end of the world" (p. 258) and he to revel in "the sense of triumphant life" she has brought to him (p. 260). Meanwhile, Peyrol has freed Arlette of the outworn terror of her past by the simple expedient of taking Scevola along as an unwilling passenger on his suicidal mission. Peyrol and his "crew," Michel, form a kind of human continuum in their final commitment: Peyrol stands at the head of the symbolic universe in *The Rover*, and Michel has long since accepted "his own insignificant position at the tail of all mankind," since " 'somebody must be last in this world' " (p. 253). Finally, Lieutenant Réal, in his own way, duplicates the personal history of Peyrol and seeks finally the same quietude that Peyrol had sought at the beginning of the novel: "Lieutenant Réal, wounded at Trafalgar . . . retired with the rank of Capitaine de Frégate and vanished from the eyes of . . . the world altogether. Whatever sign brought him back to Escampobar on that momentous night, was not meant to call him to his death but to a quiet and retired life, obscure in a sense but not devoid of dignity" (p. 283). *The Rover* thus ends as *Chance* had, with a symbolic parallel suggesting the renewed energies of life even in the face of self-destructive moral necessities.

In an excellent article, Elizabeth Cox Wright has pointed out other aspects of this allegorical structure. As she observes, the style of the novel moves away from the factual precision of the opening passages toward an "intermingling of fact and suggestion"; and as these symbolic and interpretative overtones accumulate, Peyrol himself awakens to his responsibility, becoming aware finally of "the certainty of his achievement and the inevitability of his death" [4]—features which make *The Rover* look even more like *Victory*. But Peyrol, who clearly represents Conrad in his final moral attitudes, is a more relaxed and seasoned Heyst, with "a fund of self-command amounting to placidity" (p. 33). Lieutenant Réal is "daunted by Peyrol's mildness. . . . Even physically he had an impression of the utter futility of his effort, as though he had tried to shake a rock" (p. 67). And Peyrol's reserve is thoroughly self-aware; at work fitting out his tartane, he recognizes the ultimate purposelessness of his chore: "This congenial task had all the air of preparation for a voyage, which was a pleasing dream, and it brought every evening the satisfaction of something achieved to that illusory end" (pp. 87–88). Passages like this give the tartane's suicidal mission a kind of metaphysical pathos. And when Peyrol's final commitment is seen against the background of his own sexual interplay with Arlette, his "quiet vitality," and his "robust personality . . . antagonistic to the notion of death" (p. 72), the novel's pathos comes as close to tragedy as it can, under the terms of Conrad's existential commitments. Conrad's final moral affirmation has been severely tested, and the record of that testing is preserved implicitly in *The Rover,* just as it had been declared more rhetorically in *Chance* and recorded symbolically in *Victory*. If the epigraph from Spenser—"Sleep after toyle, port after

---

[4] Elizabeth Cox Wright, "The Defining Function of Vocabulary in Conrad's *The Rover*," *South Atlantic Quarterly,* LIX (Spring 1960), pp. 271, 266–267.

stormie seas,/ Ease after warre, death after life, does greatly please"—is taken too sentimentally, so that Peyrol is seen as a mere seeker of peace, both Conrad and his novel are done an immense disservice.

In a moving and poignant little story entitled simply "The Tale," published in 1917 and included in the posthumous *Tales of Hearsay*, Conrad's autobiographical interests and allegorical techniques fuse completely for the first and only time; and the story serves as a fitting climax to an account of his artistic growth. The story's frame is simple: the Captain of a man-of-war, home on five days' leave, tells his woman a personal parable as she reclines wearily in a room filling gradually with "the irresistible tide of the night" (p. 59). " 'Tell me something,' " she commands.

"You used to tell—your—your simple and—and professional—tales very well at one time. Or well enough to interest me. You had a—a sort of art—in the days—the days before the war."

. . . . .

"It could be a tale not of this world," she explained.

"You want a tale of the other, the better world?" he asked, with a matter-of-fact surprise. "You must evoke for that task those who have already gone there."

"No, I don't mean that. I mean another—some other—world. In the universe—not in heaven."

. . . . .

"As you will. In that world, then, there was once upon a time a Commanding Officer and a Northman. Put in the capitals, please, because they had no other names. It was a world of seas and continents and islands——"

"Like the earth," she murmured, bitterly.

"Yes. What else could you expect from sending a man made of our common, tormented clay on a voyage of discovery? What else could he find? What else could you understand or care for, or feel the existence of even?" (pp. 60–61)

The Captain's abrupt questions reaffirm Conrad's hard existential awareness, and his "world" is like the world of *Chance*'s Marlow:

"There was comedy in it, and slaughter."

"Always like the earth," she murmured.

"Always. And since I could find in the universe only what was deeply rooted in the fibres of my being there was love in it, too. But we won't talk of that."

"No. We won't," she said, in a neutral tone which concealed perfectly her relief—or her disappointment. Then after a pause she added: "It's going to be a comic story."

"Well——" he paused, too. "Yes. In a way. In a very grim way. It will be human, and, as you know, comedy is but a matter of the visual angle." (pp. 61–62)

The tale the Captain finally tells, however, is comic only in the highest and grimmest philosophic sense—a measure of the extraordinary detachment and depth of Conrad's final "affirmation." The Commanding Officer of the tale is sent out "along certain coasts to see—what he could see" (p. 63). (The reader remembers here the Preface to the *Nigger*: "The Tale" is an allegory of Conrad's esthetics, as well as of his moral affirmation.) But the Commanding Officer knows that his "preliminary information" is "about as useful as information trying to convey the locality and intentions of a cloud, of a phantom taking shape here and there and impossible to seize, would have been" (p. 63). And as in the earlier work, this problem of knowledge rests on a metaphysical uncertainty: " 'What at first used to amaze the Commanding Officer was the unchanged face of the waters, with its familiar expression, neither more friendly nor more hostile. . . . It is impossible to believe that the familiar clear horizon traces the limit of one great circular ambush' " (p. 63). Like Jim aboard the *Patna* and the narrator of "The Secret Sharer," however, the Commanding Officer encounters a submarine threat which makes him "believe." And in opposing this threat—in following Stein's pragmatic dictum that the destructive element must be made to keep him up—the commander is faced with an impossible moral test. Moving into a cove to wait through a thick fog, he discovers a neutralist ship which he suspects of helping to replenish the stores of enemy submarines at sea. There is little direct evidence for his suspicion; but the apparent attempt of the neutral to lie quietly in the fog, unseen by the man-of-war; the drunken bravado of its Captain; and the uniformity of its crew's responses all reinforce the commander's conviction that he is faced with a lie. Uncertain whether he is about to " 'litter the bed of the unreadable sea [with] the bodies of men completely innocent or basely guilty,' " he nevertheless orders the steamer to leave on a course which he knows will lead it straight onto a deadly reef. In this decision, and in the commander's grim awareness that he will never know the truth, lies the full extent of Conrad's final affirmation. If the commander, like Conrad himself, can still find meaning in the "gospel" of "sincerity—frankness—passion" (p. 64), and "an infinity of absolution" in the word "duty" (p. 61), it is only from a profound conviction of the significance of mankind even in an enigmatic universe.

"Achievement and Decline":
A Bibliographical Note

The idea of Conrad's achievement and decline was first developed at length in Douglas Hewitt's *Conrad: A Reassessment* (Cambridge: Bowes and Bowes, 1952), and received its chief impetus from Thomas Moser's *Joseph Conrad: Achievement and Decline* (Cambridge: Harvard University Press, 1957) and Albert J. Guerard's *Conrad the Novelist* (Cambridge: Harvard University Press, 1958). These valuable critical works have recently been buttressed by Bernard C. Meyer, M.D., *Joseph Conrad: A Psychoanalytic Biography* (Princeton: Princeton University Press, 1967). The notion had been suggested as early as 1927, however, in John Galsworthy's "Reminiscences of Conrad," in *Castles in Spain and Other Screeds* (New York: Scribners, 1927); and Vernon Young had anticipated most of the argument, including the Moser-Meyer analysis of Conrad's misogyny, in "Joseph Conrad: Outline for a Reconsideration," *Hudson Review*, II (Spring 1949), 5–19.

Hewitt, who dates Conrad's decline from the end of 1909 (when he had just finished "The Secret Sharer"), believes that at that point Conrad "started to suppress those aspects of his sensibility which give value to such works as 'Heart of Darkness,' 'Falk,' *Nostromo, The Secret Agent,* 'The End of the Tether,' *Lord Jim* and 'The Secret Sharer.' It is strange that Conrad . . . should in the latter part of his life have written so much which obscures the valuable qualities of his early works. . . . I [have been] forced to the conclusion that, despite his conscious attention to his craft, he was—particularly after the deterioration set in—far less aware of his real powers than one would expect" (p. 4). In the later works Conrad represses his earlier high awareness of human complexity, and more specifically of "the darker side of even our good feelings"—an "evasion" which accounts for the "obvious flaws" in a novel like *Chance:* "its clichés, its defensive irony, its imprecise rhetoric" (p. 89), and so on. The later fiction is populated with characters who are either all good or all bad, and as a result is marred by a sentimental tone and melodramatic structure. Conrad's sense of evil returned to the depths with Leggatt, never to reappear in the same form: "There seems to have been within him a continual war between the recognition of the 'heart of darkness' and the desire to rest securely on unquestioned values. His letters tend to show that the desire for security was the more conscious, but in the best of the early works the 'other self' cannot be denied. . . . With 'The Secret Sharer' Conrad seems to resolve this conflict for his peace of mind, and we must now consider the works which follow it" (p. 79). Of all these later works, only *The Shadow-Line,* in Hewitt's view, is free "from all the flaws of lush rhetoric and moralizing which disfigure the others" (p. 112).

Moser's chief purpose is not so much to establish Conrad's decline (which he sees as beginning a little later, with *Chance* in 1912), as to explain it. To do this, he adds a psychoanalytic dimension to Hewitt's theory. At the same time that Conrad was "turning his back on moral judgment" (p. 130), Moser tells us, he was also devoting himself to a subject he secretly feared and therefore could not successfully dramatize—namely, love: "Conrad's decision to finish *Chance* determined his decline. In his early major period, he had, as we have seen, either evaded love or subordinated it to other subjects. *Chance* has love for its central subject, as do *Victory, The Arrow of Gold, The Rescue, The Rover,* and the unfinished *Suspense.* Of the later novels, only *The Shadow-Line* does not deal with love. Such a radical shift in subject naturally raises the unanswerable question: why? Why did Conrad cease those explorations into moral failure in the masculine world that had enabled him to achieve artistic success?" (p. 102). Besides sharing Hewitt's view of the moral tone and technique of the later works, Moser holds that "love," as it appears in these works, is essentially destructive: "The world is full of evil, except in certain characters whom Conrad likes," and the greatest good for these "figures of purity afflicted by an external evil" is to "lose themselves in a love that will blot out all awareness of the world and bring the semblance of death" (pp. 141, 143). Moser points to a variety of evidence in Conrad's fiction—the absence of children borne from his love affairs and marriages, the paucity of dramatic give-and-take between his lovers, the persistence of threatening imagery in his sexual scenes, and so on—to show that Conrad could not really face up to his subject.

Guerard accepts the broad outlines of the Hewitt-Moser view. But his chief purpose is to provide detailed readings of Conrad's best fiction; he therefore spends less time analyzing Conrad's failures, and his explanation of the "decline" is more cautious: "Is the uncongeniality of love as a subject, and Conrad's later determination to present it 'affirmatively,' the most important cause of his serious anticlimax, as Moser affirms? Perhaps. I should insist more than he does, however, on the understandable exhaustion following upon the astonishing creative labors of 1894–1903, on the turn to European settings and a more conventional realistic manner, above all on the effects of dictation. But I could not agree more warmly that the best work of Conrad is the work of a tragic pessimist, concerned with other kinds of masculine failure than sexual" (p. 55). Like other readers who find an achievement and decline in Conrad, Guerard objects to the apparent lack of psychological and moral complexity in his later work; and he finds the later style too rhetorical, too sentimental, and too often faulty in syntax and grammar—characteristics which, along with the relative frequency of Gallicisms in the later prose, are taken as evidence of Conrad's flagging energies.

Meyer's volume is the final product of a series of articles in psychiatric and literary journals; quite understandably, it supersedes Moser's as a psychoanalytic study; and it is unquestionably one of the most valuable biographical sources on Conrad. Conrad's artistic decline, according to Meyer, was brought about "not by physical ill health, mental fatigue, or financial worries, not by the necessity to dictate his novels, not by his 'relative isolation' or other environmental factors, but rather by the inevitable consequence of the specific psychological defenses adopted by him after his mental illness [in 1910]." No longer able to afford those "introspective journeys into the self" that had characterized the best of his earlier work, Conrad elected to "confine his art to the surface of life," willfully cutting himself off from "the dream source of poetic invention" and "the rich lode of his own well-guarded fancy" (p. 243). Meyer's evidence for these assertions, and for his broader theories about the conflicts and fetishes that "played a crucial role in facilitating or diminishing the fullest expression" of Conrad's gift (p. 14), is detailed and impressive. But having started with Moser, Guerard, and Frederick Karl (another achievement-and-decline critic) as his literary authorities, Meyer accepts the "patent deterioration of [Conrad's] artistry during the second half of his literary career" (p. 4) as a donnée, thus foreclosing the essential critical question from the beginning.

Within these broad areas of agreement, certain specific value judgments have also come to be shared by achievement-and-decline critics—the greatness of "Heart of Darkness" and Nostromo, for example, or the near-total failure of The Arrow of Gold. Victory, since it has traditionally been viewed as the best of Conrad's later novels, is a crucial case. "It would be tempting to pass over it in silence," Guerard says, "could one only be sure that readers would eventually reach the excellent critiques of Douglas Hewitt and Thomas Moser. For this is one of the worst novels for which high claims have ever been made by critics of standing: an awkward popular romance built around certain imperfectly dramatized reflections on skepticism, withdrawal, isolation," and including story elements appealing chiefly to the "adolescent" mind—the "rudimentary but exciting adventure story, the romantic pose of world-weary detachment, the simple yet vague erotic fantasy of the island shared with a grateful uneducated girl." Like Hewitt and Moser, Guerard objects to the novel's shifting point of view, its implausibly rhetorical dialogue, "flat and unenergized" prose, and "sentimentality and vagueness," and believes that "the time has come to drop *Victory* from the Conrad canon" (pp. 272 ff.)—a judgment since echoed by other influential critics (e.g., David Daiches, *New York Times* Book Review, August 17, 1958, p. 4; R. W. Stallman, "Conrad Criticism Today," *Sewanee Review*, LXVII [Winter 1959], 137). Similarly, it is fashionable among achievement-and-decline critics to reject Conrad's later letters and prefaces as clues to his art, especially where they are in the reductive vein of the "few very simple ideas" passage. Hewitt holds that to read the early works in the light of the prefaces would be "to miss almost everything which they have to give us" (p. 4); but on matters of artistic method Conrad may be trusted: "Though . . . Conrad often seems to misunderstand the nature of the issues with which his early work deals, his more specifically technical comments are far more acute and reliable" (p. 6). According to Frederick Karl, the Author's Notes are "docile," rooted in fact instead of imagination, and show the same decline of conceptual power as the later fiction (*A Reader's Guide to Joseph Conrad* [New York: Noonday Press, 1960], p. 41). In its extreme form, the idea that Conrad's self-criticism is misleading becomes a charge of coyness or dishonesty: Conrad's declaration that "I did not wrap [*Victory*] up in very mysterious processes of art" is, Stallman says, "nothing less than a strategic feint to conceal the secret intentions of *Victory*, and it is characteristic of that cunning strategy by which he everywhere conceals what his books are really about" ("Conrad and 'The Secret Sharer,'" *Accent*, IX [Spring 1949], 132); Conrad's "disclosures about his literary aims are highly deceptive, often deliberately misleading," and his Author's Notes are planted with "bogus trade secrets" and "false clues" (pp. 135, 136). Meyer, taking it for granted that Conrad's later self-criticism is simplistic and self-deprecatory, views it as one more of Conrad's postpsychotic defenses against complexity, thus avoiding Stallman's moralistic tone, but reinforcing the essential point.

Some mutterings against the tyranny of "achievement and decline" have recently been heard in the journals; *Victory*, in particular, coming in for some sympathetic reassessment (for citations, see Chapter 5). No work has yet appeared to place all these matters in perspective, however, or to answer Moser's "unanswerable question" by relating the later stages of Conrad's career thematically to the earlier—tasks that the present study, however successfully, has undertaken. Guidance on specific points has been acknowledged in the text and notes. It remains only to acknowledge some further general sources which have influenced the description of Conrad's career given here. The most obvious of these sources, of course, are Conrad's own letters and prefaces (both early and late); particularly where their tone seems self-controlled, and where the calculated prefaces and comparatively unguarded letters are in accord. The idea that his career can profitably be viewed as growth within a fixed frame of reference, for example, is Conrad's own: "My writing life extends . . . over twenty-three years . . . and all that time has been a time of evolution. . . . Some critics have found fault with me for not being constantly myself. But they are wrong. . . . Certain conclusions remain immovably fixed in my mind, but . . . my attitude to subjects and expressions, the angles of vision,

my methods of composition will, within limits, be always changing—not because I am unstable or unprincipled but because I
am free" (*Life and Letters,* II, p. 204). Similarly, as Zabel has
pointed out, the idea that this growth is not merely technical, but
is part of a growing self-awareness, is Conrad's also: "The letters
he wrote Mme. Poradowska between 1890 and 1900 reveal . . .
[that] he was already groping for the means and courage to
translate [his] experiences into fictional form, to objectify them
dramatically, and thus to come into an intelligent realization of
their meaning: to save himself, as he once expressed it, 'from the
madness which, after a certain point in life is reached, awaits
those who refuse to master their sensations and bring into coherent form the mysteries of their lives' " (Morton Dauwen Zabel,
"Joseph Conrad: Chance and Recognition," *Sewanee Review,*
LIII [Winter 1945], as revised for his *Craft and Character in
Modern Fiction* [New York: The Viking Press, 1957], p. 158).
It has frequently been observed how insistently Conrad referred
to the moral center of his work, but the point is worth repeating
once again, since it has been the tendency of recent critics to
ignore it: "I think I've got the theme for a Mediterranean novel
with historical interest, intrigue and adventure. . . . All I want
now is to discover the moral pivot"; or again, "I have been called
a writer of the sea, of the tropics, a descriptive writer, a romantic
writer—and also a realist. But as a matter of fact all my concern
has been with the 'ideal' value of things, events and people. That
and nothing else. The humorous, the pathetic, the passionate,
the sentimental *aspects* came in of themselves—*mais en vérité
c'est les valeurs idéales des faits et gestes humains qui se sont
imposés à mon activité artistique*" (*Life and Letters,* II, pp. 42,
185). And in line with the development of his later fiction,
Conrad's later letters display more frequent literary allusions,
more frequent philosophical and political disquisitions, more
frequent expressions of a refined skepticism, and the like. Disre-
garding its rather elegant theses, Edward W. Said's *Joseph
Conrad and the Fiction of Autobiography* (Cambridge: Harvard

University Press, 1966) furnishes some support for this point, arguing that the letters are "Conrad's spiritual history as written by Conrad himself" (p. 5), and that "the intellectual and spiritual climax of the letters . . . coincided not only with the fulfillment of his desire for self-discovery, but also with . . . the period of World War One" (pp. vi–vii), which is to say, the period of *Victory*.

The bias of early writers like Aubry and Mégroz toward biography and "personality" helped them to observe the ethical coherence of Conrad's work; but beyond that they see very little of Conrad's artistic growth. Muriel Bradbrook's brief *Joseph Conrad: Poland's English Genius* (Cambridge: At the University Press, 1941), divides Conrad's work into three stages: "The Wonders of the Deep," from *Almayer's Folly* through the *Typhoon* volume; "The Hollow Men," from *Nostromo* through *Victory;* and "Recollections in Tranquility" for all the work after *Victory*. More valuable than these categories, perhaps, is her awareness of the growing technical complexity of Conrad's work, and of the near-allegorical quality of *Victory*, which she singles out, along with *The Rover*, for special praise. More recently, Paul L. Wiley's *Conrad's Measure of Man* (Madison: University of Wisconsin Press, 1954) has offered another tripartite view of Conrad's career, according to the central protagonist of each period: "Man in the World," "Man in Society," and "Man in Eden." Wiley's archetypal frame of reference and his too-vigorous pursuit of literary and intellectual relationships between Conrad and his contemporaries introduce some distortions; and he agrees with achievement-and-decline critics that romantic love is a matter of central concern in the later fiction. But there is considerable validity in his broad divisions of Conrad's career; and his inclination to resist the idea of a "decline" in Conrad, and to defend the later works against severe negative criticism, is of course shared by the present study. Of all the critics who have offered general descriptions of Conrad's career, however, the most stimulating may be Zabel, whose "Chance and Recognition" and introductions to individual volumes are standard reading for students of Conrad. The commitment to human solidarity, Zabel says, is for Conrad "a necessity which defines man as human, his moral consciousness as imperative, and his persistence in that consciousness as the fundamental law of life. From this germinal presentation of the case Conrad's drama of the self widens until, in his most ambitious books, it comes to include the larger workings of that law in society and politics, even in the destiny of nations and of races. The growth in his thought from an idealistic conception of life to a critical one, from his temperamental romanticism to his later realism of values, is the drama of his genius in its difficult emergence." ("Chance and Recognition," as revised for *Craft and Character*, p. 166). The idea that Conrad's career may be seen as an outward growth from a germinal center, toward the periphery of his intellectual vision and a more-and-more ambitious subject matter, is the theoretical spine of this book. And to see the conscious center of Conrad in an ethical view of the universe and of man's place in it, and the growth of his art as a progress in self-discovery—these points are crucial.

Bibliography

Works of Joseph Conrad

All page references are to Dent's *Collected Edition of the Works of Joseph Conrad* (London: J. M. Dent & Sons, 1946–1955). Pagination is identical with the Dent Uniform Edition and with Doubleday, Page and Company's Canterbury Edition. The following list includes only those works discussed in the text. For a complete listing, see Kenneth A. Lohf and Eugene P. Sheehy, *Joseph Conrad at Mid-century: Editions and Studies, 1895–1955* (Minneapolis: University of Minnesota Press, 1957); or Baines, *Joseph Conrad*. The titles are arranged chronologically by date of first publication. If a work first appeared in a periodical, the date of book publication is given in italics.

Almayer's Folly (1895)
An Outcast of the Islands (1896)
"The Idiots" (October 1896, *1898*)
"The Lagoon" (January 1897, *1898*)
"An Outpost of Progress" (June–July 1897, *1898*)
The Nigger of the 'Narcissus' (August–December 1897, *1898*)
"The Return" (*1898*)
Tales of Unrest (1898; includes "The Idiots," "Karain," "The Lagoon," "An Outpost of Progress," "The Return")

[269]

"Youth" (September 1898, 1902)

"Heart of Darkness" (February–April 1899, 1902)

Lord Jim (October 1899–November 1900, 1900)

"Amy Foster" (December 1901, 1903)

Typhoon (January–March 1902, 1902)

"The End of the Tether" (July–December 1902, 1902)

"Tomorrow" (August 1902, 1903)

Youth, and Two Other Stories (1902; includes "Youth," "Heart of Darkness," "The End of the Tether")

"Falk" (1903)

Typhoon, and Other Stories (1903; includes "Typhoon," "Amy Foster," "Tomorrow," "Falk")

Nostromo (January–October 1904, 1904)

"Anatole France, (i) *Crainquebille*" (article; July 1904, 1921)

"Cobwebs and Gossamer" (article; June 1905, 1906)

"Autocracy and War" (article; July 1905, 1921)

The Mirror of the Sea (1906)

"Gaspar Ruiz" (July–October 1906, 1908)

"An Anarchist" (August 1906, 1908)

"The Informer" (December 1906, 1908)

The Secret Agent (October 1906–January 1907, 1907)

"The Duel" (January–May 1908, 1908)

"Il Conde" (August 1908, 1908)

A Set of Six (1908; includes "An Anarchist," "The Brute," "Gaspar Ruiz," "The Informer," "The Duel," "Il Conde")

A Personal Record (December 1908–June 1909, 1912)

"The Secret Sharer" (August–September 1910, 1912)

Under Western Eyes (December 1910–October 1911, 1911)

"A Smile of Fortune" (February 1911, 1912)

"The Partner" (November 1911, 1915)

Chance (January–June 1912, 1913)

"Freya of the Seven Isles" (April 1912, 1912)

'Twixt Land and Sea (1912; includes "The Secret Sharer," "A Smile of Fortune," "Freya of the Seven Isles")

"The Inn of the Two Witches" (March 1913, 1915)

"The Planter of Malata" (June–July 1914, 1915)

"Because of the Dollars" (September 1914, 1915)

Victory (February 1915, 1915)

Within the Tides (1915; includes "The Partner," "The Inn of the Two Witches," "Because of the Dollars," "The Planter of Malata")
The Shadow-Line (September 1916–March 1917, *1917*)
"The Tale" (October 1917, *1925*)
The Arrow of Gold (December 1918–February 1920, *1919*)
The Rover (September–December 1923, *1923*)

Other Sources

The following list includes everything cited in the notes, plus a dozen other items that seemed especially pertinent to points discussed in the text.

Aubry, Georges Jean. *Joseph Conrad: Life and Letters.* 2 vols. Garden City, N.Y.: Doubleday, Page, 1927.
———. *The Sea Dreamer: A Definitive Biography of Joseph Conrad.* Translated by Helen Sebba. Garden City, N.Y.: Doubleday, 1957.
Baines, Jocelyn. *Joseph Conrad: A Critical Biography.* New York: McGraw-Hill, 1960.
Beach, Joseph Warren. "Impressionism: Conrad," in his *The Twentieth Century Novel: Studies in Technique.* New York: Appleton-Century, 1932, pp. 337–365.
Bradbrook, Muriel C. *Joseph Conrad: Poland's English Genius.* Cambridge: At the University Press, 1941.
Cox, Roger L. "Conrad's Nostromo as Boatswain," *Modern Language Notes,* LXXIV (April 1959), 303–306.
Curle, Richard. Introduction to *Nostromo,* in 1958 reprinting of Dent's Collected Edition, pp. vii–xiii.
D'Avanzo, Mario L. "Conrad's Motley as an Organizing Metaphor in *Heart of Darkness,*" *College Language Association Journal,* IX (March 1966), 289–291.
Day, Robert A. "The Rebirth of Leggatt," *Literature and Psychology,* XIII (Summer 1963), 74–80.
Dike, Donald A. "The Tempest of Axel Heyst," *Nineteenth-Century Fiction,* XVII (September 1962), 95–113.
Dowden, Wilfred S. *"Almayer's Folly* and *Lord Jim*: A Study in the

Development of Conrad's Imagery," *Rice University Studies*, LI (Winter 1965), 13–27.

——. "The 'Illuminating Quality': Imagery and Theme in *The Secret Agent*," *Rice Institute Pamphlets*, XLVII (October 1960), 17–33.

Fleischmann, Wolfgang B. "Conrad's *Chance* and Bergson's *Laughter*," *Renascence*, XIV (Winter 1961), 66–71.

Fleishman, Avrom. *Conrad's Politics: Community and Anarchy in the Fiction of Joseph Conrad*. Baltimore: Johns Hopkins Press, 1967.

——. "The Symbolic World of *The Secret Agent*," *ELH*, XXXII (June 1965), 196–219.

Ford, Ford Madox. *See* Hueffer.

Galsworthy, John. "Reminiscences of Conrad," in his *Castles in Spain and Other Screeds*. New York: Scribner's, 1927, pp. 99–126. Reprinted from *Scribner's Magazine*, LXXVII (January 1925), 3–10; reprinted again in his *Candelabra*. New York: Scribner's, 1933, pp. 195–212.

German, Howard. *See* Kaehele.

Gillon, Adam. *The Eternal Solitary*. New York: Bookman Associates, 1960.

Gordan, John Dozier. *Joseph Conrad: The Making of a Novelist*. Cambridge: Harvard University Press, 1940.

Gose, Elliott B., Jr. " 'Cruel Devourer of the World's Light': *The Secret Agent*," *Nineteenth-Century Fiction*, XV (June 1960), 39–51.

——. "Pure Exercise of Imagination: Archetypal Symbolism in *Lord Jim*," *PMLA*, LXXIX (March 1964), 137–147.

Greenberg, Robert A. "The Presence of Mr. Wang," *Boston University Studies in English*, IV (Autumn 1960), 129–137.

Gross, Seymour L. "The Devil in Samburan: Jones and Ricardo in *Victory*," *Nineteenth-Century Fiction*, XVI (June 1961), 81–85.

Guerard, Albert J. *Conrad the Novelist*. Cambridge: Harvard University Press, 1958.

——. Introduction to *'Heart of Darkness' and 'The Secret Sharer.'* New York: New American Library, 1950, pp. 7–15.

——. Introduction to *Nostromo*. New York: Dell, 1960, pp. 5–20.

——. *Joseph Conrad*. New York: New Directions, 1947.

Guetti, James. " 'Heart of Darkness': The Failure of Imagination," in his *The Limits of Metaphor: A Study of Melville, Conrad, and Faulkner*. Ithaca: Cornell University Press, 1967, pp. 46–68. A revised version of " 'Heart of Darkness' and the Failure of the Imagination," *Sewanee Review*, LXXIII (Summer 1965), 488–504.

Gurko, Leo. *Joseph Conrad: Giant in Exile*. New York: Macmillan, 1962.

Harkness, Bruce, ed., *Conrad's 'Heart of Darkness' and the Critics*. San Francisco: Wadsworth, 1960.

——. "The Epigraph of Conrad's *Chance*," *Nineteenth-Century Fiction*, IX (December 1954), 209–222.

Haugh, Robert F. *Joseph Conrad: Discovery in Design*. Norman: University of Oklahoma Press, 1957.

——. "The Structure of *Lord Jim*," *College English*, XIII (December 1951), 137–141.

Hay, Eloise Knapp. *The Political Novels of Joseph Conrad*. Chicago: University of Chicago Press, 1963.

Herndon, Richard. "The Genesis of Conrad's 'Amy Foster,' " *Studies in Philology*, LVII (July 1960), 549–566.

Hewitt, Douglas. *Conrad: A Reassessment*. Cambridge: Bowes and Bowes, 1952.

Hicks, John H. "Conrad's *Almayer's Folly*: Structure, Theme, and Critics," *Nineteenth-Century Fiction*, XIX (June 1964), 17–31.

Hoffman, Stanton de Voren. "Conrad's Menagerie: Animal Imagery and Theme," *Bucknell Review*, XII (1964), 59–71.

Holland, Norman N. "Style as Character: *The Secret Agent*," *Modern Fiction Studies*, XII (Summer 1966), 221–231.

Howe, Irving. "Conrad: Order and Anarchy," in his *Politics and the Novel*. New York: Horizon Press and Meridian Books, 1957, pp. 76–113. Reprinted from *Kenyon Review*, XV (Autumn 1953), 505–521; and XVI (Winter 1954), 1–19.

Hueffer, Ford Madox. *The Cinque Ports*. London, 1900.

——. *Joseph Conrad: A Personal Remembrance*. Boston: Little, Brown, 1924.

James, Henry. "The New Novel, 1914," in his *Notes on Novelists*. New York: Scribner's, 1914, pp. 314–361.

Jean-Aubry, G. *See* Aubry.

Johnson, Bruce M. "Conrad's 'Falk': Manuscript and Meaning," *Modern Language Quarterly*, XXVI (June 1965), 267–284.

———. "Conrad's 'Karain' and *Lord Jim*," *Modern Language Quarterly*, XXIV (March 1963), 13–20.

———. "Joseph Conrad and Crane's *Red Badge of Courage*," *Papers of the Michigan Academy of Science, Arts, and Letters*, XLVIII (1963), 649–655.

Kaehele, Sharon, and Howard German. "Conrad's *Victory*: A Reassessment," *Modern Fiction Studies*, X (Spring 1964), 55–72.

Karl, Frederick R. "Joseph Conrad: A *fin de siècle* Novelist—A Study in Style and Method," *Literary Review*, II (Summer 1959), 565–576.

———. *A Reader's Guide to Joseph Conrad*. New York: Noonday Press, 1960.

Kramer, Dale. "Marlow, Myth, and Structure in *Lord Jim*," *Criticism*, VIII (Summer 1966), 263–279.

Leavis, F. R. "Joseph Conrad," in his *The Great Tradition: George Eliot, Henry James, Joseph Conrad*. New York: George W. Stewart; London: Chatto and Windus, 1948, pp. 173–226.

Levin, Gerald H. "An Allusion to Tasso in Conrad's *Chance*," *Nineteenth-Century Fiction*, XIII (September 1958), 145–151.

Lodge, David. "Conrad's *Victory* and *The Tempest*: An Amplification," *Modern Language Review*, LIX (April 1964), 195–199.

Lordi, R. J. "The Three Emissaries of Evil: Their Psychological Relationship in Conrad's *Victory*," *College English*, XXIII (November 1961), 136–140.

Malbone, Raymond Gates. " 'How to Be': Marlow's Quest in *Lord Jim*," *Twentieth Century Literature*, X (January 1965), 172–180.

Mégroz, R. L. *Joseph Conrad's Mind and Method: A Study of Personality in Art*. London: Faber and Faber, 1931.

Meyer, Bernard C., M.D. *Joseph Conrad: A Psychoanalytic Biography*. Princeton: Princeton University Press, 1967.

Michel, Lois A. "The Absurd Predicament in Conrad's Political Novels," *College English*, XXIII (November 1961), 131–136.

Miller, J. Hillis. *Poets of Reality: Six Twentieth-Century Writers*. Cambridge, Mass.: Belknap Press, 1965, pp. 13–67.

Moser, Thomas. *Joseph Conrad: Achievement and Decline*. Cambridge: Harvard University Press, 1957.

Perry, John Oliver. "Action, Vision, or Voice: The Moral Dilemmas in Conrad's Tale-telling," *Modern Fiction Studies,* X (Spring 1964), 3–14.

Pilecke, Gerard A. "Conrad's *Victory,*" *Explicator,* XXIII (January 1965), Item 36.

Robinson, E. Arthur. "Conrad's 'The Secret Sharer,'" *Explicator,* XVIII (February 1960), Item 28.

Rosenfield, Claire. *Paradise of Snakes: An Archetypal Analysis of Conrad's Political Novels.* Chicago: University of Chicago Press, 1967.

Ryf, Robert S. "Conrad's Stage *Victory,*" *Modern Drama,* VII (September 1964), 148–160.

Said, Edward W. *Joseph Conrad and the Fiction of Autobiography.* Cambridge: Harvard University Press, 1966.

Scrimgeour, Cecil. "Jimmy Wait and the Dance of Death: Conrad's *Nigger of the 'Narcissus,'*" *Critical Quarterly,* VII (Winter 1965), 339–352.

Sherry, Norman. *Conrad's Eastern World.* Cambridge: At the University Press, 1966.

Smith, Curtis C. "Conrad's *Chance:* A Dialectical Novel," *Thoth,* VI (Spring 1965), 16–24.

Smith, J. Oates. "The Existential Comedy of Conrad's 'Youth,'" *Renascence,* XVIII (Fall 1963), 22–28.

Stallman, Robert W., ed. *The Art of Joseph Conrad: A Critical Symposium.* East Lansing: Michigan State University Press, 1960.

——. "Conrad and 'The Secret Sharer,'" *Accent,* IX (Spring 1949), 131–143.

——. "Conrad Criticism Today," *Sewanee Review,* LXVII (Winter 1959), 135–145.

——. "The Structure and Symbolism of Conrad's *Victory,*" *Western Review,* XIII (Spring 1949), 146–157. Reprinted in Ray B. West, Jr., and Stallman, eds., *The Art of Modern Fiction.* New York: Rinehart, 1949.

Tanner, Tony. "Butterflies and Beetles—Conrad's Two Truths," *Chicago Review,* XVI (Winter-Spring 1963), 123–140.

—— "Nightmare and Complacency: Razumov and the Western Eye," *Critical Quarterly,* IV (Autumn 1962), 197–214.

Tillyard, E. M. W. "*The Secret Agent* Reconsidered," *Essays in Criticism,* XI (July 1961), 309–318.

Tindall, W. Y. "Apology for Marlow," in R. C. Rathburn and M.

Steinmann, Jr., eds., *From Jane Austen to Joseph Conrad*. Minneapolis: University of Minnesota Press, 1959.

Van Ghent, Dorothy. "On *Lord Jim*," in her *The English Novel: Form and Function*. New York: Rinehart, 1953, pp. 229–244.

Wang, Joan Parsons. "Joseph Conrad, Proto-Existentialist: A Comparative Study of Conrad, Camus and Sartre." Ph.D. dissertation, Indiana, 1965.

Warren, Robert Penn. Introduction to *Nostromo*. New York: Modern Library, 1951. Reprinted from *Sewanee Review*, LIX (Summer 1951), 363–391.

Watt, Ian. "Conrad Criticism and *The Nigger of the 'Narcissus,'*" *Nineteenth-Century Fiction*, XII (March 1958), 257–283.

——. "Joseph Conrad: Alienation and Commitment," in H. S. Davies and George Watson, eds., *The English Mind*. Cambridge: At the University Press, 1964, pp. 257–278.

——. "Story and Idea in Conrad's *The Shadow-Line*," *Critical Quarterly*, II (Summer 1960), 133–148.

Whitehead, Lee M. "Alma Renamed Lena in Conrad's *Victory*," *English Language Notes*, III (September 1965), 55–57.

Wilding, Michael. "The Politics of *Nostromo*," *Essays in Criticism*, XVI (October 1966), 441–456.

Wiley, Paul L. *Conrad's Measure of Man*. Madison: University of Wisconsin Press; Toronto: Burns and MacEachern, 1954.

Wright, Elizabeth Cox. "The Defining Function of Vocabulary in Conrad's *The Rover*," *South Atlantic Quarterly*, LIX (Spring 1960), 265–277.

Young, Vernon. "Joseph Conrad: Outline for a Reconsideration," *Hudson Review*, II (Spring 1949), 5–19.

——. "Lingard's Folly: The Lost Subject," *Kenyon Review*, XV (Autumn 1953), 522–539.

——. "Trial by Water: Joseph Conrad's *The Nigger of the 'Narcissus,'*" *Accent*, XII (Spring 1952), 67–81.

Zabel, Morton Dauwen. "Conrad," in his *Craft and Character in Modern Fiction*. New York: Viking, 1957, pp. 147–227. Includes revised version of "Joseph Conrad: Chance and Recognition," *Sewanee Review*, LIII (Winter 1945), 1–22.

——. Introduction to *The Portable Conrad*, ed. Zabel. New York: Viking, 1947, pp. 1–47.

———. Introduction to *Lord Jim*, ed. Zabel. Cambridge, Mass.: Riverside Press, 1958, pp. v-xxxvii.

Zuckermann, Jerome. "Contrapuntal Structure in Conrad's *Chance*," *Modern Fiction Studies*, X (Spring 1964), 49–54.

Index

[279]